3 1174 00021

W9-AHQ-313

973.33
GEO

GEORGE WASHINGTON'S
GENERALS

DATE DUE

AUG 2 5 2000	
MAR 0 8 2003	

GEORGE WASHINGTON'S GENERALS

Mount Prospect
Public Library

GEORGE
WASHINGTON'S
GENERALS

Edited by

GEORGE ATHAN BILLIAS

CLARK UNIVERSITY

WILLIAM MORROW AND COMPANY

NEW YORK, 1964

This book is affectionately dedicated
to my father and mother
for their love and understanding.

Copyright © 1964 by William Morrow and Company, Inc.

All rights reserved.

Published simultaneously in the Dominion of
Canada by George J. McLeod Limited, Toronto.

Printed in the United States of America.

Library of Congress Catalog Card Number: 64-12038

73.33
GEO

Contents

vi CONTENTS

Preface

THIS BOOK presents a literary portrait gallery of George Washington's generals. Surprising as it may seem, the last book of essays devoted solely to Revolutionary War military leaders was written more than a century ago. Three developments in recent years have shed new light on America's military leadership in the War for Independence—the appearance of Douglas Southall Freeman's monumental study of Washington, the publication of a number of full-scale biographies of other generals, and the discovery of more manuscript materials. The purpose of the present volume is to re-examine the careers of the most important Continental army commanders in the light of these new findings, hoping thereby to lead the reader to a better understanding of how America won the war.

Within these pages the reader will encounter many of the outstanding military figures of the Revolution: Washington, "god of the army"; Charles Lee, the brilliant but unorthodox ex-British officer who dreamed of altering the art of warfare to suit the peculiar genius of the American people; Philip Schuyler, the New York aristocrat who was as capable as he was cool toward the Yankees in his army; Horatio Gates, the cautious but competent professional soldier; the gifted Nathanael Greene, who was, after Washington, perhaps the best general in the Continental army; John Sullivan, the contentious Irishman who spent as much time battling congressmen as he did the British; brash, ambitious Benedict Arnold, who prior to his defection proved to be one of the army's bravest and boldest battlefield commanders; Benjamin Lincoln, the steady New Englander; the fledgling Frenchman, Lafayette, who was so eager to impress Washington; portly Henry Knox, who earned Washington's rare affection by his faithful service and tireless energy; dashing Anthony Wayne, who was not "mad" but a military romanticist; and the burly frontiersman, Daniel Morgan, whose flair for guerrilla warfare bedeviled the British.

This set of essays does not pretend to account for all the major commanders of the Continental army. The generals treated here were selected on the basis of two criteria: the significance of their contribution to the war effort; and the fact that they served alongside Washington in some capacity or campaign—hence the title of this volume. Had space permitted, essays might have been included on at least three other figures who also meet these criteria—Rochambeau, Putnam, and von Steuben.

Every one of the essays is by a specialist in his subject. Each contributor was asked to prepare an essay covering primarily one man's military career in the Continental army and placing proper emphasis upon the relative importance of his contribution to America's victory. The authors were not always in agreement, but in the best interests of scholarship I have allowed their judgments to stand unaltered.

As editor, I must express my appreciation to many persons who improved this volume in a number of ways. To my contributors, I am grateful for the good grace with which they accepted my suggestions and criticisms. Of the historians who helped me, I relied most upon the literary talents of two close friends—Professor Herbert J. Bass, of the University of Maine, and Dean Milton M. Klein, of Long Island University. They gave most generously of their time in reading these essays and I profited immensely from their wise advice. I am indebted also to Lois Dwight Cole—my co-worker and editor at William Morrow and Company—for her sympathetic and imaginative assistance in preparing this book for press. Messrs. Nathan Cohen and Stanley Shapiro, of Worcester, Massachusetts, patiently drew the maps for this volume. The following fellow historians shared their ideas with me, read parts of the manuscript, or offered expert advice in certain areas: Professor John R. Alden, of Duke University; Professors Gerald N. Grob and George H. Merriam, of Clark University; Dr. Clifford K. Shipton, of the American Antiquarian Society; and Dr. John D. R. Platt, of Independence National Historical Park. Staff members of the American Antiquarian Society, Clark University Library, and Worcester Public Library eased the burdens of my research. My wife, Joyce B. Billias, as in the past, shared my labors; without her loving help, cheerful encouragement, and patience this book could not have been completed.

G.A.B.

Introduction

AMERICA's victory in the Revolutionary War came as a surprise to many people. Even some of the combatants were amazed at the war's outcome. Washington himself predicted in 1783 that posterity might one day label the patriot triumph as "fiction" rather than fact. "For it will not be believed," he went on to say, "that such a force as Great Britain has employed for eight years in this Country could be baffled in their plan for Subjugating it by numbers infinitely less, composed of Men oftentimes half starved; always in Rags, without pay, and experiencing, at times, every species of distress which human nature is capable of undergoing."

Behind Britain's defeat lay many factors—French aid, flaws in British strategy, the distance of three thousand miles between England and America, the rugged terrain of the New World, and the necessity of having to reconquer a vast territory in order to win. But America's victory could not have been achieved without the efforts of George Washington and his generals. Despite defeats, an undisciplined army, and supply shortages, these officers stubbornly fought on until they brought to a successful conclusion the longest war this country has ever waged.

America's success appears all the more surprising when one considers that the Continental army leaders were essentially military amateurs at the outbreak of the war. How amateur American generals managed to defeat trained British professionals puzzles some military historians to this day. It is true, of course, that many Americans had had previous combat experience in the French and Indian War. But field operations in the French War provided valuable training only for enlisted men and officers in the lower echelons; they did little to prepare provincial officers for the problems of high command.

Consider, for a moment, Washington's own case. Having served five years as regimental commander along the Virginia frontier, he had, by 1775, a more active war record than most colonists. Yet in spite of his military background, he was poorly prepared to assume the post of commander-in-chief and confessed his "want of experience to move upon a large Scale." Commanding a regiment of several hundred men along a 300-mile frontier was hardly adequate training for the huge task of handling an entire American army numbering in the thousands on a continent encompassing 200,000 square miles. His combat experience was scanty at best and confined for the most part to small-scale operations against French and Indians in woodland warfare. His firsthand knowledge of certain branches of the army was extremely limited—he had never commanded a cavalry unit, employed massed artillery, or administered medical or supply installations of any great size. Because British regulars relegated him to a comparatively junior rank, he was never called upon to help formulate strategy.

Younger generals such as Henry Knox, Anthony Wayne, and Nathanael Greene, who were not of age to serve during the French War, had even less experience. These men came into the army straight from civilian life and were forced to acquire most of their military expertise from books. Propelled into the higher ranks of the Continental army with lightning rapidity, they continued to rely heavily upon book learning to solve many of their military problems. History offers few more comic examples of amateurs in combat than the scene that took place in front of the Chew House at Germantown in the fall of 1777. When the attack was momentarily held up, Washington began debating with his generals as to what the next move should be. Significantly, it was Henry Knox who settled the argument. Having owned a book store in Boston before the war, Knox was well-read in matters of tactics and strategy; he won his point simply by quoting from the writings of one of Europe's leading military men.

ǂ Of the generals appointed to the Continental army in 1775, only three could properly be regarded as professional soldiers— Charles Lee, Horatio Gates, and Richard Montgomery. All had been officers in the British army, had seen service in the French War, and had remained with the regulars in the postwar period. Yet even among these professionals, experience in the upper echelons of command was quite limited. Charles Lee reached the rank of lieutenant colonel in the British regulars long after his active service in America and Portugal—though he did gain more knowledge and experience while serving with foreign armies in Central Europe and the Balkans. Gates, who became a major, spent most of his time in military administration and never commanded a considerable body of troops. Montgomery rose only to the rank of captain. Nor was the advice of the professionals available to Washington for very long. Of the three, only Gates was still with the Continental army at the close of the conflict; Montgomery was killed in the first year of fighting and Lee held no important post after 1778.

Throughout the war, Washington was joined by other professionals and soldiers of fortune from the armies of Europe. Such officers frequently proved to be more trouble than they were worth. The commander-in-chief was forced to find places for them in order to placate Congress; at the same time he had to be careful not to disappoint jealous American generals who were equally deserving of higher rank. The commission given to the Frenchman, Phillipe du Coudray, for example, brought forth letters threatening resignation from three Americans— Nathanael Greene, John Sullivan, and Henry Knox. Thomas Conway and Johann de Kalb, who had both been in the French service, caused difficulties of a different sort; they hinted or proposed that Washington be replaced as head of the army.

Although certain foreign generals had much to offer in the way of expert military knowledge, their contributions to final victory on the whole were rather limited. The Comte de Rochambeau influenced strategy by pressing upon Washington, in 1781, the idea of attacking Cornwallis in Virginia rather than Clinton in New York. Louis du Portail, the efficient Frenchman, became the army's most competent engineer, and von Steuben, the Prussian drillmaster, its finest disciplinarian. Lafayette arrived in America innocent of battle and stayed on to win his spurs in combat as well as the affection of his commander-in-chief. But with the possible exception of Rochambeau, none of these officers made a contribution so decisive as to affect the outcome of the war. It is safe to say that, despite the presence of foreign professionals, the generalship of the American army maintained its amateur standing during the early war years.

Yet this very amateurism at the outset contributed, in part, to America's success, and enabled the colonists to make a contribution to the art of warfare. By refusing to fight according to the formal rules employed by professional soldiers in the eighteenth century, Americans developed new techniques of fighting. In an era when Europeans were still depending upon Prussian tactics that emphasized massed linear formations, the Americans frequently resorted to the thin skirmish line. The British put a premium on volley firing, which made up in firepower what it lacked in accuracy; the Americans encouraged individually aimed fire and showed a greater appreciation of military technology by substituting rifles for muskets in some of their units. The colonials were quick to recognize the value of fast, light infantry and demonstrated more military flexibility in employing swiftly moving forces for hit-and-run tactics. Their readiness to carry on winter campaigns and to march and fight at night also violated to some degree the code by which Europeans normally conducted warfare.

The American approach to warfare, however, was no conscious effort to introduce new military methods. For the most part, the amateurs tried to ape the professionals. Washington sought to model the Continental army along the lines of the British army by stressing drill and discipline, emphasizing distinctions in rank between officers and enlisted men, and insisting upon longer terms of enlistment. His aim was to create an army of regulars capable of meeting British troops on their own terms. An amateur himself, Washington had little faith in militia forces unless they were properly trained. Paradoxically, it was professionals like Lee and Gates who saw some military potential in short-term irregulars.

If George Washington and his generals were not military men primarily, where did they hail from and what was their background? A glance at the first group of fourteen generals commissioned by Congress in June, 1775, is revealing. Only three of this number—Washington, Lee, and Gates—had lived in the South. Of the remaining eleven generals, nine were Yankees and two Yorkers. This sectional imbalance was to continue throughout the war; most of the eminent military leaders were born or resided in the North. All fourteen men emerged from the upper or middle classes—some, like Washington, were great aristocratic landowners; others, like William Heath, owned less land but were prosperous; one was a lawyer, another a doctor, and a third a well-to-do artisan. Only three, so far as is known, held a college degree. Although a high number—about three-fourths—had seen active military service before the Revolution, relatively few had held a rank above major or commanded a unit larger than a battalion.

Their civilian activities were often of as much importance in preparing these men for a military career as was their active service in the field. The executive ability which Washington developed as a plantation owner—by supervising men, planning complex agricultural and commercial activities, and directing the efforts of a slave labor force—served him well as commander-in-chief. Philip Schuyler's previous experience as a part-time merchant along the Hudson eased his task of collecting supplies for the Continental army. And the habit of command demanded of men who led New England town meetings was precisely the same quality of leadership needed to take troops into battle. This ability of American generals to put their peacetime pursuits to good wartime use helps to account in part for the success of the patriots against British professionals.

Politics as well as peacetime experience played an important part in qualifying many men for an appointment in the army. Washington, as is well known, was picked primarily for political rather than military reasons. Similar motives governed the selection of many of his colleagues. Congress could rarely commission a general solely on the basis of merit. Conditions in the Continental Congress being what they were, state, not national, considerations were paramount. In certain instances—as in the case of Benedict Arnold in February, 1777—deserving individuals were passed over for promotion because of such political pressures.

Although political influence was a factor in selecting generals, remarkably few misfits reached that rank. The few who did, like old Israel Putnam, were rapidly replaced in responsible positions by younger and more able men. Others, such as the cantankerous John Sullivan, prepared the way for their own downfall by antagonizing congressmen. Most generals, however, showed an unusual capacity for learning. By conducting combat operations, they slowly mastered the art of warfare and by 1783 had become as professional as their adversaries in most respects.

Despite their growing professionalism, almost none of the military leaders of the Revolution emerged as first-rate generals. Amateurism, politics, and prudence resulting from feelings of inferiority when faced by British regulars inhibited the development of any outstanding commanders. Few had an opportunity to command forces of sufficient size to enable them to demonstrate a grasp of precise tactics or grand strategy. Of those who served for more than half the war, only Washington, Greene, and Arnold could be considered above average in ability.

Washington towered above his colleagues and deserved the title "Atlas of America" bestowed upon him by a French officer. To the position of commander-in-chief he brought great traits of character—an unflinching sense of responsibility, tenacity of purpose, and steady courage. His qualities of leadership alone must be reckoned among the more important influences in winning the war. But he also had serious shortcomings. His portrait as revealed in the pages that follow is often an unflattering one; he sometimes tried to shift the blame for his errors onto the shoulders of others, suspected that a "junto" was out to unseat him, and proved overly sensitive to criticism. As an army commander, he was inclined to rely too much upon his staff for advice and to employ faulty tactics on occasion. He never once defeated the enemy's main army in a major engagement on the open field. Despite these deficiencies, Washington was probably the man best qualified for the post of commander-in-chief in terms of military ability and temperament. While he was by no means as indispensable as historians sometimes have represented him to be, it is unlikely that the Continental army would have fared better under any one of its other top-ranking commanders.

One of Washington's greatest attributes was his genius in the art of managing men. Although he could not inspire genuine affection among the rank and file because of a certain hauteur and coldness in his personality, Washington had a profound effect upon the members of his official family. His ability to contend with jealous colleagues, to assess the relative strengths and weaknesses of his subordinates, and to cope with misfits and malcontents enabled him to weld a few fellow officers into some semblance of an American high command. It is not too much to suggest that Washington's gifts as a general were more political than military and that his unique contribution to the Continental army resulted not from his grasp of strategy and tactics but rather from his skill in handling America's military leaders. By shaping some of these men in his own image, he produced commanders who could rightly be called George Washington's generals.

GEORGE ATHAN BILLIAS

Clark University

TWO NORTHERN CAMPAIGNS 1775-1777

SCALE (APPROX)
0 10 20 30 40

QUEBEC

St. Lawrence R.

Etchemin R.

Chaudière R.

C A N A D A

Sorel R.

MONTREAL

ST. JOHNS

GREAT CARRYING PLACE

Kennebec R.

N E W

Lake Champlain

BURGOYNE 1777

Y O R K

Connecticut R.

N E W   H A M P S H I R E

FT. HALIFAX
FT. WESTERN

HAMPSHIRE GRANTS

CROWN POINT

FT. TICONDEROGA

MOUNT INDEPENDENCE
HUBBARDTON

Lake George

CASTLETON
SKEENSBORO

FT. ANNE

FT. EDWARD

SARATOGA

Mohawk R.

BEMIS HEIGHTS

North R.

BENNINGTON

ARNOLD 1775

NEWBURYPORT

M A S S A C H U S E T T S

SCALE (APPROX.)

PRINCETON

McCONKEY'S FERRY

Delaware R.

Assunpink Creek

TRENTON

NEWTOWN   WASHINGTON 1776

BORDENTOWN

WHITEMARSH   BURLINGTON

Skippack Creek

WASHINGTON Oct. 1777

GERMANTOWN

PENNSYLVANIA

NEW JERSEY

VALLEY FORGE

PAOLI

PHILADELPHIA

CHESTER

CHAD'S FORD

SEPT. 1777 HOWE

CORNWALLIS

NEW JERSEY
1776 and 1777
PHILADELPHIA
CAMPAIGNS

CHARLOTTESVILLE

VIRGINIA

RICHMOND

WASHINGTON

YORKTOWN
PORTSMOUTH

Dan R.

NORTH

GUILFORD

HALIFAX
HILLSBORO

CAROLINA

CHARLOTTE
MORGAN

Yadkin R.

COWPENS

SOUTH

WINNSBORO

CHERAW
HILL

CORNWALLIS

Cape Fear R.

CORNWALLIS 1781

Santee R.

CAMDEN

NINETY-
SIX

CAROLINA

WILMINGTON

Pee Dee R.

AUGUSTA

Eutaw
Spr.

Savannah R.

GEORGIA

BRITISH 1780

CHARLESTON

SOUTHERN
CAMPAIGNS
1780-1781

SAVANNAH

0   20   40   60   80   100
SCALE IN MILES
(Approx.)

GEORGE WASHINGTON'S GENERALS

George Washington:

GEORGE WASHINGTON'S GENERALSHIP

MARCUS CUNLIFFE

University of Manchester, England

AT first sight there is not much to be said about George Washington's generalship. At least, there is little new to be said. With hardly an exception, his contemporaries and biographers alike have agreed that he was an exemplary leader. Not even his few detractors have denied that he possessed certain essential attributes. To begin with, he was personally brave. In the fighting on Manhattan in September 1776, at Princeton in the following January, and at Germantown in September 1777, he displayed conspicuous courage. Tall, handsome, dignified, an expert horseman, he *looked* the part of a commander. He had great physical stamina; unlike some of his generals he was able to survive years of arduous campaigning without a serious illness. While less well educated than a number of his associates, he managed to express himself, in conversation and correspondence, with clarity and vigor. He was a methodical and energetic administrator. However despondent he might appear in private correspondence, he never wavered in his public insistence that the American cause was righteous and would triumph. Nor did he ever waver in his loyalty; the British admiral, Rodney, hopelessly misread his character in assuring Lord George Germain (as late as December 1780) that "Washington is certainly to be bought—honours will do it." [1] Then, early in the struggle he realized that crisis could

3

be defined as peril plus opportunity. The limitations of his command—miscellaneous and inexperienced troops, inadequate equipment and supplies, lack of naval vessels—must determine military
policy. "[W]e should on all occasions," he told the President of
Congress in September 1776, "avoid a general Action, or put
anything to the Risque, unless compelled by a necessity, into
which we ought never to be drawn." [2] But these words were
written at a time of grave danger, when his troops were raw,
hard-pressed and considerably outnumbered. He never ceased to
seek out the possibility of what he liked to call a "brilliant
stroke": a sudden assault, that is, like the one across the Delaware
in December 1776. And when he felt more confidence in the
quality of his men, he did not shun large-scale encounters. Finally, though he had a high sense of his own reputation, he resisted the temptation to abuse his authority. No scandal, financial
or moral, attached to his name. If he kept a punctilious record
of the expenses owed him by the United States, he took no pay
for his services. If British propaganda alleged that he had a
mistress, the *canard* gained no credence. More important, he
made it plain beyond doubt that he cherished no overweening
dream of military dictatorship. In emergency Congress twice
entrusted him with exceptional powers. Some of his officers were
prepared to hint in 1783 that he might become king of the new
nation. In such situations he responded with the utmost rectitude.
No wonder that the contrast was so often drawn between his
own career and that of Napoleon Bonaparte.

On all this there is virtually no argument. But to probe deeper,
to offer any reassessment of Washington's relative military talent,
or of his standing vis-à-vis his brother generals or the Continental Congress, is difficult. Some of the evidence we need—for
example, on the true nature of the so-called Conway Cabal—
is lacking and probably never will be available. And the story has
become too fixed in its main outlines. Between us and what might
be a fresher truth lie all the famous tableaux, apocryphal or
authentic. Through portraiture we see Washington as elegant,
severe, unruffled. We recall a whole sequence of static scenes:

Washington being placed in nomination for the chief command by John Adams at Philadelphia in June 1775; Washington reviewing his army on Cambridge Common a couple of weeks later; Washington sharing the miseries of the Valley Forge winter of 1777–78 with his men, yet (in our minds' eye) less affected by the cold than they; Washington rebuking Charles Lee at Monmouth Court House in June 1778, his soldiers broiled and parched, yet himself neither thirsty nor perspiring though angry enough with Lee; Washington superb in triumph at Yorktown, when Cornwallis surrenders to him in October 1781; Washington equally superb in his fatherly wisdom, when he puts on his spectacles to reply to the Newburgh Address of his discontented officers in March 1783; Washington bidding farewell to his officers, who now weep, at Fraunces Tavern in December of the same year. With such scenes are associated smaller vignettes: of nice young Lafayette, gruff old Steuben, jealous Gates and Conway, robust John Stark, comical Artemas Ward, villainous Arnold, loyal Greene, fat Knox; of Major André the British spy, so polite as to be almost masochistic; and of the Continental Congress, peevish, erratic, self-important. The total effect is like that of an old-fashioned engraving in which a central subject or person (Washington) is surrounded by a decorative border of tiny subordinate figures. The achievements of others are dwarfed, and made to seem dependent upon Washington's direction.

An awareness of this disparity accounts for much of the carping or malicious comment about him that circulated among such prominent soldiers and civilians as Joseph Reed, Charles Lee, Benjamin Rush, James Lovell, and John Adams. Admired, deferred to, secure in seniority, Washington (as they saw it) could easily afford the luxury of *noblesse oblige,* just as the wealthy, well-born Lafayette could easily rise to a nobility of conduct that endeared him to Washington but made him an exasperating example for a hard-up comrade like "Baron" de Kalb.

The nature of the war itself creates further difficulties of interpretation. Though we call it the Revolutionary War, or the

War of Independence, it was also a civil war—less so than the War Between the States, but enough to blur conventional military evaluations. It was an improvised, ambiguous struggle. We do well to remember, for instance, that John Stark, the hero of Bennington, had a brother William who fought on the opposite side and was killed in the Battle of Long Island in August 1776.[3] The British were not sure how to regard the conflict. The simplest answer was to call it a rebellion. Indeed, the British might have noted that such disturbances were apparently subject to a thirty-year cycle: 1775 was preceded by the Jacobite risings of 1745 and 1715, and by Monmouth's rebellion of 1685. The difference was that the American rebels were more remote, and the extent of their threat to British power less starkly obvious. So George III's advisers and generals fell into confusions over strategy and policy comparable to those that were later to perplex Abraham Lincoln. Both sides complained bitterly, and with reason, that they did not know where they stood, or where they ought to stand in a war that was much easier to lose than to win.

In the circumstances, British generalship was so hesitant and mediocre at major moments that Washington's own prowess is not easy to determine. When he tried to write this portion of his biography of the American commander-in-chief, Washington Irving confessed his bewilderment. The military campaigns, he said, reminded him of two drunk men trying to hit one another yet failing to connect. An English observer (in *The Gentleman's Magazine* of August 1778), while seeking of course to denigrate Washington, admitted to a similar inability to make sense of events:

> Nature has certainly given him some military talents, yet it is more than probable that he will never be a great soldier. . . . He is but of slow parts, and these are totally unassisted by any kind of education. Now, though such a character may acquit itself with some sort of eclat, in the poor, pitiful, unsoldierlike war in which he has hitherto been employed, it is romantic to suppose he must not fail, if ever it should be his lot to be opposed by real military skill.

The anonymous commentator continues:

> He never saw any actual service, but in the unfortunate action
> of Braddock. He never read a book in the art of war of higher value
> than Bland's Exercises; and it has already been noted, that he is
> by no means of bright or shining parts If, then, military knowledge
> be not unlike all other; or, if it be not totally useless as to all the
> purposes of actual war, it is impossible that ever Mr. Washington
> should be a great soldier. In fact, by the mere dint and bravery
> of our army alone, he has been beaten whenever he has engaged;
> and that this is left to befall him again, is a problem which, I be-
> lieve, most military men are utterly at a loss to solve.

The author is ungenerously inaccurate Washington had had several years of soldiering in the French and Indian War. He had
"heard the bullets whistle" more than once, before and after
Braddock's disaster at the Monongahela. And it would strain the
imagination to see the actions at Trenton and Princeton as proofs
of British military superiority. Still, the commentator's puzzle-
ment is understandable. For whatever reasons, and with the
doubtful exception of Monmouth Court House, Washington *did*
get the worst of all the major engagements he had a hand in during the first half of the war. The English writer goes on:

> It should not be denied . . . that all things considered, [Washington]
> really has performed wonders. That he is alive to command an army,
> or that an army is left him to command, might be sufficient to
> insure him the reputation of a great General, if British Generals any
> longer were what British Generals used to be. In short, I am of the
> opinion . . . that any other General in the world than General
> Howe would have beaten General Washington; and any other Gen-
> eral in the world than General Washington would have beaten
> General Howe.[4]

Without taking the last observation too seriously, perhaps we can
agree that Washington came very near to catastrophe in the latter
part of 1776. With a little more persistence and audacity from
Howe, the army led by Washington might have been destroyed.
If so, and if he himself had fallen into British hands, the struggle

might have continued and Washington would have been dismissed by posterity as a well-intentioned but outmatched amateur.

The situation—to return to the perspective of the period—was certainly novel. As this *Gentleman's Magazine* assessment indicates, the war defied measurement according to European standards. It was a civil war, or a rebellion, or a popular patriotic rising, or a mixture of all three. Washington was a novice, with a reputedly limited intelligence; and yet he had "performed wonders."

In the final analysis the two most decisive factors were perhaps not personal but geographical: the huge extent of America and the width of the Atlantic. We have said that Washington's own eminence has made the activities of his officers seem minuscule. Geography, as Washington Irving came to feel, had a similar diminishing effect upon the commanders of both sides. A third factor, the French alliance, could be held almost equally decisive. Its inception might be counted as a diplomatic rather than a military success, while the all-important victory at Yorktown may be seen primarily as a Franco-British affair—a blow struck in a century-long contest.

If we attach some weight to such elements, what are we left with by way of an estimate of George Washington's generalship? It seems that there must be some scaling-down of the wilder claims: claims, it must be said, that he did not advance on his own behalf and that have not been asserted by reputable historians in the past half-century. We must discard the legend, disproved but still lingering on in folklore, that Frederick the Great ever sent Washington a sword with the engraved inscription, "From the oldest soldier in Europe to the greatest soldier in the world." [5] Instead, let us consider dispassionately his stature as a fighting general, or field commander; and secondly, as an organizing general, or commander-in-chief.

Washington's talents as a field commander were in truth not tested often enough, or upon a big enough scale, to rank him automatically with the prodigies of military history. Like the other American generals at the beginning of the war, he was after all deficient in experience. At the outset this recognition weighed upon them to a perhaps undue extent. None of them had had much formal training on the European pattern. They were at best veterans of colonial warfare, unaccustomed to the handling of large bodies of troops or to the employment of special arms such as cavalry. Washington never had the responsibility for campaigns on the Napoleonic scale, not to mention those of the American Civil War. This is not to maintain that he would have failed to rise to the occasion, but simply to note that the giant occasion did not present itself. We can only guess what his "ceiling" of achievement might have been in the tactical disposition of one big army confronting another.[6]

On the debit side, military historians tend to agree that Washington made mistakes. Possibly he was too ready to shift the blame for a reverse onto a subordinate. This has been said of his treatment of Nathanael Greene after the loss of Fort Washington, and of his more peremptory reaction to Charles Lee at Monmouth Court House. The evidence against him is by no means conclusive; and indeed few senior soldiers in history could be held entirely innocent of such a charge. Washington's record is, for example, no worse and probably better than that of Stonewall Jackson in this respect. As for actual mistakes, he is most commonly accused of the following:

Long Island (August 1776): Splitting his army between New York and Brooklyn; failure to appreciate the value of cavalry for reconnaissance purposes, and so being taken by surprise through a flank attack; failure to give close supervision to General Israel Putnam's dispositions, which led to raw troops fighting without benefit of entrenchments.[7]

Fort Washington (November 1776): The loss of 3,000 men when the Fort was captured through his own indecision.[8]

Brandywine (September 1777): Failure to use his Light Horse to gather information of enemy moves, or in other ways to anticipate Howe's flank attack; general lack of firm direction.[9]

Germantown (October 1777): Reliance upon too intricate a plan of battle.[10]

Campaigns of 1777: A strategic error in deciding to march south against Howe's invasion of Pennsylvania, instead of joining Gates and Schuyler so as to crush Burgoyne in the north and then swing south, with reinforcements from the Northern army, against Howe.[11]

These charges are not without substance. In extenuation, it should be said that most soldiers, even celebrated ones, make mistakes. Stonewall Jackson, brilliant in the Shenandoah Valley in 1862, was abominably sluggish in the Peninsula fighting a few weeks later. Washington's errors, significantly, were concentrated in the first half of the war, when he was a learner in command of learners, face to face with professionals. Probably Howe could have destroyed him at the end of 1776. But Howe hesitated; Washington's response was the splendidly impudent *coup* at Trenton. It was a raid rather than a battle; part of the plan miscarried; but the effect upon American morale was tremendous. It was as needed a victory, at the time, as was the more ripely comprehensive and more thoroughly professional victory at Yorktown five years later. The difference in the scope and context of the two engagements defined the distance that Washington and his army had traveled in skill, in offensive capacity, and in assurance. Valley Forge and the French alliance represent the turning point. After the winter of 1777–78, the troops close to Washington began to correspond to the notion he had always stressed: namely, that America must have a disciplined national force, as trained and tried as the best European ranks that could be brought against them.

Here we come to a point that is worth stressing. Ever since the Revolution, Americans have been debating the respective merits of professional and of amateur soldiery. It has been a heated debate, for it embodies quite fundamental divisions of opinion as to the true nature of American nationalism and democracy. The contenders have both managed to find ammunition in their interpretation of the Revolutionary War. The professionals cite Washington's highly critical references to the militia, and to all short-term enlistments; the conflict was won, they believe, by the Continental regiments. The amateurs dwell upon the battles in which the militia fought stoutly, and upon the superior qualities of initiative, patriotism, and ingenuity which derive from an amateur tradition. George Washington, the Virginia planter, could be seen as the highest product of this essentially civilian approach to warfare.[12]

That he retained some "civilian" characteristics is undeniable. His deference to Congress, and to civilian authority generally, may be seen in this light. It is arguable that the tactics to which he sometimes resorted show a refreshing freedom from military orthodoxy, and that the British generals were hopelessly hidebound. No doubt the achievements of Washington's lieutenants —Greene, Knox and Morgan especially—are striking illustrations of amateur proficiency. But the professional-amateur debate is misleading in various ways. On the British side, many of the officers prided themselves on a dilettante approach to warfare. Nor do we give proper credit to the Americans if we caricature the British conduct of operations as a series of brutally stupid frontal attacks on the Bunker Hill pattern. On occasion the British showed considerable enterprise. One example of this would be Grey's night assault on Anthony Wayne at Paoli in September 1777, when the British killed, wounded, or captured nearly 400 Americans for the loss of only 8 of their own men. On the American side, amateurishness may have been evident—perhaps all too evident—in the war's initial stages. But after two or three years of campaigning, Washington, his officers, and his Continental rank-and-file had become professionals in all important respects.[13]

This was what Washington himself ardently desired. He did not visualize himself as a guerrilla leader, a will-of-the-wisp harassing the stolid British like some brigand chief. From the

start he strove to build an army able to meet the British in open
battle and beat them at their own game.[14] He knew that this was
only a dream in the early stages, and acted accordingly. But it
was no idle dream; it was an ambition that he labored to fulfill.
As his correspondence shows, he hammered away at the task of
creating an army officered (as far as possible) by gentlemen, observing strict discipline, properly armed, accoutered, paid, rewarded, punished. His was no doubt a sensible conservatism:
even the most revolutionary armies discover the advantages of
well-established procedures and hierarchical distinctions. "Let us
have a respectable Army," was his plea from 1776 onward, "and
such as will be competent to every exigency." In other words, an
army much like that of Howe or Rochambeau.[15]

But George Washington was not merely a field commander,
though he maintained his headquarters in the field with whatever troops seemed to be best placed for his manifold purposes.
He was commander-in-chief. The limits of his authority could
not be exactly defined, in a situation without precedent. Even if
a precise definition could have been formulated, much else would
have remained hazy. He had a large but vague jurisdiction. His
commission came from the Continental Congress, a body speaking for a then nonexistent nation. Congress entrusted him with
considerable powers. But Congress itself was only a comity, or
perhaps more accurately a committee, of thirteen semi-sovereign
states. Washington was clearly senior in rank to all the other
generals. But what control was he to exercise, theoretically or
actually, over armies that might be several hundred miles away
from his own headquarters? To what extent could he give orders
to the French military and naval leaders when their expeditions
began to arrive in 1778? Who was to formulate strategy? With
whom was he to communicate, and on what terms—governors
of states, other commanders, the President of Congress, the
Board of War? If he lost favor, was he removable?

Like the rest of his countrymen, Washington had to proceed
by trial and error. That he did err now and then seems both
undeniable and forgivable. His appointment was meant to sym-

bolize the spirit of union. In 1775 such spirit was more an as-
piration than a reality. Through indiscreet early letters he let it
be known that he, the Virginian, was not much impressed by
New England's military prowess. Some harm was done. He had
one or two awkward passages with the French, again through
indiscreet and possibly disingenuous correspondence which fell
into the wrong hands. For a prudent man he sometimes expressed
himself with dangerous candor in letters to his family and to
friends in and out of Congress. Yet he learned by his mistakes.
He shed all trace of Virginia localism, until he, more than any
other person or any institution or symbol, became synonymous
with America's cause. And compared with most of his prominent
fellow countrymen—soldiers and civilians—he was a model of
discretion. His letters are sometimes angry and self-righteous;
they are never whining, silly or malicious.

It was both a strength and a weakness of his position that he
seemed, in more than one sense, irreplaceable. In retrospect the
critical mutterings of 1776–77, in Congress and among certain
army officers, strike us as petty and perhaps even treasonable.
We find it absurd that Washington's military policy should be
subject to the scrutiny of the five men whom Congress constituted as the Board of War and Ordnance in June 1776. What
assistance could be rendered by such a member of the Board as
the utterly unmilitary John Adams? It was replaced in 1777 by
a new Board not composed of congressmen. But was this not
even worse, when intrigue might place disgruntled army officers
upon it? Or what of the six special committees sent by the Continental Congress to inquire into the army's affairs? Knowing
what befell Gates at Camden—or thinking we know—we wonder how anyone could have entertained the notion of substituting
him for Washington in the supreme command.

But this is hindsight, and a hindsight which may be cruelly
unfair. On the whole Congress and Washington worked together
well—fantastically well if we compare their relations with those
between Congress and Lincoln's wretched generals in the Civil
War. The boards and special committees of Washington's day

had next to nothing in common with the inquisitorial Committee on the Conduct of the War. They were anxious to help, and rendered all the aid within their power. It is doubtful whether there was any serious and concerted scheme to supplant Washington. There was something of a crisis of confidence in 1777–78. His more demonstratively enthusiastic supporters may have persuaded him that an organized plot existed. In the subsequent jockeying for position certain officers—Conway, Gates, Mifflin— may have been identified as a coalition hostile to Washington. Whether they were is dubious. Washington and posterity have treated them with marked disdain.

Whatever the inner history of a situation that may have had *no* inner history, Washington emerged as the undisputed commander, at the head of a group of competent and devoted officers. If there was a plot, it hardly deserves the name. If there was a counterstroke by Washington, it was far from being a Putsch.[16] In the long run, the effects of the entire episode were probably beneficial. The army could rely on Washington to put its case before the country; Congress could feel reasonably sure that with Washington in command there was no risk of subversion by a military junto. It would have been amazing if there had been no friction, no dissension, no backbiting. Once his position was secure, Washington was able to display a remarkable magnanimity. True, he complained unceasingly of the difficulties in his path. The war dragged on and on. The French had their own views of fruitful strategy. There were ominous mutinies in the Continental line. Yet there was a good deal more acrimony in the British camps and council chambers, and far more in that later American conflict of 1861–65.

Washington's ultimate success may owe as much to British limpness as to his own firmness. It has been plausibly maintained that the British situation was impossible from the start, and that no amount of brilliance in leadership could have offset the formidable disadvantages of having to fight an unpopular war, with resources strained by other global commitments, in a terrain in which merely to feed or move an army—let alone fight major battles—was an administrative problem of daunting dimensions.[17] The surrender of Cornwallis could not have been encompassed without the French fleet and army. Washington's own growing military capacity would have counted for little if his generals, junior officers, and enlisted men had not grown commensurately in competence and assurance. The heroic efforts of Greene, Knox, Lafayette, and others ought not to be underrated in the apportionment of credit. Greene was accurate as well as warmhearted in writing to Knox after Yorktown:

> Colonel Lee who has lately returned from the Northern Army says you are the genius of it, and that everything is said of you that you can wish. . . . Your success in Virginia is brilliant, glorious, great and important. The commander-in-chief's head is all covered with laurels, and yours so shaded with them that one can hardly get sight of it.[18]

As Washington himself was quick to acknowledge, there was room for more than one set of laurels.

Nevertheless, his devoted subordinates and his admiring French allies gladly yielded to him a major share of the glory. We may discount some of their compliments as flattery or as formal rhetoric. Yet they knew him, closely and testingly, from day to day and month to month. If he had been indecisive, or unduly arrogant, nervous, or reckless, he could not have won and held their respect. The British army no doubt labored under handicaps; yet those of Washington's army were sometimes very similar. Long after the war, John Adams is said to have growled that Washington was "a block of wood!" [19] If he really made the remark, which is likely enough, it can be understood as an oblique commendation, a grudging testimony to the vital elements of straightforwardness, consistency, and reliability in Washington's character. He won, that is, by taking to the field and staying there: by tenacity rather than by Napoleonic *brio*. Though he could be dashing in action, his overriding service to America lay in his steadfastness. He was a fixed point in a shifting universe.

Washington's role in the War of Independence was extraordinary. There are no close historical parallels. Yet two comparisons can be made, each of which helps to remind us that the commander-in-chief was only in part a military leader. The two comparisons are with Charles de Gaulle and Dwight D. Eisenhower. Like de Gaulle, though with less conscious purpose on his part, George Washington symbolized his country and its will to resist. The new nation insisted upon endowing "His Excellency" George Washington with charismatic glamour.[20] He was able to sustain the role with remarkable modesty, all things considered, as well as with remarkable dignity. Like the French leader, he was a figure of exceptional strength of purpose. And like General Eisenhower, he was a coalition general for a large part of the war. A great proportion of his work went on in conference and in correspondence. Some of his activities were political, or diplomatic, rather than military, as when he had to deal with British offers to negotiate, or with French military and naval chiefs. As with General Eisenhower, major strategic plans usually lay outside his scope; but their implementation often depended upon his advice. Despite his charismatic authority, he was more a mediator than a dictator. He communicated with governors of states, with Congress, with the Board of War, with the whole gamut of overlapping jurisdictions. In this respect, indeed, we might say that he was a dictator: a dictator of letters, not of decisions. If his charismatic symbols were those of the flag, the sword, the beautifully caparisoned horse, his day-to-day responsibilities were more appropriately symbolized by the chairman's gavel, the memorandum, the agenda, and the secretary's quill. It was his task, and his talent, to preside, to inform, to adjudicate, to advise, to soothe, to persuade, to anticipate, to collaborate. He had to weld the states together, as far as he could; to co-operate with the French, harmonizing America's aims and theirs; to reconcile the competing claims of different theaters of war; to face the consequences, in terms of mounting pride and estrangement, of having managed to create a professional army; to remember that though a master of men, he was the servant of his country and of Congress.[21] A co-ordinator, he had to learn how to stay near the scene of military action and yet not allow local problems to narrow his vision. A more mercurial figure might well have lost patience. A more genial one might have found his popularity was too cheaply purchased, and so too rapidly dispersed. For most of the war he had to stand on the defensive, reacting to British pressures. But when the chance came, in 1781, he showed that years of parleying had not eroded his spirit. At a vital moment he seized the initiative, like an ideal coalition leader, in ensuring that he and the French for once acted in entire harmony. In earlier episodes he may perhaps now and then have picked the wrong alternative in what he called his "choice of difficulties." Should he, for instance, have marched north instead of south in 1777? Should he, failing that, have retained the 3,000 men he sent to reinforce Schuyler and Gates? He made up his mind and acted, without vain regrets. He sent help to another army at the expense of his own immediate command. Can we imagine such a response from, say, General George B. McClellan?

What irony has accrued to those grudging judgments from *The Gentleman's Magazine!*

> Now, though such a character may acquit itself with some sort of eclat, in the poor, pitiful, unsoldierlike war in which he has hitherto been employed, it is romantic to suppose he must not fail, if ever it should be his lot to be opposed by real military skill. . . .

If and perhaps. History can only answer that it was Washington who stayed the course; it was Howe and Clinton and Cornwallis who headed back home to their firesides and their extenuating speeches and memoirs.

FOOTNOTES

1. Quoted in Henry S. Commager and Richard B. Morris, eds., *The Spirit of 'Seventy-Six: The Story of the American Revolution as told by Participants,* 2 vols. (Indianapolis, 1958), II, 703.
2. Letter of September 8, 1776, in John C. Fitzpatrick, ed., *The Writ-*

ings of George Washington, 39 vols. (Washington, D.C., 1931–44), VI, 28.

3. Maldwyn A. Jones, *American Immigration* (Chicago, 1960), pp. 53–54.

4. "Particulars of the Life and Character of General Washington, Extracted from a Letter in Lloyd's Evening Post of Aug. 17, Signed An Old Soldier," *The Gentleman's Magazine,* Vol. XLVIII (August 1778). This is conveniently reprinted in Martin Kallich and Andrew MacLeish, eds., *The American Revolution Through British Eyes* (Evanston, 1962), pp. 111–13.

5. The results of various scrutinies of the legend are summarized in Francis V. Greene, *The Revolutionary War and the Military Policy of the United States* (New York, 1911).

6. "His courage is calm and brilliant, but to appreciate in a satisfactory manner the real extent of his . . . ability as a great . . . captain, I think one should have seen him at the head of a greater army, with greater means than he has had, and opposed to an enemy less his superior. At least one cannot fail to give him the title of an excellent patriot, of a wise and virtuous man, and one is . . . tempted to ascribe to him all good qualities, even those that circumstances have not yet permitted him to develop." This is the rather feline opinion of Colonel de Broglie, a young French nobleman who joined his regiment in 1782. W. S. Baker, *Character Portraits of Washington* (Philadelphia, 1887), pp. 18–21. Perhaps its coolness, unusual for this late stage of the war, has something to do with family history. Four years earlier, another de Broglie was being hinted at as a candidate for what would in effect have been the chief command in America. See Douglas S. Freeman, *George Washington,* 6 vols. (New York, 1948–54), IV, 99.

7. F. V. Greene, *op. cit.,* p. 41; Christopher Ward, *The War of the Revolution,* 2 vols. (New York, 1952), I, 229; George F. Scheer and Hugh F. Rankin, *Rebels and Redcoats* (Cleveland, 1957), p. 174.

8. This criticism has been most sharply formulated by Bernhard Knollenberg, in *Washington and the Revolution: A Reappraisal* (New York, 1940), pp. 129–39.

9. For some representative comments, see Willard M. Wallace, *Appeal to Arms: A Military History of the American Revolution* (New York, 1951), p. 139; John R. Alden, *The American Revolution, 1775–1783* (New York, 1954), p. 123; Freeman, *op. cit.,* IV, 488; and Scheer and Rankin, *op. cit.,* pp. 240, 293–94.

10. Ward, *op. cit.,* I, 364–71; Alden, *op. cit.,* p. 125; Scheer and Rankin, *op. cit.,* p. 244.

11. One of the first books in Washington historiography to express serious reservations as to the commander-in-chief's military prowess (including his failure to understand the value of cavalry) was Charles Francis Adams, Jr., *Studies Military and Diplomatic, 1775–1865* (New York, 1911). For the campaigns of 1777 see pp. 132–49.

12. One stout upholder of this view is John A. Logan, *The Volunteer Soldier of America* (Chicago, 1887), p. 484: "No amount of preliminary technical education could have made a greater general of the hero of Trenton, Princeton, and Yorktown. His genius was natural, and bloomed into the perfection attained under the developing influence of actual warfare."

13. There are intelligent comments on these matters in Walter Millis, *Arms and Men* (New York, 1956), pp. 32–33; Daniel Boorstin, *The Americans: The Colonial Experience* (New York, 1958), pp. 364–71; Theodore Ropp, *War in the Modern World* (Durham, 1959), pp. 71–80; and Alfred Vagts, *A History of Militarism,* revised ed. (New York, 1959), pp. 92–101.

14. An excellent recent study is Russell F. Weigley, *Towards an American Army: Military Thought from Washington to Marshall* (New York, 1962). See especially pp. 1–7.

15. By the closing stages of the war he had gone far enough in this direction to astonish discriminating Frenchmen, although previously Mifflin and other generals had enjoyed a reputation for being somewhat more effective disciplinarians. "I had expected to see," wrote the Comte de Ségur, "unkempt soldiers and officers without training. . . . I saw a well-disciplined army presenting in every detail the very image of order, reason, training and experience." Chastellux was equally impressed: "When one sees . . . the General's guards encamped within the precincts of his house; nine waggons, destined to carry his baggage, ranged in his court; . . . grooms taking care of very fine horses belonging to the General Officers and their Aides de Camp; when one observes the perfect order . . . within these precincts, . . . one is tempted to apply to the Americans what Pyrrhus said of the Romans: *Truly these people have nothing barbarous in their discipline!*" Gilbert Chinard, ed., *George Washington as the French Knew Him* (Princeton, 1940), pp. 37, 57. If these officers had visited Washington's headquarters in 1776 or 1777, instead of 1781 or 1782, they would of course have found a more rough-and-ready atmosphere.

16. The undercurrents of hostility and rivalry are closely analyzed in Knollenberg, *op. cit.*, pp. 30–77, and in Kenneth R. Rossman, *Thomas Mifflin and the Politics of the American Revolution*

(Chapel Hill, 1952), pp. 91–139, as well as in Freeman, *op. cit.*, IV, 581–611. An older account, which assumes that opposition to Washington was organized, is Louis C. Hatch, *The Administration of the American Revolutionary Army* (New York, 1904), pp. 23–34.

17. See Eric Robson, *The American Revolution in its Political and Military Aspects* (London, 1955), pp. 93–152.
18. Greene to Knox, December 10, 1781, quoted in North Callahan, *Henry Knox: General Washington's General* (New York, 1958), p. 190.
19. An anecdote relating to *circa* 1816, recorded by John G. Palfrey; see *William & Mary Quarterly*, 3rd series, XV (January 1958), 93–94.
20. Seymour Martin Lipset, *The First New Nation: The United States in Historical and Comparative Perspective* (New York, 1963), pp. 16–23.
21. Edmund C. Burnett, *The Continental Congress* (New York, 1941), has some fascinating detail on Congress and the army. See for example pp. 442–67 for the period in 1780 when a committee of Congress visited Washington's headquarters.

BIBLIOGRAPHY

Burnett, Edmund C., *The Continental Congress*. New York, 1941. Explores the complicated relationships of the commander-in-chief with his civilian colleagues and mentors.

Cunliffe, Marcus, *George Washington: Man and Monument*. Boston, 1958. Treats Washington's symbolic as well as military role.

Fitzpatrick, John C., ed., *The Writings of George Washington*, 39 vols. Washington, 1931–44. Perhaps the best way of putting oneself in Washington's place is to read selected letters from these volumes. The portions dealing with the war years number some 10,000 pages.

Freeman, Douglas S., *George Washington: A Biography*, 6 vols. New York, 1948–54. The essential work on Washington. Volumes IV and V relate to the Revolutionary War and they are thorough, dispassionate, and admirably indexed. Washington's military qualities are interestingly assessed at the end of Volume V.

Frothingham, Thomas G., *Washington, Commander in Chief*. Boston, 1930. An older work that is laudatory in tone but still of some value.

Knollenberg, Bernhard, *Washington and the Revolution: A Reappraisal*. New York, 1940. The most searching critical comment to be found on Washington.

Miller, John C., *Triumph of Freedom, 1775–1783*. Boston, 1948. A solid contribution as a general account of the war.

Sparks, Jared, ed., *Correspondence of the American Revolution, Being Letters of Eminent Men to Washington, 1775–1789*, 4 vols. Boston, 1853. Supplements the work of Fitzpatrick.

Charles Lee:

THE SOLDIER AS RADICAL

———•—•———

JOHN W. SHY

Princeton University

THE reputation of Charles Lee has long suffered by comparison with that of George Washington. He is traditionally remembered as a troublemaker—one who confounded Washington by disobeying orders, intriguing for the position of commander-in-chief, and calling for a court-martial with the hope of casting his superior into oblivion. Lee may have even betrayed the Revolution itself because of his malice toward Washington. His conduct after dismissal from the army has been debated so long as a political, not a military, question that Lee's modern biographer has subtitled his book, *Traitor or Patriot?* [1] But in all these evaluations, the result has been to judge rather than to understand an extraordinary human being.

To understand Lee in depth, a psychiatrist instead of a historian is probably required. Certainly he would have benefited from psychiatry had such a medical practice existed in his day. Born as the youngest child of a prominent family near Chester, England, he grew up in a home environment created by the early death of five out of seven children. The only other survivor was his elder sister Sidney. Disliked by his mother, he lavished much of his affection on Sidney, who like himself never married. He grew to be a tall, skinny, ugly young man, remarkable for his slovenly personal habits and coarse speech. His sex life seems to have been of the transient kind, and in those instances where he became interested in some woman he seems to have been rebuffed. There were hints, but no more than that, of homosexuality.[2] Besides his sister, the only serious rivals for his affection were his dogs. It may be that Lee's love for dumb animals was the only kind of uncomplicated relationship of which this most complex personality was capable.

If Charles Lee conversed as he wrote, then the mid-twentieth-century label for him would be "compulsive talker." It appears that Lee would say almost anything. He was equally unrestrained in his letters. Rarely did he include a request that his views be kept confidential. More often than not, he suggested his letters be printed. His published attacks on Washington after the court-martial caused even Lee's remaining friends to turn away in disgust. When Lee turned sour, and his frenetic energy that had helped sustain the American cause in 1776 was turned against the commander-in-chief two years later, then another modern label is suggested: the "true believer," the fanatic whose very strength lies in his lack of balance, judgment, and self-restraint.[3]

Washington, with all the understatement of a Virginia gentle-man, called Lee "fickle" long before he knew the worst about him. Washington's biographer, Douglas Southall Freeman, an-other Virginia gentleman who understood perfectly the vocabu-lary of his subject, hated Lee with a passion that he had some difficulty in controlling.[4] At best, Freeman ceased to take Lee seriously, treating him as a two-dimensional, unbalanced man. Many historians, led on perhaps by Lee's own admission of "the distemper of my mind," have been willing to do likewise.[5]

Members of the Continental Congress took Lee with utter seriousness, however, when the time came to organize an Ameri-can army in June, 1775. For a man of forty-three, and a citizen of an empire at peace for more than a decade, he had an impres-sive military record. At the age of fourteen he had received a commission in his father's regiment. While still in his early twen-ties, he served as lieutenant in one of two British regiments sent to America from Ireland in early 1755 under the command of Major General Edward Braddock. Scanty evidence suggests that Lee first met Washington that spring on the disastrous expedition against Fort Duquesne, when Lee's regiment was shot to pieces and Braddock killed in an ambush by French-led Indians.[6]

Lee's regiment, the 44th Foot, moved northward into New York as Britain's war with France expanded in North America. Vigorous recruiting, by Lee and others, brought the 44th back to strength, so that it soon was composed primarily of native Americans. The regiment was in the Albany area during 1756, where Lee had time to study Iroquois culture, acquiring an Indian consort and a Mohawk name—"Boiling Water"—in the process. In 1757, he went on the abortive expedition against Louisbourg, but service the next summer was more rugged. By then a captain and company commander, Lee had two ribs smashed by a musket ball before the French earthworks around Ticonderoga. He was several months recovering from his wounds, but spent some of his convalescence criticizing his superior for the conduct of a campaign that ranks with Braddock's march for misfortune and bloodshed.

The next two campaigns in which Lee participated brought about the fall of Canada. He was at the siege of Niagara, went on a hazardous mission from Niagara to Fort Pitt, and then accompanied the main attack in 1760 down the St. Lawrence which ended with the taking of Montreal. With the capture of Montreal, fighting came to an end on the American mainland.

Lee got leave to go to England, rather than vegetate with his messmates in the American wilderness, and soon was promoted to major in a newly-raised regiment. When Spain jumped into the war in early 1762, the British response was an expedition to the Iberian Peninsula. Lee served there under Brigadier General John Burgoyne, and each won his brightest victory when Burgoyne ordered and Lee led a daring and successful raid upon a Spanish encampment.

Peace came to Britain in 1763, but by 1765 Lee was off to other wars. He went to Poland where civil strife threatened, carrying letters of introduction to Stanislas Poniatowski—King of Poland, former lover of Catherine the Great, and reputedly one of the most enlightened and liberal minds of his age. Though Lee became royal aide-de-camp, he saw no action and, after a visit to Constantinople, returned to England. In 1769, when Stanislas lost control of his kingdom as the result of a revolt, and Russian armies began moving into Poland to give him "support," Lee returned to Warsaw. Commissioned a Polish major general without command, he joined the huge Russian army in Moldavia, and watched it grapple with an even larger Turkish army. Then, sick and disgusted, he went slowly home to England by way of Hungarian spas and Italian beaches. He had seen in his travels through Poland what civil war could be: rebel bands so active that "it is impossible to stir ten yards without an escort of Russians," and vicious fighting methods "about as gentle as ours was in America with the Shawenese and Dellawars." [7]

During the years after 1755, while Washington was patrolling a comparatively quiet Virginia frontier and worrying about the price of tobacco, Lee had been exposed to a variety of military experiences. More important, his experience had profoundly affected him, because he was that rarity in any age—the soldier who is also an intellectual. He had attended good schools, knew classical and modern languages and literature, and was especially fond of Shakespeare. But above all, he had studied military theory and tactics. John Adams, who came to know Lee "very thoroughly," modestly admitted that Lee was the only American officer who had read more than he had on the history and art of war.

If the active service which guided his military study was deficient in any respect, it was in its comparative lack of experience with the "conventional" warfare epitomized by Frederick the Great. Lee had seen the highly disciplined Prussian battalions move slowly through their intricate linear tactical formations, but no document records that he was especially impressed. On the contrary, he expressed contempt for "Hyde Park tactics" and recollected that British regulars became effective in the French and Indian War only after they had forgotten everything they had learned on the parade grounds at home. His less studious and stay-at-home contemporaries were apt to regard Prussian military methods as the proper models for warfare, but Lee knew better. Between his books, travels, and combat experience in irregular warfare, he had become something of a military radical, prone to doubt the accepted practices of his day.[8]

His radicalism was not solely the product of experience and study, nor was it confined to military affairs. By temperament he was disposed to attack or question the assumptions and conventions that most men lived by. Quiet loyalty did not stand high in his scale of values and three British commanders in America had felt the sting of Captain Lee's tongue and pen. The King of England himself was not immune. When George III granted Lee an audience in order to receive a letter from Stanislas of Poland, and began to apologize for his inability to offer Lee military preferment, the latter stopped him short by coolly observing: "Sir, I will never give your Majesty an opportunity of breaking your promise to me again." [9]

Some have used this broken promise to explain Lee's readiness to serve on the American side in the Revolution. But the truth lies deeper. Lee's personal and family connections were with the Whig politicians who opposed the policies of young King George in the 1760's. He was not satisfied, however, with the narrow ground of opposition taken by the Whig aristocrats. Instead, Lee repeatedly attacked the very principle of monarchy itself. He called Switzerland "those bless'd regions of manly Democracy" (when *democracy* was still a dirty word), and darkly alluded to making himself a good soldier "for purposes honest, but which I shall not mention." [10] It was not only a disgruntled half-pay officer who tendered his services to Congress in 1775, but a man whose whole life seemed preparation to fight against arbitrary, corrupt monarchical authority in the name of American freedom.

Members of Congress were impressed by Lee, for political as well as military reasons. Shrewd, learned men like John Adams would have detected a mere military adventurer. But Lee talked to them earnestly and knowledgeably about Rousseau and the rights of man; he shared their fondness for the now-forgotten Whiggish historian, Mrs. Catherine Macaulay; and he wrote a biting pamphlet explaining why American militiamen could fight more effectively than British regulars. Once Virginia had been placated with the appointment of Washington as commander-in-chief and Massachusetts was satisfied by the naming of Artemas Ward, some delegates from these two provinces proposed Lee as third-ranking general. When Congress hesitated, Washington himself requested Lee's appointment and the issue was settled in June, 1775.[11]

From that time until the early fall of 1776, there can be no question that Lee lived up to the highest expectations of his supporters. To the Boston siege in the summer of 1775 he brought the organizational, tactical, and engineering skills that were so badly needed. There are glimpses in the records of Lee working tirelessly to improve the new American army—riding, observing, writing, correcting, and commending. James Warren, who was disturbed by Lee's lack of conventional manners, described Lee's activity for Sam Adams: "[Lee] came in just before dinner, drank some punch, said he wanted no dinner, took no notice of the company, mounted his horse, and went off again to the lines."[12]

Washington, dividing his army into three divisions, gave Lee the northernmost command, facing the Charlestown peninsula and British position on Bunker Hill. Lee's brigadiers were Nathanael Greene, of Rhode Island, and John Sullivan, of New Hampshire. In late July, he was exhorting Sullivan to use all his manpower to complete the fortifications, adding: "For God's sake finish and strengthen the abattis." By late August, when a British attack over the Charlestown neck against Lee's position seemed imminent, the Americans were able to move first. With 1,200 men as a work party and twice as many to cover them, Sullivan moved forward and in a single night entrenched Ploughed Hill, within point-blank range of Bunker Hill. The

British countered with a violent artillery and naval bombardment, but the work had been done too well; Lee's division stood fast.[13]

Confidence in Lee's abilities soon spread throughout the army. Greene wrote of Lee's "genius and learning," and William Thompson, colonel of riflemen, reported that he was "everyday more pleased with General Lee." [14] As winter came on and the likelihood of British naval raids on American ports grew, Washington ordered Lee to Rhode Island to lay out defensive positions, and later to New York on a similar mission. It is clear that Lee was a trouble shooter, a key man to be sent to points where danger threatened.

When it became apparent in February, 1776, that the American expedition against Canada had failed, and that the British soon would withdraw from Boston to attack somewhere to the southward, American leaders were in a quandary as to what to do with Lee. "We want you at N. York— We want you at Cambridge— We want you in Virginia—" wrote John Adams. "But Canada seems of more Importance than any of those places," he continued, "and therefore you are sent there." [15] But the estimate of the situation changed almost before Lee received this letter, and Congress ordered him south instead. At Baltimore, Williamsburg, and Norfolk, Lee did all he could to strengthen defenses. Then in May came definite word that a British fleet was moving off the Carolinas, probably toward Charleston. Lee set out immediately for that city.

From Boston to Norfolk, Lee had contributed his military expertise at the crucial, formative stage of American resistance. The defenses that he had planned and begun at Newport and New York would later crumble before determined British attacks, but he had made those places far stronger than they had been before. Of greater importance, however, was his political activity between December, 1775, and May, 1776. During those trying months, people on the American seaboard outside Boston were wavering. There had been little fighting and many people, caught up in the shadowy state between war and peace and loyalty and

treason, made small compromises with British officials. There
seemed to be a tendency to listen more closely to loyalist neighbors now that an abstract argument had become immediate and
concrete, and to postpone any violent or decisive action as long
as possible. Lee moved through this murky world of indecision
like a flame. In Newport and New York, he made suspected
Tories swear an elaborate oath.[16] In New York and Virginia, he
disarmed them or moved them from militarily sensitive areas.
When fence-sitters living under the guns of British ships used
their vulnerability as an excuse for inaction, Lee told them to
move out where they could not be threatened. He demanded
that the Revolutionary authorities in New York, Maryland, and
Virginia stop communicating with their royal governors, and
make a clean break.

Lee antagonized and upset civil officials wherever he went, but
he also shocked them out of their lethargy. He had been an outspoken advocate of an immediate declaration of American independence since October, 1775. Lee supported the idea of
independence partly for diplomatic reasons, but primarily as a
means of crystallizing the popular will to fight before it was
eroded by confusion and delay. He saw clearly that a successful
Revolution needed much more than an army in the field; it required action at the grass-roots level—determination and effi-
ciency among its supporters, and firm control over its enemies.
The extralegal political bodies that had sprung up since 1774
were to provide the basis of this action, but their members in
general had been unwilling to usurp the essential function of
government by using coercion in a systematic way. Everywhere
he went, Lee pushed the new holders of power toward this last
and decisive step—the step that meant treason and no turning
back.[17]

He made an effort to be tactful in his direct dealings with
Revolutionary officials, but he let himself go in his reports to
Congress and to Washington. Wherever he saw vacillation, or
interest in conciliation with the British government, it sickened
him and he said so. When he could not obtain civilian co-opera-

tion in New York, he moved against Tories and suspects on his own initiative and justified his conduct on the basis of military necessity. Congress, frightened by any encroachment of the military on civil authority, reprimanded him gently.[18]

What Washington thought about Lee and his behavior at this time is more interesting. When he sent Lee to New York, he had accurately predicted that Congress would not support Lee, but would be "duped" by the lukewarm New York government. Two months later, as if in response to Lee's rhetorical question, "Are we at war or are we not?", he wrote: "It is a great stake we are playing for, and sure we are of winning if the Cards are well managed. Inactivity in some, disaffection in others, and timidity, in many may hurt the Cause; nothing else can. . . ." And of Lee himself: "General Lee . . . is the first Officer in Military knowledge and experience we have in the whole Army. He is zealously attach'd to the Cause, honest and well meaning, but rather fickle and violent I fear in his temper. However as he possesses an uncommon share of good Sense and Spirit I congratulate my Countrymen upon his appointment. . . ." [19] Whatever his doubts, Washington was equally uncompromising in the face of fear and uncertainty.

When Lee arrived at Charleston in early June, 1776, he found less trouble with Tories and more preparation for defense than he had elsewhere. But Charleston was not ready to resist the British force that had appeared on the horizon almost as Lee rode into town. Islands, rivers, marsh, shoal and deep water created a problem for the defender nearly as complex as the one Lee had met in fortifying New York.[20] There was a half-finished fort on Sullivan's Island, east of the city and commanding the entrance to the harbor. Both Lee and the British commanders saw its weaknesses: it could not protect the city from a determined attack, could be flanked by sea from the west and by land from the east, and might well be a trap for its garrison. Lee wanted to abandon the fort, but too much labor and prestige were invested in it. The hour was late and he finally agreed to complete the fort and to make it as defensible as possible, though he was still dubious about its strength. By erecting batteries, building bridges, digging trenches, and clearing fields of fire, he managed to keep pace with the slow-moving councils of the invaders.[21]

Lee angered more than one Charleston worthy with his "hasty and rough" manners, his demands for speed and obedience, and his insistence that white men do work usually reserved for Negro slaves. He made life miserable for Colonel William Moultrie, the easy-going commander of the fort, and alienated William Henry Drayton, future chief justice of South Carolina. When the British finally launched their attack on June 28, it came in the form of a naval assault on the fort itself. The enemy plan was both unimaginative and badly executed. In part, this was because Lee had managed to eliminate most other tactical choices. Moultrie's men drove off the attackers with heavy losses and suffered few casualties themselves.

In the report he submitted after the battle, Lee gave full credit to the Carolinians for the victory. He admitted he "had once thoughts of ordering the Commanding officer to spike his guns," but that the "cool courage" of the garrison, which "astonished and enraptured" him, had made it unnecessary. Moultrie, he concluded, "deserves the highest honors."[22] Lee, in fact, had been on the verge of replacing Moultrie when the attack began, and after its repulse continued to harass the colonel with directions and questions—"Is your Gate finish'd? How is the Bridge? I beg you will inform me. . . ."[23] After Lee's disgrace and death, Moultrie and Drayton's son each wrote memoirs of the Revolution, and one might expect to find in them two hostile witnesses. But John Drayton thought that "however disagreeable General Lee's manners were, . . . there is much reason for being thankful, that he was sent on to command. . . ."[24] Moultrie concurred: ". . . his coming among us was equal to a reinforcement of 1000 men . . . he taught us to think lightly of the enemy, and gave a spur to all our actions."[25]

Lee was at the peak of his career when Congress ordered him, on August 8, to return to New York. The war was going badly.

Before Lee arrived, Washington suffered a sharp reverse in the Battle of Long Island in late August and was forced to evacuate his position. Many in the American army began comparing Washington's dark defeat with Lee's shining victory in Charleston. Washington's army was then driven from New York City and lower Manhattan. The army retreated to Harlem Heights, where it was exposed on both flanks to envelopment by British amphibious attack, and Congress was directing the commander-in-chief to hold the forts located near the ends of the present George Washington Bridge. More than one American officer looked to Lee's arrival as the only salvation of the army.

When he finally reached New York and saw the situation, Lee responded to it just as he had responded to every new turn in his life—sharply. He wrote to Horatio Gates that he disliked the position of the army and that Congress was a herd of stumbling cattle. Washington, said Lee, was wrong to let the legislators interfere with military strategy.[26]

As at Charleston, Lee seemed to appear just in the nick of time. In a well-executed amphibious operation, Howe landed most of his force on the north shore of Long Island Sound on October 12, threatening Washington's left flank and rear. Lee took command in that sector on the fourteenth. Tench Tilghman, one of Washington's aides, described the effect: "You ask if General Lee is in Health and our people feel bold? I answer both in the affirmative. His appearance among us has not contributed a little to the latter." [27] The troops in Lee's command fought a skillful delaying action, Howe co-operated by not pressing too hard, and Washington was able to extricate his army from Manhattan and march safely to White Plains.

As soon as Lee joined Washington at White Plains, the two generals reconnoitered the lines together. Lee saw serious flaws in the position and recommended a movement northward to the next ridgeline. Washington agreed, but immediately received a report that British troops were preparing for an attack. There was no time to deploy, and Washington could only alert his command and tell his generals, rather lamely, "do the best you can." [28] Their best was not good enough to hold a faulty position, and the American army was again driven back.

There was a lull in the fighting in early November until Howe suddenly turned southward to swoop down upon the American garrison at Fort Washington, which had been left as a pocket in the British rear on upper Manhattan. When Washington was sure that Howe had left White Plains, he crossed the Hudson with all the troops who came from states south of that river, leaving Lee with about 7,500 New Yorkers and New Englanders on the east side. From that day—November 12—there was never again a meeting of the minds between the two men, and Lee's career began its downward run.

It may well be that their minds had never met at all. When they had first inspected the troops around Boston in June, 1775, both had agreed that the officers as a group were woefully incompetent. But their reports showed a significant difference in evaluating the rank and file. Washington seemed to doubt whether Yankees could ever be good soldiers; ". . . an exceeding dirty and nasty people," he wrote to Lund Washington, and to Richard Henry Lee he described "an unaccountable kind of stupidity in the lower class of these people." [29] Nothing comparable is to be found in Lee's correspondence.

Lee explained in one letter that British officers were fatally underestimating Yankee soldiers as a result of the French and Indian War. In that conflict, "the regulars attributed to a difference of materials in their men what, in fact, ought to have been attributed solely to ignorance of method." [30] This letter to Edmund Burke was admittedly propaganda, but his reports to Benjamin Rush can be trusted. In one of them, he stated his belief in a close connection, not separation, between military and civil affairs: "Duke Ferdinand," who reportedly had criticized the failure to assault the British garrison inside Boston, "is beyond dispute a very great soldier," wrote Lee. "But if he is at the same time a Philosopher he wou'd not dictate the same measure to different Troops—if the Army before Boston had been Russians, Boston must have been ours . . . but They are not Russians

. . . the men (as I observ'd before) are excellent materials. . . .
Our new Army will I hope and believe be good." [31] The military
virtues of a free people were different in kind from those of a
peasant army, he observed, and military organization and tactics
had to take account of the differences. Among the American
troops, Lee had doubts only about the southern soldier because
Virginians and Carolinians seemed not quite ready for republicanism; but even on this point he had soon changed his mind.[32]

Nearly every step taken by Lee as general in the American
army had shown a consciousness of the political aspects of the
war. He was obsessed with the idea of maintaining the morale
of his men and creating the proper attitude among the civilian
population. He even capitalized upon his own eccentric behavior
in order to gain these ends. Whether recommending that a pro-
American Jesuit be sent to the army in Canada, or suggesting
that unarmed Virginians be trained in the use of spears, Lee constantly emphasized the psychological aspects of warfare.[33] Washington, on the other hand, was far more in tune with the
mid-eighteenth-century concept of warfare—an era in which
war and society were carefully separated and the soldier fought
primarily because he was more afraid to disobey than to die.
Washington and Lee looked at the same troops, but where the
Virginia planter saw only surliness and disobedience, the British
radical saw alertness and zeal.

If the war had not gone badly, perhaps the divergence of their
views never would have been of any consequence. During the
first year of the Revolution, when the two men played comple-
mentary rather than clashing roles, their assignments were nicely
suited to their respective attitudes. But Lee's success and rising
reputation, coupled with Washington's record of failure from
August to November, were bound to bring a change. Relations
between the two had remained friendly, and Lee's barbs had been
aimed only at Congressional interference with Washington. It
is likely, however, that the incident on the lines at White Plains
in late October had shaken Lee's confidence in his commander.

By the end of November, it is certain that this confidence was destroyed.

On November 16, Lee expressed an opinion which he directed to Joseph Reed, Washington's adjutant general: "I cannot conceive what circumstances give to Fort Washington so great a degree of value and importance as to counterbalance the probability or almost certainty of losing 1400 of our best Troops." [34] Washington had decided not to evacuate Fort Washington when Nathanael Greene convinced him that the fort was defensible, and that the troops could be withdrawn across the river whenever necessary. Greene was soon proved wrong on both points. On the day that Lee wrote his letter to Reed, Howe assaulted the fort, capturing not 1,400 but 3,000 men, and inflicted one of the worst American defeats of the Revolution. Several years later, Washington confessed there had been "warfare in my mind and hesitation which ended in the loss of the Garrison." [35] Lee, when he heard the news, by all accounts went wild. Someone told Benjamin Rush that he cried out in anger and grief, ". . . had it been called Fort Lee, it would have been evacuated long ago." [36] His first letter to Rush after the loss was certainly indiscreet, though a close reading reveals the principal target of his wrath was Congress, not Washington.

Before Lee could recover from this shock, he learned that the garrison of Fort Lee, on the New Jersey side, had almost been surprised by a similar attack. Washington at this time was known to be fleeing across the Hackensack River. On the heels of this news Lee received an incredible letter from Joseph Reed, dated November 21: "I do not mean to flatter," wrote Washington's most trusted staff officer, "nor praise you at the Expence of any other, but I confess I do think that it is entirely owing to you that this Army & the Liberties of America so far as they are depending on it are not totally cut off. You have Decision, a Quality often wanting in Minds otherwise valuable. . . ." [37] There was more in the same vein, including the hint that Reed was speaking for the whole army. It is hardly surprising that Lee, upon reading these words, lost his equilibrium, never to regain it.

From the time he received Reed's letter until his capture by the British on December 13, Lee was no longer the subordinate ready to give unquestioning obedience to his commander.

The events of Washington's retreat across New Jersey are usually treated as the prelude to the Trenton–Princeton campaign—the most brilliant stroke of his military career. In this context, Lee's failure to join him becomes just one more gloomy aspect of a situation so dismal that it provoked Thomas Paine to begin a pamphlet with the words, "These are the times that try men's souls." It is as difficult to quarrel with success as it is with some traditional ideas about George Washington. But the traditional view does less than justice to the actual course of events.

After the fall of the Hudson forts, Washington repeatedly urged Lee to move west of the river and join him, although the wording of these orders was more or less equivocal. The truth is that Lee did not want to move, and he used every possible excuse to delay. Some of the excuses seemed good ones: enlistments throughout the American army expired at the end of the year, but Lee's troops, unlike Washington's, would be marching farther from home rather than closer to it. Lee was afraid, with reason, that his army would simply fall apart. It was winter, many of the men were sick and some were literally naked, and there seemed little chance to find adequate shelter on the other side of the Hudson. Washington's retreat was along the main road between New York and Philadelphia, but Lee would have to follow a longer and rougher route and perhaps expose his army to capture. Was Washington's order militarily sound? He justified it by expressing fear that Howe's objective was Philadelphia; Lee disagreed, and thought that Howe wanted no more than to clear East Jersey for use as winter quarters. We know now that Lee was right in his estimate, Washington wrong.[38] The excuses make an impressive list, but the fact remains that Lee disobeyed.

Lee had never before allowed obstacles to stand in his way when he thought some course of action was necessary. In fact, he took pleasure in overcoming such obstacles. In this case, the explanation is that he considered the orders given by Washington not only unnecessary but unwise. When Washington scuttled back across New Jersey, resistance in the state collapsed. British observers were delighted by the submissiveness of the inhabitants, loyalists came out of hiding everywhere, and there were even reports of Tory militia units rounding up known "rebels." Washington himself knew why this had happened; he had written to Lee that the people of New Jersey "will expect the Continental Army to give what support they can, or failing in this, will cease to depend upon or support a force, from which no protection is giv'n to them." [39] But the need to maintain popular support by protecting people and property, and the need to keep a Continental army intact and united, had become conflicting demands on American strategy. It was obvious to Washington that, however painful the choice, the army was more important than the people if the war were to be won. To Lee, it was not at all obvious. He had a different conception of what to do with a revolutionary war on the brink of failure, and being no longer willing to trust Washington's judgment, he intended to be guided by that conception. Lee meant, as he so incautiously phrased it, to commit a "brave, virtuous kind of treason," and "to reconquer . . . the Jerseys." [40]

His plan for doing so, from all indications, was based on the use of militia forces. The militia was the last line of local defense. When militiamen did not fight to defend their locality or at least to make existence there dangerous for small bodies of the enemy, then the rest of the people were sure to submit, hoping for gentler treatment at the hands of the British and Germans in return for good behavior. But militiamen would not automatically spring to arms in time of danger. They were afraid. They lacked the confidence that comes with training and experience, and their companies and regiments were much too small to fight without help. Militiamen had to be encouraged, they had to be organized, and they had to be supported by Continental troops until there were enough active militia units to support one another. Lee would co-operate with Washington, but he would do so by creating zones of resistance that could deny General Howe the fruits of his recent victories. As the end of the year approached and one-year soldiers prepared to go home, Washington damned the militia and called on Congress for a professional army of long-service volunteers.[41] Lee was doing the opposite. Forget long-service enlistment, he wrote Benjamin Rush, and get soldiers on any terms you can. Draft every seventh man from the militia, Lee begged James Bowdoin of Massachusetts, and he praised a "people" who had "virtue enough to . . . oblige every citizen to serve in his turn as a soldier." [42]

Lee knew on November 21 that he was supposed to join Washington. From his camp north of White Plains, he could have had his whole command across the Hudson at Peekskill no later than November 26. He actually completed the crossing nine days later, on December 5. He was at Morristown, about fifty miles away from the crossing, on December 8—not an unreasonable rate of march for men "so destitute of shoes that the blood left on the rugged frozen ground, in many places, marked the route they had taken." [43] The delay east of the Hudson had been used to re-enlist soldiers, to clear upper Westchester of Tories and irregulars like Robert Rogers and his "Queen's Rangers," and to give Massachusetts and Connecticut time to replace the departing Continentals with militia. As Lee moved through New Jersey, he arrested Tories and called out the militia. He established a base for the militia in the Morristown area. Some successful raids were conducted and the New York militia under George Clinton started moving to join him. Northern New Jersey began to present a considerably different picture from the one Washington had seen as he retreated south to the Delaware leaving the state to the mercy of the British.

Three times—on December 3, 5, and 7—Washington sent messengers to find Lee. There can be no doubt that the commander-in-chief was exasperated by the tardiness of his subordinate. But there was once good evidence, of which only traces remain, that Washington was not sure himself of just what he should do next. Unfortunately, the letters have disappeared that could prove this indecision beyond a doubt. On December 3, Lee wrote a reply to accompany the messenger sent by Washington on December 5. In his letter, Lee said he had learned that Washington was "considerably reinforced," and he referred to "your Excellency's idea of surprising [New] Brunswick." If such a letter was sent to Lee with the messenger on December 5, it no longer exists. The implication that Washington had proposed or agreed to some plan of raids on the British flanks and rear is borne out by a second letter from Lee, on December 8. The third messenger, sent by Washington the day before, had just arrived, and Lee expressed surprise that his information about reinforcements had been wrong. Lee then wrote: "Your last letters proposing a plan of surprises and forced marches convinced me that there was no danger of your being obliged to pass the Delaware; in consequence of which proposals I have put myself in a position the most convenient to cooperate with you by attacking their rear."

Lee had referred to "letters" from Washington. These may have been the letters of December 2 and 3, which Washington said he wrote but which no longer exist, or the letter of December 5, if there ever was one. Likewise the letter sent by the messenger on December 7 is not to be found. But the internal evidence is unmistakable; some or all of these missing letters must have presented to Lee an image of a commander still unsure and wavering between alternatives.[44]

None of this, of course, can excuse Lee. After he received the peremptory order on December 8 to make haste, he remained near Morristown. In his last letter to Washington before his capture, he revealed himself in the final sentences: "The Militia in this part of the Province seem sanguine. If they could be assured of an army remaining amongst 'em, I believe they would raise a considerable number."[45] Apparently he had tried to swing Washington around to his view, and failing, he was ready to disobey. On December 12, he unwisely accepted an invitation to stay at an inn at Baskingridge, several miles from his camp. That night, he complained about Washington to his old comrade, Horatio Gates: ". . . *entre nous*, a certain great man is most damnably deficient— He has thrown me into a situation where I have my choice of difficulties—if I stay in this Province I risk myself and Army and if I do not stay the Province is lost for ever." [46]

The next morning Lee was taken prisoner by a patrol of British cavalry. Ironically, he was captured by members of a unit he had once commanded in Portugal. For a time, there was danger that he would be hanged as a British officer waging war on his King. Instead, he was finally exchanged in April, 1778. Had he been put to death, he probably would have gone down in history as one of America's heroes.

But it was not to be. In the mid-nineteenth century, a document was found, unquestionably in Lee's handwriting, dated March 29, 1777, in the family papers of one of the British commissioners then in New York. It called into question Lee's whole career in the Revolution because it was a plan to end the war. The document began by expressing concern for continued bloodshed on both sides. It then proposed that British sea power be used to support an army controlling a line from the upper Chesapeake Bay to Narragansett Bay, or Alexandria–Annapolis–Philadelphia–New York–Newport. Such a deployment was supposed to rally the Tories, to "unhinge and dissolve the whole system of defence," and to end the war two months after its execution.

The discoverer of the plan believed it proved Lee's treason. His chief biographer, however, is of the opinion that it was intended to trick Howe into his fruitless expedition to Philadelphia in 1777.[47] Curiously enough no reference to the plan has ever been found in any other contemporary document. But Lee's recommendations to Congress after his release were based on a similar analysis of the strategic situation, so there is little room to doubt its authenticity. The plan itself seemed sound, though rather ambitious for the forces available to Howe. It was characteristic of Lee to argue that encouragement and protection of loyalists were the true keys to pacifying America. From the American point of view, the plan was fairly humane, for it proposed no raids or harsh policies. One can only guess why Lee wrote it: to save his neck, to mislead Howe, to strike at Washington, perhaps simply to become a participant again instead of a bystander—it would have been perfectly in character for Lee to do such a thing.

Upon his release, Lee had another plan ready, this one for Washington and Congress. In it, he proposed a reformation of army organization and tactics, and analyzed the strategic choices for the campaign of 1778. His discussion of tactics and organization showed that his ideas had not changed. He stressed the value of simplicity and the need for American warfare to fit the American genius. "If the Americans are servilely kept to the European Plan," he wrote, "they will make an Awkward Figure, be laugh'd at as a bad Army by their Enemy, and defeated in every Rencontre which depends on Manoeuvres." The exact meaning of these ideas became clearer when he discussed strategy. He believed that it was madness to think of fighting British regulars on their own terms; to do so would be to forsake the natural advantages of the American position. The idea "that a Decisive Action in fair Ground may be risqued is talking Nonsense." Instead, "a plan of Defense, harassing and impeding can alone Succeed." If necessary, the Americans could base their operations on the rough country west of the Susquehanna, where British regulars would not dare penetrate. In short, Lee had driven his earlier thinking toward its logical conclusion, and was proposing a war waged along guerrilla lines.[48]

Nothing could have been further from Washington's mind. Throughout the winter and spring at Valley Forge, he and Steuben had planned and trained the army according to the "European Plan," as Lee had put it. Steuben has often been quoted on the difference between Europeans and Americans as soldiers, but if he learned to explain to Americans why they were being trained, it was only to shape them better to the conventional European form of tactics. It is likely, in fact, that Lee's plan was aimed directly at Steuben's program, for Lee had hardly arrived in the American camp when he succeeded in having Steuben's powers as inspector general curtailed.[49]

Lee, however, could arouse little interest in his own plan. Both in Congress and among the senior officers of the army, he had gained a following among those men who disliked Washington or doubted his ability. But their preference for Lee was a matter of personalities rather than military theories. If any of them fully understood Lee's military arguments, they probably were puzzled or dubious. Although they preferred Lee, they lacked his radical perceptions, and they must have been attracted more by the promise of an army composed at last of *real* soldiers, able to fight redcoats and Germans in the open field. During his year in New York, the war seemed to have moved beyond Charles Lee.

Washington received Lee warmly, but may not have been altogether happy to have him back. By this time Washington had learned of the disloyal letters exchanged by Lee and Joseph Reed. Because of illness and a desire to visit Congress, Lee did not join the army until May 20. Sir Henry Clinton, who had succeeded Howe, sat in Philadelphia with the bulk of the British forces. The crucial questions for Washington were: when and where would Clinton move, and what should the American army do once the British began to march? Lee had been back on duty less than a month when, on June 18, Clinton evacuated Philadelphia, crossed the Delaware, and began marching across New Jersey toward New York City. Within a few hours, the American vanguard under Lee's command had begun to move from Valley Forge on a parallel course.

The events of the next ten days were complicated and remain controversial.[50] Washington twice called a council of war, on June 17 and 24, both of which revealed that he and his generals were torn between two desires: one was to fight; the other, not to get hurt. Most wanted some "partial attack," but all agreed that a "general action" was to be avoided. The key issue was whether a "partial attack" would necessarily entail a "general action." [51]

Lee advised caution, and for the record, most of the council went along with him. But Wayne, Lafayette, Greene, Knox, and certainly the young aide, Alexander Hamilton, wanted to strike a blow before Clinton reached New York. Hamilton described

the council of war at Hopewell, New Jersey, on the twenty-
fourth, as doing "honor to the most honorab[le] body of midwives and to them only." [52] No one was completely happy with
the compromise that was reached. When Washington decided to
detach 1,500 men from his 10,000 to harass the British flank and
rear, the detachment seemed either too large or too small.

Lee, at first, declined the command of the force. But then
Washington decided to send another 1,000 and to put Lafayette
in charge of all detached forces—over 4,000 Continentals and
1,000 New Jersey militia. At this point, Lee asserted his right as
senior major general and asked for the command because it now
included almost half the army. Washington agreed, and on
June 27 Lee caught up with his troops around Englishtown.

Six miles east, at Freehold, lay the flank of the British column,
stretching four miles along the road to Sandy Hook. The weather
continued suffocatingly hot. Lee had argued against any action
east of Princeton, down in the lowland where British cavalry
superiority could prove decisive. Even Hamilton, so ardent for
battle, suddenly feared that the main body, at Cranbury ten
miles west of Englishtown, was not close enough to support the
vanguard effectively. But now it was too late. On the twenty-
seventh, Washington ordered Lee to attack the British rearguard
over terrain that neither general had reconnoitered.

The approach to Freehold from Englishtown was along a road
that ran on the high ground between two branches of swampy,
westward-flowing Wemrock Brook.[53] In order to reach the British flank, Lee had to pass three ravines, created by the brook and
its tributaries, that crossed the American axis of advance. The
plan was to wait until the British column was on the march. But
conflicting reports about British movements caused some confusion as Lee's command got under way from Englishtown early
on the morning of the twenty-eighth. Soon after, the leading
American units made contact with the British beyond the far-
thest, or eastern, ravine. Lee ordered Wayne to the front with reinforcements and told him to keep the enemy engaged. The
action was on the left, with Freehold and the roads through it

on the American right flank. The British were marching away toward the northeast. Lee meant to send most of his remaining troops behind and to the left of Wayne, thus cutting off and enveloping Clinton's rearguard, which Wayne had pinned down. But Clinton, to whom the attack was no surprise, anticipated the American maneuver. He held Wayne with minimum forces, halted the rearmost of the two British divisions and sent it back down the road through Freehold against the American right.

The action took on a pinwheel pattern, with Clinton, able to use the road, outracing Lee, who had to cross rough, wooded, and boggy ground. The American general, Charles Scott, who led the first element following Wayne, ran into Wayne in the woods instead of going behind and to Wayne's left. Neither Scott nor Wayne seemed to understand Lee's concept of the operation, and in the rapidly changing situation the system of mounted aides carrying messages merely added to the confusion. Lee was forced to order troops to Scott's right, toward Freehold, and placed Lafayette in charge of them. As Lafayette advanced and then fell back before the returning British division, Scott watched from across the 1,000-yard gap that separated him from Lafayette. Afraid that he was going to be cut off when he saw the American troops moving rapidly back toward Freehold, Scott began moving his own men to the rear without orders and without informing Lee. Wayne soon followed.

Once the American half of the pinwheel had ceased to turn, a large part of Lee's command was in danger of being cut off. It might be trapped against one of the ravines and wiped out. With most of his force now marching instead of fighting, Lee had to move all of his units across the middle ravine and take up a defensible position. He gave the necessary orders, but in the noise and confusion he was unable to contact his scattered subordinates. At this point Washington arrived on the scene, and he and the hot and exhausted Lee exchanged some sharp words. The day ended better than the Americans deserved. They finally retreated to a strong position on the westernmost ravine and fought off repeated British attacks. Washington could claim a victory, but it was a soldier's victory; none of the senior commanders—Scott, Wayne, Lafayette, Lee, or Washington—had performed with distinction. Clinton smiled at the American claim. From his point of view, the British had conducted a model rearguard action.[54]

Without doubt, Washington's sharp words precipitated Lee's ruin. Lee had reached the end of his patience: his advice on strategy had been rejected; his opinion in council was ignored; and while he was in the process of saving the army from a defeat he had foreseen, he was insulted. This was too much! Lee wrote to Washington, demanding an explanation of the treatment accorded him. He had not been dealt with fairly, he claimed. No doubt, he said, Washington's behavior had been "instigated by some of those dirty earwigs who will forever insinuate themselves near persons in high office." Washington replied that Lee would be given an opportunity to clear or hang himself. Lee fired back a letter referring to the "tinsel dignity" of Washington's office. In a third letter, Lee demanded a court-martial. His wish was soon granted.[55]

Lee was tried on three charges: disobedience of orders by not attacking; "making an unnecessary, disorderly, and shameful retreat"; and disrespect toward the commander-in-chief. No one who carefully reads the record of trial, examines the ground, and considers the British side of the battle would find Lee guilty of the first two charges. But no one who reads his letters to Washington will believe him innocent of the third. Under the circumstances an acquittal on the first two charges would have been a vote of no-confidence in Washington. Lee was convicted on all counts, with the wording of the second charge considerably softened. He was given the absurd sentence of suspension from command for one year.

The rest of the story is not pretty. Lee and his friends lobbied in Congress to disapprove the findings of the court-martial. A number of delegates must have squirmed, as did Gouverneur Morris when he wrote to Washington: "General Lee's Affair hangs by the Eye Lids. . . . Granting him guilty of all the

Charges it is too light a Punishment. And if he is not guilty . . .
there would be an Injustice in [delegates] not declaring their
Opinion." John Laurens expressed his fear to Alexander Hamilton that "the *old faction*," meaning Richard Henry Lee and Sam
Adams, might recruit a majority in Charles Lee's favor. But
Benjamin Rush was soon complaining that delegates had begun
to "talk of *state necessity* and of making justice yield in some
cases to policy." The sentence was confirmed, though the vote
was surprisingly close.[56]

Lee retired to his Virginia farm and vented his spleen for the
rest of his life. He was subsequently dismissed from the army for
a disrespectful letter to Congress and had to fight a duel with
John Laurens for his public attacks on Washington. To Lee and
his few remaining intimates, Alexander Hamilton was "the son
of a bitch" who had been out to ruin him and who had perjured
himself at the trial.[57]

Lee's few remaining years were rather pathetic ones. He lived
in quarters that were more like a barn than a house. There was
no glass in the windows, and the rooms were marked out by chalk
lines on the floor. In a pitiful letter to his sister, he recalled being
asked years ago when he would stop wandering, and reminded
her of his reply—". . . whenever I could find a Country where
power was in righteous hands." He felt further from his goal
than ever, and concluded, "I may be a pilgrim to all eternity." [58]
And so he was. Not long before his death in 1782, he was busily
drawing up Utopian plans for a military colony in the West.

The contribution of Charles Lee to the Revolution was substantial, though perhaps difficult to measure. His services should
not be minimized in the light of what finally happened to his
career. As the partisan Rush recalled, "He was useful in the beginning of the war by inspiring our citizens with military ideas
and lessening in our soldiers their superstitious fear of the valor
and discipline of the British army." [59] At a glance, this would
seem to contradict the judgment of Alexander Graydon: ". . . if
he committed a fault it was because he was too respectful of the
enemy; and that he was too scientific, too much of a rea-

soner . . ." [60] But Graydon's statement contains the link between these two views of Lee: ". . . too much of a reasoner." Intellectual that he was, Lee tried to see the Revolution as a consistent whole, with every aspect in rational harmony with every other. It was a fight by free men for their natural rights. Neither the fighters nor the cause were suited to the military techniques of despotism —the linear tactics, the rigid discipline, the long enlistments, the strict separation of the army from civic life that marked Frederick's Prussia. Lee envisioned a popular war of mass resistance, a war based on military service as an obligation of citizenship. He sought a war that would use the new light-infantry tactics already in vogue among the military avant-garde of Europe, the same tactics the free men at Lexington and Concord had instinctively employed.[61] Such men could not be successfully hammered into goose-stepping automatons and made to fire by platoons, but properly trained and employed, they could not be defeated. Here lay the solution to any apparent contradiction in his opinion of American soldiers as against British regulars.

Nathanael Greene's campaign in the South, and, on a far larger scale, the early campaigns of the French Revolutionary War, were to confirm Lee's prophetic insight.[62] But to Washington—a practical man not given to theorizing—this was all madness. He never seriously considered resorting to a war of guerrilla bands drawn from the militia. He would have recoiled with horror from such an idea.[63] Such strategy would change the war for independence into a genuine civil war with all its grisly attendants—ambush, reprisal, counterreprisal. It would tear the fabric of American life to pieces. It might even undermine the political process, and throw power to a junta—a committee of public safety with a Lee, not a Washington, as its military member.

Historians have often noted that the American Revolution was a "conservative" revolution, with surprising stability of institutions and continuity of leadership. But few have noticed that it was also militarily conservative, and that its conventional strategy served as a buffer for American society and politics. If

Washington's strategy had failed, as it almost did in 1776, then the Revolution would have collapsed or turned sharply leftward. Charles Lee was one who, by his alienation from the world to which other men were adjusted, could dimly see the full range of possibilities. He might then have had a chance to translate his vision into reality. Probably the true blessing of his unhappy career is that he never got the chance.

FOOTNOTES

1. John R. Alden, *General Charles Lee, Traitor or Patriot?* (Baton Rouge, 1951).
2. There are three hints, all of which are susceptible to other interpretations. One is in a letter to his sister, December 23, 1763, *Lee Papers, New York Historical Society Collections*, 1871–74, I, 48; hereinafter referred to as *Lee Papers*. Another is in a letter about Lee when he was staying at Lucca, during his return from the second journey to Poland; it is quoted in a note by Alden, *op. cit.*, p. 317, n. 15. The third is the attempt by his first biographer, Edward Langworthy, to prove that Lee liked women, rumors to the contrary notwithstanding; in *Lee Papers*, IV, 163–64.
3. The description is borrowed from Eric Hoffer, *The True Believer* (New York, 1951).
4. Douglas Southall Freeman, *George Washington* (New York, 1948–57), especially Vols. IV and V.
5. Lee to Sidney Lee, March 28, 1772, *Lee Papers*, I, 110.
6. See Lee to Washington, May 9, 1776, *ibid.*, II, 12, for an indication that Lee was on Braddock's march with Washington.
7. Lee to George Colman (the elder), May 8, 1769, *Lee Papers*, I, 81–82.
8. He mentioned a proposed visit to Silesia to see a Prussian military review in a letter from Warsaw to the Earl of Charlemont, June 1, 1765, *ibid.*, 41. His view of the French and Indian War is best expressed in his influential pamphlet, *Strictures on . . . A "Friendly Address to All Reasonable Americans . . ."* (Philadelphia, 1774), in *Lee Papers*, I, 162.
9. The three commanders were Loudoun, Abercromby, and Amherst. For the encounter with the King, see Horace Walpole, *Last Journals* (London, 1910), I, 404–05.
10. Lee to Sidney Lee, March 28, 1772, *Lee Papers*, I, 111.
11. In particular, see the letters of John Adams in Edmund C. Burnett,

ed., *Letters of Members of the Continental Congress* (Washington, D.C., 1921–36), I, 136–37; hereinafter, Burnett, *Letters.*

12. James Warren to Sam Adams, July 9, 1775, in William V. Wells, *The Life and Public Services of Samuel Adams* (Boston, 1866), II, 316.

13. Lee to Sullivan, July 24, 1775, *Lee Papers,* I, 199. Historians usually credit Washington or Sullivan with the movement forward to Ploughed Hill, but contemporary accounts describe it as Lee's action. See the *Virginia Gazette,* October 21, 1775, and *The Magazine of American History,* VIII (1882), 125.

14. George W. Greene, *The Life of Nathanael Greene* (New York, 1867), I, 131; Thompson to his brother, September 10, 1775, in William T. Read, *The Life and Correspondence of George Read* (Philadelphia, 1870), 112.

15. John Adams to Lee, February 19, 1776, *Lee Papers,* I, 312.

16. For a sympathetic eye-witness account of Lee's effect in Newport, see Franklin B. Dexter, ed., *The Literary Diary of Ezra Stiles* (New York, 1901), I, 646–47.

17. Letters expressing his attitude during these months are in *Lee Papers,* I, 233 ff. Curtis Nettels, *George Washington and American Independence* (Boston, 1951), describes the problems of this period and puts Lee's activity in proper perspective.

18. For the politics of this resolution, see Burnett, *Letters,* I, 329, 339, 354, 389, 405, and 408.

19. To John Augustine Washington, March 31, 1776, in John C. Fitzpatrick, ed., *The Writings of George Washington* (Washington, D.C., 1931–44), IV, 450–51. All quotations from Washington's letters are from the Fitzpatrick edition unless otherwise noted. This work is referred to hereinafter as Washington, *Writings.* Lee's question was asked in a letter to Robert Morris, January 23, 1776, *Lee Papers,* I, 255.

20. Lee to Washington, February 19, 1776, *ibid.,* 309.

21. See Eric Robson, "The Expedition to the Southern Colonies, 1775–1776," *English Historical Review,* LXVI (1951), 535–60, for the British side.

22. Lee to Washington, July 1, 1776, *Lee Papers,* II, 100–03.

23. Lee to Moultrie, July 7, 1776, *ibid.,* 126.

24. John Drayton, *Memoirs of the American Revolution* (Charleston, 1821), II, 313 and 280 ff.

25. William Moultrie, *Memoirs of the American Revolution* (New York, 1802), I, 141.

26. Lee to Gates, October 14, 1776, *Lee Papers,* II, 261–62.

27. Tilghman to Duer, October 17, 1776, quoted in Henry P. Johnston,

The Campaign of 1776 Around New York and Brooklyn (New York, 1878), p. 271. See also note on p. 270.

28. The incident is recounted by Major General William Heath, who was not sympathetic to Lee in general, in Rufus R. Wilson, ed., *Heath's Memoirs of the American War* (New York, 1904), pp. 87–88; hereinafter Heath, *Memoirs*.

29. Washington to Lund Washington, August 20, and to Richard Henry Lee, August 29, 1775, Washington, *Writings*, III, 433 and 450.

30. Lee to Burke, December 16, 1774, *Lee Papers*, I, 147.

31. Lee to Rush, November 13, 1775, *ibid.*, 216.

32. Lee to Rush, October 10, 1775, *ibid.*, 212.

33. *Ibid.*, 332, and 417–18.

34. *Ibid.*, II, 283.

35. Washington to Reed, August 22, 1779, Washington, *Writings*, XVI, 152.

36. Rush to John Adams, September 21, 1805, in Lyman H. Butterfield, ed., *Letters of Benjamin Rush* (Princeton, 1951), II, 906; hereinafter, *Letters of Rush*.

37. Reed to Lee, November 21, 1776, *Lee Papers*, II, 293–94.

38. Howe to Germain, November 30, 1776, in Peter Force, ed., *American Archives*, 4th series (Washington, D.C., 1837–53), V, 926.

39. Washington to Lee, November 21, 1776, *Lee Papers*, II, 296.

40. His words about "treason" were used in another connection to James Bowdoin, November 22, 1776, *ibid.*, 303, but they do indicate his state of mind. He wrote of reconquering New Jersey to Heath, December 9, 1776, *ibid.*, 340.

41. See Freeman, *op. cit.*, IV, 232–90.

42. Lee to Rush, November 20, 1776, and to Bowdoin, November 30, 1776, *Lee Papers*, II, 289 and 324.

43. Heath, *Memoirs*, 107.

44. The sequence of letters, and the indications that some letters are missing, are found in *Lee Papers*, II, 326–44, and Washington, *Writings*, VI, 318–42. For further evidence that Washington was neither quite as desperate in early December nor as certain about what Lee should do as tradition suggests, see the letters in Greene, *op. cit.*, I, 280–85.

45. Lee to Washington, December 11, 1776, *Lee Papers*, II, 345.

46. Lee to Gates, December 12/13, 1776, *ibid.*, 348.

47. The document is printed in *Lee Papers*, II, 361–66. It is discussed by George H. Moore, *The Treason of Charles Lee* (New York, 1860); in *Lee Papers*, IV, 335–427; and by Alden, *op. cit.*, pp. 174–79.

48. "A Plan for the Formation of the American Army . . . [April, 1778]," *Lee Papers*, II, 383–89.
49. Alexander Hamilton to Elias Boudinot, July 26, 1778, in Harold C. Syrett and Jacob E. Cooke, eds., *The Papers of Alexander Hamilton* (New York, 1961–), I, 528–29; hereinafter, *Hamilton Papers*.
50. There is no satisfactory account of the Monmouth campaign. What follows is based on the record of Lee's court-martial except where noted (*Lee Papers*, III, 1–208) and on several visits to the ground itself.
51. Nathanael Greene best expressed the optimistic view of the American strategic dilemma to George Washington, June 24, 1778, quoted in Theodore Thayer, *Nathanael Greene, Strategist of the American Revolution* (New York, 1960), p. 244. Greene wrote: "People expect something from us. . . . I think we can make a partial attack without suffering them to bring us to a general action."
52. Hamilton to Boudinot, July 5, 1778, *Hamilton Papers*, I, 510.
53. Every published sketch map of the battle of Monmouth that I know of is misleading and inaccurate. The best one, surprisingly, is in Jared Sparks, ed., *The Writings of George Washington* (Boston, 1834–37), V, 430. William S. Stryker, *The Battle of Monmouth*, William S. Myers, ed. (Princeton, 1927), makes no attempt to plot the battle graphically. The most important contemporary map is reproduced in Louis Gottschalk, *Lafayette Joins the American Army* (Chicago, 1937), p. 222.
54. William B. Willcox, ed., *The American Rebellion; Sir Henry Clinton's Narrative of His Campaigns, 1775–1782* (New Haven, 1954), pp. 91–98. Clinton, who did not like Lee, thought Lee had been unjustly treated.
55. The letters are in *Lee Papers*, II, 435–38.
56. Morris to Washington, October 26, 1778, Burnett, *Letters*, III, 465; Laurens to Hamilton, December 5, 1778, *Hamilton Papers*, I, 593; Rush to William Gordon, December 10, 1778, *Letters of Rush*, I, 220; Alden *op. cit.*, pp. 253–54.
57. The epithet was used by Major John Eustace, Lee's aide; Eustace to Lee, November 23, 1779, *Lee Papers*, III, 394.
58. Lee to Sidney Lee, December 11, 1781, *ibid.*, 464–65.
59. Benjamin Rush, *Autobiography*, George W. Corner, ed. (Princeton, 1948), pp. 155–56.
60. Alexander Graydon, *Memoirs of a Life* (Edinburgh, 1822), pp. 337–39.
61. Lee had expressed keen interest in light infantry to Sidney Lee,

March 1, 1761, *Lee Papers*, I, 29. For the rapidly growing European interest in light infantry tactics and partisan warfare at this time, see Max Jähns, *Geschichte der Kriegswissenschaften* (Munich and Leipzig, 1889–91), III, 2710–20.

62. For a brilliant account of the military revolution that accompanied the political revolutions of the late eighteenth century, see Robert R. Palmer, "Frederick the Great, Guibert, Bülow: From Dynastic to National War," in Edward M. Earle, ed., *Makers of Modern Strategy* (Princeton, 1941), pp. 49–74.

63. Marcus Cunliffe, *George Washington: Man and Monument* (Boston, 1958), in the third chapter of his book was the first to develop the idea of Washington as a military conservative.

BIBLIOGRAPHY

Alden, John R., *Charles Lee, Traitor or Patriot?* Baton Rouge, 1951. The thorough, sympathetic study that Lee deserves.

Bunbury, Sir Henry, "Memoirs of Charles Lee," in *The Life and Correspondence of Sir Thomas Hanmer*. London, 1838. A brief account, inferior to Langworthy's, but containing some information not available elsewhere because Sir Henry was a maternal second cousin to Lee.

Fiske, John, "Charles Lee, The Soldier of Fortune," in *Essays Historical and Literary*, 2 vols. New York, 1902, I, 55–98. Fiske, a great popularizer of American history, built his unfavorable interpretation of Lee on Moore's essay; probably Lee's reputation will never recover.

Langworthy, Edward, *Memoirs of the Life of the Late Charles Lee, Esq.* London, 1792. The first biography of Lee, by an admiring Georgian who, as a delegate to Congress, voted to disapprove the findings of the court-martial.

Lee Papers, 4 vols. *New York Historical Society Collections*, 1871–74. New York, 1872–75. Unusually important because of the subsequent loss of many of the originals. The works by Langworthy, Bunbury, Sparks, and Moore, listed here, are conveniently reprinted in Volume IV.

Moore, George H., *The Treason of Charles Lee*. New York, 1860. Not a biography, but a tract using the recently discovered Plan of March, 1777, in an uncritical way to prove Lee a traitor.

Patterson, Samuel W., *Knight Errant of Liberty: The Triumph and Tragedy of General Charles Lee*. New York, 1958. The latest biography, but comparable to Alden's only in its sympathy for its subject.

Sparks, Jared, *Life of Charles Lee*. Boston, 1846. Although Sparks has a
bad reputation as an uncritical admirer of George Washington, his
life of Lee shows careful research and balanced judgment on Washington's worst enemy.

Philip Schuyler:

THE GENERAL AS ARISTOCRAT

———•———

JOHN H. G. PELL

Long Island University

PHILIP SCHUYLER enjoyed George Washington's friendship, high regard, and complete loyalty as did few other generals in the Continental army. Some commanders, like Gates and Lee, started out as trusted colleagues, but soon fell from Washington's favor. Others, like Putnam and Sullivan, were given important positions by the commander-in-chief, but were found lacking in ability. Schuyler, however, remained in the esteem of his fellow aristocrat, Washington, throughout the entire war.

Washington and Schuyler first met on May 15, 1775, when Schuyler arrived to attend the Second Continental Congress in Philadelphia. The two men took an instant liking to one another because they had so much in common: both were in their early forties; both had been large landowners; and both had acquired managerial experience in running huge estates—Schuyler in New York and Washington in Virginia. The similarities did not end there. Both men had been amateur soldiers of long standing prior to 1775. They had served in the French and Indian War, enduring the rigors of frontier campaigning, learning the ways of the colonial militia, and fighting alongside British regulars. Both men were also political leaders in their communities, having served in their respective provincial assemblies. It was little won-

der, then, that they became fast friends and remained close for
the rest of their lives.

Philip Schuyler was born in Albany on November 11, 1733,
the eldest son of Johannes and Cornelia Van Cortlandt Schuyler.
The Schuylers, one of the great landed families in upper New
York, were generally regarded as the first family in Albany in
terms of wealth, social standing, and political prestige. To say
that Schuyler was born with a silver spoon in his mouth was, if
anything, an understatement.

As befitted a member of the Dutch aristocracy, he received a
fine education. At the age of fifteen, he was sent to New Ro-
chelle to study under a talented minister of the French Protestant
Church. He soon mastered the French language and became so
proficient in mathematics that in later years he corresponded
with David Rittenhouse, the famed astronomer, about the mathematics of astronomy. Besides his formal education, Schuyler
learned to converse in the tongue of the Mohawk Indians after
taking numerous trading trips into the wilderness of western
New York.

By the time Schuyler was twenty, he was tall—as tall as
George Washington—thin, with aquiline features, brown eyes,
and reddish brown hair. He was powerfully built and had the
commanding presence required of a good soldier. Despite his fine
physique, he was rarely in excellent health. He kept suffering
attacks of rheumatic gout—a disease that dogged him throughout his entire life.

When the French and Indian War broke out, Schuyler was
commissioned a captain, in 1755, and raised a company of militia
to join General William Johnson's expedition against Crown
Point. The campaign got underway in late August, and Schuyler
had his first taste of combat in a skirmish against the French at
Lake George on September 8, 1755. Because of his knowledge of
French, the young captain was assigned the duty of escorting
prisoners back to Albany. While he was at home, Schuyler
took advantage of a brief furlough to marry Catherine Van
Rensselaer, the talented daughter of Colonel Johannes Van Rens-

selaer of Greenbush. Within a few weeks after his wedding, however, the new bridegroom was back at Fort Edward trying to build up a depot of military stores.

In the spring of 1756, Schuyler served under Colonel John Bradstreet on an expedition to carry provisions to Oswego. This meant traveling almost due west from Albany mostly by canoe up the Mohawk River, through Lake Oneida, down the Oswego River into Lake Ontario. During this campaign Schuyler learned a great deal about transporting men and supplies by canoe and bateau through wilderness waterways. Although he resigned his commission the following year, he continued to supply provisions to the army and earned a substantial income.

Schuyler returned to the military service in 1758, this time as deputy commissary. He was with General James Abercromby when the ill-fated attempt was made to take Ticonderoga in early July. This disaster was counterbalanced by the capture of Fort Frontenac in late August, during which Schuyler served under Colonel Bradstreet. Both campaigns provided Schuyler with an opportunity to learn more about military organization and the problems of logistics.

He served the following year when another army gathered at Albany, under the leadership of General Sir Jeffrey Amherst. Schuyler's logistical talents by now were widely known, and during this expedition he was employed for the most part at Albany in collecting and forwarding supplies to the army. Occasionally he made trips to the forts on the frontier. On one of these visits, Schuyler met Paul Revere, who presented him with a beautifully inscribed rum horn.[1]

Altogether Schuyler participated in four major campaigns during the French and Indian War. He had ample opportunity to study at first hand the problems of feeding, housing, and transporting supplies to troops stationed on the New York frontier. This experience was to prove valuable, for the future general was to face similar situations in the same region during the Revolutionary War.

The year 1763 marked not only the close of the French and

Indian War but the final settlement of the estate of Philip Schuyler's father. Schuyler inherited thousands of acres in the Mohawk Valley and along the Hudson River. From his Uncle Philip's estate he received even more land in the Saratoga patent and the old Schuyler homestead near West Troy. The Saratoga patent was to become Schuyler's favorite area of all his estates. He conducted lumbering operations there, developed water power for his sawmills and gristmills, maintained a small fleet of vessels on the Hudson for trading purposes, and leased a group of small farms to tenants.

Successful in business, Schuyler soon began to take a serious interest in politics. In 1768, he was elected to the Assembly and quickly became identified with those who were hostile to Parliament's interference with colonial commerce and industry. He sat in the Assembly for the next seven years. Although he never openly sympathized with the radicals among New York's Sons of Liberty, Schuyler constantly fought against the pro-British faction in the colony—the DeLancey–Colden coalition.

In January, 1775, Schuyler introduced a motion in the Assembly calling for repeal of the recent acts of Parliament for raising a revenue in America, extending the admiralty courts, and depriving American subjects of trial by jury. The resolution was adopted and sent as a petition to the King. It was forwarded to Edmund Burke, who was then serving as colonial agent for New York in England.

When the New York delegates were named to the Second Continental Congress, Schuyler was among those appointed. By the time Congress convened in Philadelphia in May, 1775, fighting had already broken out at Lexington and Concord. In forming an army to fight the British, Congress asked the New York Provincial Congress that an officer be nominated to command the American troops in that province. The answer was not long in coming:

> Courage, prudence, readiness in expedients, nice perception, sound judgment, and great attention, these are a few of the natural qual-

ities which appear to us to be proper. To these ought to be added an extensive acquaintance with the sciences, particularly the various branches of mathematical knowledge, long practise in the military arts, and above all a knowledge of mankind. On a general in America, fortune also should bestow her gifts that he may rather communicate lustre to his dignities than receive it and that his country, his property, his kindred and connections, may have sure pledges that he will faithfully perform the duties of his high office and readily lay down his power when the general weal requires it. Since we cannot do all that we wish, we will go as far towards it as we can. And therefore you will not be surprised to hear that we are unanimous in the choice of Colonel Philip Schuyler.[2]

Acting upon this recommendation, Congress appointed Schuyler as one of the four major generals under Washington on June 19, 1775.

Washington and Schuyler left Philadelphia together and rode toward New York City. After remaining in New York for a few days, Washington continued on his way to Cambridge. Before leaving, however, he handed Schuyler his orders:

You are to take upon you the command of all the troops destined for the New York department and see that the orders of the Continental Congress are carried into execution, with as much precision as possible. . . . Your own good common sense must govern you in all matters not particularly pointed out as I do not wish to circumscribe you within narrow limits.[3]

Thus, Schuyler became commander of what came to be called the Northern Department and commandant of the Northern army.

Schuyler spent the next few weeks in New York City organizing supply lines and recruiting troops to strengthen the garrisons at Ticonderoga and Crown Point. These two northern outposts constituted New York's first line of defense. The British forces in Canada under the command of Sir Guy Carleton were stationed at three places—St. Johns, the principal British stronghold between Lake Champlain and the St. Lawrence River, Montreal, and Quebec. Realizing that if Carleton invaded New York he would sail down Lake Champlain, Schuyler began build-

ing an American fleet. The same craft that were built to defend
against a British invasion might also be employed to transport
troops to the north if the Americans decided to mount an offensive against Canada.

Schuyler left New York City early in July and traveled north
in order to be present as the building of the fleet got underway.
Upon reaching Lake George, he was shocked at the lack of discipline and vigilance shown by the troops guarding the area:

> About ten o'clock last night I arrived at the landing place, at the
> north end of *Lake George,* a post occupied by a captain and one
> hundred men . . . the whole guard, like the first, in the soundest
> sleep. With a penknife only I could have cut off both guards. . . .[4]

Despite this discouraging reception, Schuyler quickly went
about putting the American defenses in order. By the end of
July, he was able to report to Washington: "I have now one boat
on the stocks, which I hope will carry near three hundred men;
another is putting up today."[5] Orders were issued to the commanding officers at Crown Point and Fort George warning them
to exercise greater vigilance in guarding their posts.[6]

In the weeks that followed, Schuyler showed many of the same
qualities of organization and planning in building up the defenses on Lake Champlain that had enabled him to become such
a success in civilian life as a businessman. Soldiers were sent into
the forests to fell choice timbers for building boats and making
oars. A field hospital was organized to care for the sick and
wounded. Schuyler also located a powder mill on the Hudson
and proceeded to make arrangements to have powder shipped up
the river to Albany and thence to Ticonderoga. His correspondence for this period was filled with requests for carpenters, tools,
pitch, oakum, nails, rope, and numerous other items required for
building sailing vessels.

At the same time, Schuyler kept up a constant stream of correspondence with Washington, the New York Provincial Congress, and the Continental Congress in Philadelphia. Alarmed

by reports received from the north, the Continental Congress practically granted Schuyler dictatorial powers in mid-July:

> The dispatches from General Schuyler being taken into consideration, *Resolved*, that Gen[era]l Schuyler be empowered to dispose and employ all the troops in the New York department, in such manner as he may think best for the protection and defense of these colonies, the tribes of Indians in friendship and amity with us, and most effectually to promote the general Interest, still pursuing, if in his power, the former orders from this Congress, and subject to the future orders of the commander in chief.[7]

Schuyler then turned his attention to the problem of winning the friendship of the powerful Iroquois Indian tribes in New York. This was not an easy thing to do. The Iroquois had traditionally sided with the British in their wars with the French, and it would be difficult to woo and hold their affections. But Schuyler had been dealing with the Indians since boyhood days and understood the redmen as few whites did. He invited the Indian chiefs to meet him at Albany, and a number of them arrived early in August accompanied by 700 braves. Many of the Indians attended the parley wearing ruffled shirts, Indian moccasins and stockings, and blankets trimmed with silver and wampum.

After a few days of opening festivities, the conference got underway. Before long, Schuyler was able to report to Washington that he had been successful. "[A]pprehensive that we should request them to take arms in our cause, they explicitly declared that it was a family quarrel," he wrote, and that "they would not interfere." [8] Under the circumstances, this settlement was the best that could be expected. The treaty cleared the way for the major military operation in northern New York which the Americans had planned.

Congress for some time had been proposing an invasion of Canada with the hope of inducing a fourteenth colony to revolt. Schuyler, along with his energetic second in command, Brigadier General Richard Montgomery, were ordered to seize any points in Canada vital to the security of the colonies. Launching an ex-

pedition from Crown Point, Montgomery went north in the
direction of St. Johns in August, with Schuyler following on
his heels. At about the same time, a second small army led by
Benedict Arnold set out from Massachusetts to march through
the Maine woods to meet the force from New York at Quebec.
If the two armies succeeded in linking up at Quebec, Arnold
was instructed that "in case of a union with General Schuyler
you are by no means to consider yourself as upon a separate and
independent command but are to put yourself under him and
follow his directions." [9]

Schuyler and Montgomery advanced toward St. Johns during
the early days of September. After reaching their objective, the
Americans retired a few miles south and laid siege to the British
garrison.[10] At this point Schuyler fell sick and was forced to
return to Ticonderoga, leaving the Northern army under the
command of Montgomery.[11]

What appeared at first to be a misfortune for the Americans
in losing their ranking officer soon proved to be a blessing.
Schuyler's skillful handling of supply problems from Ticonderoga prevented a complete collapse of the Northern army
from starvation. As Montgomery wrote to his superior officer
from "Camp South Side St. Johns" a few weeks later: "Your
diligence and foresight have saved us from the difficulties that
threatened us; we are no longer afraid of starving. . . ." [12]

Although his condition improved, Schuyler decided to remain
at Ticonderoga. It was well that he did, for the flow of supplies
to Montgomery's force might have ceased from sheer neglect.
As he noted in one letter:

> Near a thousand barrels of provisions lay exposed to the weather at
> Lake George and such was the laziness of the scoundrels that in
> twenty two days preceding my arrival here they had not brought
> over more than they have since done in six. The same negligence
> had prevailed in building batteaux at this place. I have been under
> the necessity of employing the blacksmiths in making nails. In
> short, I am as crusty as an old woman at all this rascality.[13]

Schuyler could not stand the inefficiency of the undisciplined soldiers under his command and wrote to Washington: "If Job had been a General in my situation, his memory had not been so famous for patience." [14]

Montgomery, a brilliant and resourceful officer, went on to capture St. Johns and Montreal in quick succession, but lost his life in a futile attempt to take Quebec on December 30, 1775. With the failure to capture Quebec, the Canadian offensive came to a halt and the Americans could only maintain a weak cordon around the city throughout the rest of the winter. Although Schuyler had not been present during most of the campaign, the failure of the Canadian offensive discredited the New York general with many of the New Englanders. Behind this antagonism lay the sectional jealousies between Yankees and Yorkers that had been evident all along in the Northern army. Most New Englanders disliked Schuyler because he had supported New York's land claims in a boundary dispute between Massachusetts, New Hampshire, and New York over the region that was later to be the state of Vermont. Moreover, Schuyler's haughty ways and aristocratic airs did not set well with Yankee troops, who entertained more democratic ideas.

Despite his waning popularity, Schuyler continued to serve the army stranded in Canada to the best of his ability. He divided his time between Ticonderoga and Albany doing what he could to help the beleaguered troops. By keeping the lines of supply open, he was able to send them food, supplies and reinforcements. When Congress appointed commissioners to evaluate the political situation in Canada, Schuyler entertained them and provided vital information.[15] By this time it was clear that Canada was irretrievably lost and that the remnants of the army before Quebec would have to retreat back to New York.

Congress sent out a succession of new commanders to head the forces in Canada. The first was Brigadier General John Thomas, who decided to raise the siege against Quebec in May, 1776. When Thomas died of smallpox, Brigadier General John Sullivan, a New Hampshire lawyer, was named commander. Then, in June,

1776, Congress appointed Horatio Gates as head of the retreating
army. This last appointment touched off a bitter dispute between
Gates and Schuyler as to just who was in command of the
Northern Department. Congress had left the matter vague by
stating that Gates was to command those forces stationed in
Canada, but making no mention of what was to happen once the
troops reached American soil. The two generals quarreled constantly, since each had some basis for his claim.

During the last days of June, Schuyler and Gates began meeting in Albany to plot the future strategy of the army. Realizing
that the command of Lake Champlain was the key to the strategic situation, Schuyler wrote to General Sullivan, who was
still in command of the retreating American army at the time:
"By keeping a naval superiority on the lake we shall be able to
prevent the enemy from penetrating into the inhabited part of
these colonies . . ." [16]

Sullivan by this time had retreated farther southward down
Lake Champlain and had encamped his army at Crown Point, a
few miles north of Ticonderoga. Schuyler, accompanied by Gates
and Benedict Arnold, met him there early in July and reviewed
the remnants of the exhausted army. After a council of war was
held on July 6, the army was ordered to retreat even farther, to
Ticonderoga and Mount Independence on the opposite shore of
Lake Champlain.

In Philadelphia, Congress became increasingly aware of the
delicate situation that had arisen regarding the command of the
Northern Department. The army in Canada no longer existed
as a separate entity, and on July 8, Congress resolved:

> . . . that General Gates be informed, that it was the intention of
> Congress to give him the command of the troops whilst in Canada,
> but had no design to vest him with a superior command to General
> Schuyler.[17]

Thus the issue between the two jealous generals was settled for
the time being.

Through the summer and fall of 1776, the generals worked in

harmony. This was fortunate for the Americans because a British army led by Sir Guy Carleton had started to move south from Canada to invade New York at that time. Dividing their duties, the American commanders made preparations to stop Carleton. Schuyler, maintaining his headquarters at Albany for the most part, sought to recruit some militia to throw against the invaders. Gates took command of the field forces inside the fortress at Ticonderoga. Benedict Arnold was put in charge of building the fleet at Skenesborough.

Carleton in the meantime halted his advance to build a British fleet at the northern end of Lake Champlain. On October 11, 1776, the American fleet commanded by Benedict Arnold engaged the British fleet off Valcour Island. Although Arnold's fleet was destroyed, it served its purpose—the British had delayed so long in building their own naval force that Carleton was forced to return to Canada because winter was coming. Schuyler's role in turning back this first major British invasion from the north was an important one: he had suggested the strategy of maintaining naval superiority on Lake Champlain and had begun building the fleet that made it necessary for the British to stop and construct one of their own.

Despite the fact that his efforts had been successful, Schuyler continued to be harassed by New Englanders. In the course of the summer campaign he had ordered Crown Point evacuated on the grounds that the post was too weak to be held. Some of the officers at Crown Point, all of whom were Yankees, signed a remonstrance declaring that the abandonment of the post would leave Lake Champlain open to the enemy and expose the New England colonies to an invasion. Washington also expressed his disapproval of the removal of the troops from the fort. Indignant that his judgment had been questioned, Schuyler demanded a court of inquiry into his conduct of the campaign. When his request was not met, he submitted a letter of resignation in mid-September. Congress, however, refused to accept his resignation and sent him assurances of respect and appreciation.

In the spring of 1777, Schuyler was attacked again by New

Englanders—this time by the Yankee delegation in Congress. As a result of two flimsy charges brought against him, Schuyler was reprimanded by the Congress. In March, 1777, he was actually deprived of his command of the Northern army and Gates was put in charge. Two months later, the legislators reversed themselves and reinstated Schuyler.

Throughout these ordeals, Schuyler continued to do the best he could for the Northern army with the slim resources available to him. In the spring of 1777, he even went so far as to furnish some of his own funds to buy food for the troops. Since Gates and Arnold had departed, Schuyler sent his most able field officer, Major General Arthur St. Clair, to Ticonderoga to take command of the fort and garrison there. After looking the situation over, St. Clair wrote back: "If the enemy intend to attack us, I assure you, sir, we are very ill-prepared to receive them. The whole amount of Continental troops, fit for duty is one thousand five hundred and seventy-six . . . we cannot reckon upon more than twenty-two hundred men . . ." [18]

Schuyler also sent scouts into Canada to try to find out what the enemy were doing. On their return, on June 10, 1777, he wrote to General Washington: "Last evening two Canadians who had been sent into Canada returned . . I cannot believe that there are so many troops in Canada as they report nor do I believe that General Burgoyne was there on the 10th of May." [19] Unfortunately the report was all too true General Burgoyne with a force of British and German soldiers was scheduled to leave Three Rivers in May to launch the second major British invasion from the north.

Schuyler proceeded to Ticonderoga because it was here that the Northern army was expected to make its stand. The fortress, described as the "American Gibraltar," was assumed to be an unassailable citadel. But Schuyler's report on its condition was gloomy:

> I was in hopes to have found the post in a better state of defense than it is . . . I was very disagreeably disappointed to find the

troops at Ticonderoga so miserably clad and armed . . . many are literally barefooted and most of them ragged . . . the huts built last campaign . . . consumed in the course of the winter . . . as fire wood . . . the enemy cannot be ignorant how very difficult if not impossible it will be for them to penetrate to Albany unless in losing Ticonderoga we should lose not only all our cannon but most of the army designed for this department.[20]

After determining the situation at Ticonderoga, Schuyler returned to Fort George to gather provisions and to make certain that his supply lines were in good working order. A brief time later, he was at Saratoga, writing to Pierre Van Cortlandt, president of the New York Provincial Congress: "Having brought affairs at Tyconderoga in some better train than I found them I left the necessary directions for carrying on the work . . . St. Clair . . . does not imagine they mean a serious attack on Tyconderoga." [21]

St. Clair was mistaken. General Burgoyne arrived before Ticonderoga on July 3 with a splendidly equipped army of more than 7,000 men. St. Clair had only 3,000. On July 5, he held a council of war and decided to evacuate Ticonderoga.[22] Burgoyne had hauled heavy artillery to the summit of Sugar Loaf Hill, about a mile from the fortress, and was in a position to bombard it.

Schuyler was amazed to learn that St. Clair had withdrawn from Ticonderoga. He knew that the fortress had been insufficiently manned, but the thought that it would be abandoned without a fight simply had not occurred to him. When he wrote to Washington, he communicated the bare facts of the evacuation and nothing more.[23] Unaccompanied by any explanation, the news of the fall of Ticonderoga spread throughout the country and Schuyler soon found himself subjected to severe criticism. In New England and elsewhere, he was accused of treachery for presumably delivering the fortress over to the enemy.

Although discouraged by this turn of events, Schuyler continued his efforts to halt Burgoyne's advance. He established his headquarters at Fort Edward, a strategic location on the upper

Hudson. From this post he could command both the main routes leading south from Ticonderoga: one by Lake Champlain, Skenesborough, and Wood Creek; the other by Lake George and the Hudson. When Burgoyne decided upon the former route, Schuyler made ready to stop him at Fort Anne some fifteen miles north of Fort Edward.

Writing to Colonel Long, commander of Fort Anne, Schuyler urged him, on July 7, to make a stand: "I have sent a detachment to your assistance with some ammunition and doubt not but it will be well expended. . . . I expect General Nixon with a Brigade tomorrow or next day. I hope when General St. Clair and General Nixon and the other troops from below arrive that we shall be able to do a little more than merely keep them at Bay." [24] But two days later, Schuyler had to report to Washington: "The enemy followed the troops that came to Skenesboro as far as Fort Ann where they were yesterday repulsed notwithstanding which Col. Long contrary to my express orders evacuated that post. . . . I am here at the head of a handful of men not above fifteen hundred without provisions. . . ." [25]

Burgoyne had advanced from Canada to Skenesborough at the southern end of Lake Champlain—a distance of nearly one hundred and fifty miles—in a few weeks. It was to take him a full month to advance the few miles from Skenesborough to a position south of Fort Edward. It was this month—from July 7 to August 7—that ultimately cost him the campaign. If Schuyler was not Washington's equal as a great military leader or Arnold's equal as a dashing field officer, he was the perfect commander for a delaying operation. He did everything in his power to slow down Burgoyne's progress. Trees were chopped down across the wagon tracks the British were to use. Bridges were removed or destroyed. Huge boulders were rolled into Wood Creek, diverting its waters across Burgoyne's route. Cattle were driven off and crops put to the torch to deny the enemy any food. Although Burgoyne's main column was not attacked, his advance parties were harassed unmercifully.

While slowing down Burgoyne's army, Schuyler made every

effort to build up his own forces. Most of St. Clair's Continentals who had retreated from Ticonderoga were soon able to join him. Washington sent a brigade under General John Nixon to Schuyler's support.[26] Even some of the local militia were persuaded to turn out to fight. The shock of losing Ticonderoga soon began to wear off in Schuyler's army. "The troops are recovering their spirits," he wrote, "[and] mine were never better." [27]

Schuyler's strategy was to impede the British advance and to permit the new levies of militia that were being raised to harass Burgoyne with guerrilla warfare.[28] His commanders actually were ordered to retreat before the British, taking care to destroy any bridges so that pursuit would be impossible.[29] But before Schuyler's plans could be put into effect, Congress decided to relieve him of his command.[30] The loss of Ticonderoga had shaken the faith of the legislators in Schuyler's generalship.

Washington begged to be excused when it came to naming Schuyler's successor.[31] He believed that under the circumstances Schuyler could not have defended Ticonderoga successfully and that St. Clair had reached the right decision in abandoning the fortress to save his men. Despite Washington's views, however, the congressmen were determined to change commanders. On August 4, they named Horatio Gates to supersede Schuyler.[32]

While Schuyler was still in command of the Northern army, Burgoyne's invasion plans were dealt two serious blows. The first occurred when Burgoyne, desperate for food supplies, decided to send a diversionary expedition to Bennington where the Americans were said to have assembled stores of grain and beef cattle. Two German contingents led by Lieutenant Colonel Baum and Colonel Breymann were defeated sharply by Brigadier General John Stark and Colonel Seth Warner. In this repulse alone, Burgoyne lost almost 10 per cent of his entire force, and Colonel Baum, an experienced and excellent officer, was killed.

The second setback took place well to the west of the Hudson River Valley. While Burgoyne was driving south from Canada, another task force of about 1,800 men, made up mostly of loyal-

ists and Indians, advanced eastward from Lake Ontario intending
to join up with the British general at Albany. Led by Lieutenant
Colonel Barry St. Leger, this force marched down the Mohawk
Valley until it reached Fort Schuyler. There the American garrison put up a stout defense and St. Leger was forced to place the
fort under siege. Learning of the garrison's plight, Schuyler sent
off a relief expedition under Benedict Arnold. When the siege was
raised, St. Leger abandoned his efforts to reach Albany and
turned back to Lake Ontario. These three parts of Schuyler's
strategy—delaying the advance of Burgoyne's main army, protecting the Northern army's eastward flank in the vicinity of
Bennington, reinforcing and rescuing the garrison of Fort Schuyler to the westward—all were successful, but they occurred just
prior to Gates's assumption of command. As Nathanael Greene
wrote: "This Gentleman is a mere child of fortune. The Foundation of all Northern Successes was laid long before his arrival
there!" [33]

The people of Albany remained loyal to their leading citizen,
even though his military career had suffered an eclipse. Upon
Schuyler's return to the community, they addressed a memorial
to him expressing their gratitude in the following words:

> . . . our warmest thanks, are justly your due, for having so eminently
> distinguished yourself in the preservation of the remains of our
> small and dispersed Army; by collecting them together, and effect-
> ing their safe retreat from Fort Edward, to their present Encamp-
> ment near Half Moon, without loss of men, Artillery, Baggage, or
> Stores, and . . . in defiance of the most strenuous efforts of a vastly
> superior Army, greatly elated by their easy acquisition of the For-
> tress of Ticonderoga.[34]

Schuyler was relieved of command of the Northern army on
August 19, 1777; almost two months later to the day, Burgoyne
surrendered to Gates. There can be little doubt that much of the
credit for the defeat of Burgoyne's expedition belongs to
Schuyler. He had delayed and harassed Burgoyne's army with a
force that was one-third of the size of the enemy's, lured the foe

far from the main base of supplies in Canada, and denied the
British any opportunity of replenishing their dwindling food
supplies. Moreover, it was largely due to Schuyler's efforts that
New York had been able to garrison the fort in the Mohawk
Valley to oppose the sweep of the British right wing under St.
Leger. But it was Gates, not Schuyler, who was destined to reap
the fruits of all these labors.

After his retirement to Albany, Schuyler was kept informed
of the course of events by his friends in the Northern army.
When the British surrendered, he made a trip to Saratoga and
was introduced to Burgoyne and other enemy generals. Despite
the fact that Burgoyne's troops had destroyed his fine country
house during the course of military operations, Schuyler greeted
the British general graciously and offered him the hospitality of
his home in Albany. He was equally kind to the families of the
vanquished enemy. Madame Riedesel, wife of the German general, left this interesting account of her first meeting with
Schuyler:

> I confess that I feared to come into the enemy's camp, as the thing
> was so entirely new to me. When I approached the tents, a noble-
> looking man came toward me, took the children out of the wagon,
> embraced and kissed them, and then with tears in his eyes helped
> me also to alight. "You tremble," said he to me, "fear nothing."
> "No," replied I, "for you are so kind, and have been so tender toward
> my children, that it has inspired me with courage." He then led me
> to the tent of General Gates, with whom I found Generals Burgoyne
> and Phillips, who were upon an extremely friendly footing with
> him. . . . The man, who had received me so kindly, came up and
> said to me, "It may be embarrassing to you to dine with all these
> gentlemen; come now with your children into my tent, where I
> will give you, it is true, a frugal meal, but one that will be accom-
> panied by the best of wishes." "You are certainly," answered I, "a
> husband and father, since you show me so much kindness." I then
> learned that he was the American General Schuyler.[35]

Madame Riedesel and Burgoyne accepted Schuyler's invitation
to spend some time with him at his home in Albany. There they

were received in a friendly manner and shown every mark of
respect. Even General Burgoyne was deeply moved by this magnanimity, and remarked to General Schuyler, "Is it to me, who
have done you so much injury that you show so much kindness!"
"That is the fate of war," replied the New Yorker, "let us say
no more about it."

Schuyler's concern with military affairs continued long after
he lost command of the Northern army. He was plagued by the
persistent rumors that he had been disloyal in losing the fortress
at Ticonderoga.[36] To clear himself of these charges Schuyler
insisted upon a court of inquiry into his conduct of the campaign. Although the Continental Congress was reluctant to hold
such a court-martial, Schuyler remained adamant, claiming that
he would not feel free until he had a hearing.[37]

The charge that Schuyler had responded to enemy efforts to
win him over has gained credence among historians after the discovery of certain data revealed by Major John Ackland a British
army officer. Ackland, who was attached to Burgoyne's staff,
accompanied the British general to Schuyler's residence in Albany. When Burgoyne departed for Boston, Ackland remained
with the Schuylers along with his beautiful wife, Lady Harriet,
who was pregnant.[38] Eventually an exchange was arranged for
Ackland so that he could take Lady Harriet to New York and
from there back to England. Early in January, 1778, with the
arrangements completed, Schuyler sent the couple to New York
in one of his sleighs.

Sir Henry Clinton, commander of the British garrison in New
York, closely questioned Ackland about Schuyler's views. Ackland revealed that in his conversations with Schuyler the American general did not appear to favor the break with Great
Britain. If the British would abandon their policy of taxation
without representation and would not insist upon unconditional
surrender by the Americans, Schuyler was said to be ready for
some kind of settlement between the two sides.

Sir Henry remembered these conversations and nearly eight
years later—in 1785—wrote a memorandum on the subject:

Among others of the Saratoga Convention army who came in to see me was Major Ackland who informed me that he had had many conversations with L.S. that he was certain he was a staunch friend to Government; and that he was authorized by him to open a correspondence between us; that he wished me to settle a cipher and said he had his authority to declare if the Commissioners would promise on their part that taxation would be given up and unconditional submission not insisted upon, he would join Government with all his force.[39]

In 1793, Sir Henry wrote a second memorandum:

General Schuyler was the Person. His motives were interested. In the first place till Ticonderoga was taken Burgoyne could not advance. It was the wish of Schuyler that he might because the Vermonters his bitter Enemys and who claim the greatest part of his Estates, would in that case be obliged to disclose themselves, if they joined the Kings troops, Schuyler would have been hearty with the Americans; if on the contrary they should oppose the Kings troops Schuyler would certainly take the opposite side for reasons in both cases very obvious. The Vermonters had acquired so much credit with the Americans by their spirited exertions against Burgoyne's army that Schuyler was decided in the part he was to take and thence his proposal to me through Major Ackland . . .[40]

Despite this damaging evidence, the charge of treason against Schuyler does not appear to rest upon a very solid foundation. There are no other scraps of evidence available on this subject, and it is not even clear that the "L.S." referred to in the first memorandum was Schuyler. Since all of the Schuyler estates lay to the west of the Hudson, these lands were not claimed by Vermont as was implied. Finally, there is the dubious credibility of Sir Henry Clinton as a witness. To provide an alibi for the failure of his campaign in America, Clinton actually forged a false order from his superiors and included it in his memoirs after the war—which raises a question of validity regarding everything that Clinton ever wrote.

Schuyler's court-martial was held on October 1, 1778, at the headquarters of Major General Benjamin Lincoln in Pawling,

New York. He was charged with neglect of duty for not being present at Ticonderoga during the crucial weeks prior to the taking of the fortress.[41] Schuyler produced an imposing array of witnesses and letters to show the steps he had taken to strengthen the Ticonderoga defenses.[42] As a result, he was acquitted with honor. The following spring, Schuyler formally resigned his commission as general.

Schuyler, however, continued to serve his country in many ways. He remained a member of the Board of Commissioners on Indian Affairs and advised Washington on the expedition that was sent against the tribes in the Mohawk Valley in 1779. When he went to Congress in 1779 and 1780 as a member of the New York delegation, he used his influence to emphasize the Indian menace along the northern frontier. His intimate knowledge of Indian affairs proved most valuable because many of the members of Congress had not dealt with such matters at first hand.

Although he was no longer in the army, Schuyler rendered great service to General Washington on military matters. During the spring and summer of 1780, he served as chairman of the committee at Washington's headquarters, helping to reorganize the army's staff departments and to devise ways of gaining more effective co-operation with the French forces stationed in America.[43] When Washington suggested that Schuyler accept another position in 1781, the New Yorker replied:

> Your Excellency draws too favorable a conclusion when you suppose me competent to the business of the War Department . . . I cannot suppose that Congress will offer it . . . since I have . . . in writing declared my intention never to hold any office under them unless accompanied with a restoration of my military rank . . .[44]

During July, 1781, General Washington maintained his headquarters at Peekskill, where he could keep an eye on nearby New York City. Contemplating an offensive action against the British garrison there, he turned to his old friend Philip Schuyler to build bateaux to transport troops down the Hudson River.[45]

Although a full-scale attack on the city never materialized, Schuyler built 100 boats at Albany for the army.[46]

Washington's trust in Schuyler was demonstrated once again when he sought the New Yorker's assistance in dealing with the movement that was afoot to make Vermont a British province. When the Continental Congress hesitated to admit the independent Republic of Vermont to the Confederation, General Haldimand of the British army contacted the authorities in Vermont and proposed that they rejoin the empire. Washington decided to keep a close eye on the situation, and he turned to Schuyler for advice. To open correspondence with Thomas Chittenden, the president of Vermont, Washington sent a letter addressed to him through Schuyler. The commander-in-chief asked Schuyler to look the letter over before forwarding it. All these moves were conducted in the greatest secrecy because Washington noted: "I do not wish to have my writing to him publicly known." [47] Eventually the British negotiations with the Vermonters broke down and Haldimand's efforts failed.

After the war had come to a close, Schuyler continued to hold important public offices on the state and national levels. Like many of the great landlords in New York, he supported the movement in favor of the Federal Constitution. Co-operating with his son-in-law, Alexander Hamilton, he worked hard to secure ratification of the Constitution in his state. He went on to represent New York in the first Senate of the United States and became an ardent champion of Hamilton's financial program. After a short term, he was defeated for re-election by Aaron Burr in 1791. Six years later he defeated Burr for the same seat, but was forced to resign because of ill-health in January, 1798.

Schuyler's few remaining years were sad ones. His loyal friend George Washington died. His brilliant son-in-law, Alexander Hamilton, was killed by Aaron Burr in a duel. And his devoted wife Catherine died of apoplexy in 1803. The loss of his wife hastened his own death on November 18, 1804. On the day of his funeral, the *Albany Gazette* reported: "The streets were lined with people, doors and windows were filled and even the house tops were not without spectators to behold the melancholy procession and to pay their last offices of respect to the deceased." [48]

Those who knew Schuyler well appreciated fully his great services to the Continental army. What was his contribution to the cause of American independence? From the beginning of the Revolution to its end, the British Ministry correctly realized that the way to suppress the rebellion was to take possession of the north–south water highway extending from Montreal to New York and thus split the rebellious colonies in two. After 1775, both Montreal and New York were in the possession of the British and the target was, therefore, Albany, lying halfway between. By building a fleet, or rather a series of fleets, on Lake Champlain, Schuyler prevented a British advance in both 1775 and 1776. By obstructing Burgoyne's advance in July and August 1777, he gained valuable time to allow the patriots to assemble the militia forces required to win a victory. When Gates arrived to take command, Burgoyne's troops had been defeated at Bennington and Fort Schuyler, and the balance of power had already turned in favor of the Americans.

A general by force of circumstances rather than by choice, a revolutionary who had more to lose than to gain from change, Schuyler helped to determine the outcome of the war. Burgoyne's surrender at Saratoga has been called the turning point of the war and Schuyler's contribution to that major success entitles him to a place of prominence among the military leaders of the Revolution.

FOOTNOTES

1. The rum horn is included in the Fort Ticonderoga Museum Collection.
2. *Journals of the Provincial Congress, Provincial Convention, Committee of Safety and Council of Safety of the State of New York, 1775–1776–1777*, 2 vols. (Albany, 1842), I, 33.

3. Washington to Schuyler, June 27, 1775, Schuyler Letter Books, LV, No. 1, New York Public Library; hereinafter, N.Y.P.L.

4. Schuyler to Washington, July 18, 1775, Peter Force, ed., *American Archives* (Washington, D.C., 1837–46), 4th series, II, 1686; hereinafter, *American Archives.*

5. Schuyler to Washington, July 31, 1775, Schuyler Letter Books, I, N.Y.P.L.

6. Orders, July 25, 1775, Schuyler MSS, Henry E. Huntington Library, San Marino, California.

7. Worthington Chauncey Ford, ed., *Journals of the Continental Congress,* 35 vols. (Washington, D.C., 1905–22), II, 194.

8. Schuyler to Washington, August 27, 1775, *American Archives,* 4th series, III, 442

9. Washington to Arnold, September 14, 1775, *ibid.,* 766.

10. Schuyler to Washington, September 20, 1775, *ibid.,* 751–52.

11. Schuyler to Montgomery, September 16, 1775, Schuyler Letter Books, I, N.Y.P.L.

12. Montgomery to Schuyler, September 2, 1775, Schuyler MSS, I, N.Y.P.L.

13. Schuyler to Montgomery, September 29, 1775, Schuyler Letter Books, I, N.Y.P.L.

14. Schuyler to Washington, September 26, 1775, *American Archives,* 4th series, III, 808.

15. *Journals of the Continental Congress,* IV, 219.

16. Schuyler to Sullivan, June 28, 1776, Schuyler MSS, Massachusetts Historical Society.

17. *Journals of the Continental Congress,* V, 526.

18. William Henry Smith, *Life and Public Services of Arthur St. Clair,* 2 vols. (Cincinnati, 1882), I, 399–400.

19. Schuyler to Washington, June 10, 1777, Schuyler Letter Books, XX, N.Y.P.L.

20. Schuyler to Congress, June 25, 1777, Schuyler Letter Books, XXI, N.Y.P.L.

21. Schuyler to Van Cortlandt, June 27, 1775, Houghton Library MSS, Harvard University.

22. "St. Clair Court-Martial Proceedings," *Collections of the New York Historical Society for the Year 1880* (New York, 1881), pp. 33–34.

23. John C. Fitzpatrick, ed., *Writings of George Washington,* 39 vols. (Washington, 1931–44), VIII, 377; hereinafter, Washington, *Writings.*

24. Schuyler to Long, July 7, 1777, Schuyler Letter Books, XXV, N.Y.P.L.
25. Schuyler to Washington, July 9, 1777, *ibid.*
26. Schuyler to Washington, July 10, 1777, *ibid.*
27. Schuyler to Tenbroeck, July 10, 1777, *ibid.*
28. Schuyler to Fellows, July 11, 1777, *ibid.*
29. Schuyler to Nixon, July 11, 1777, *ibid.*
30. *Journals of the Continental Congress*, VIII, 596.
31. *Ibid.*, VIII, 603–04.
32. Washington, *Writings*, IX, 11–12.
33. Theodore Thayer, *Nathanael Greene, Strategist of the American Revolution* (New York, 1960), 214.
34. Memorial, Inhabitants of Albany to Schuyler, August, 1777, Schuyler Letters, N.Y.P.L.
35. Baroness Frederika Riedesel, *Letters and Journals relating to the War of the American Revolution and the Capture of the German Troops at Saratoga,* translated from the original German by William L. Stone (Albany, 1867), pp. 134–36.
36. *Journals of the Continental Congress*, IX, 901.
37. Schuyler to President of Congress, November 29, 1777, Schuyler Letter Books, XXII, N.Y.P.L.
38. F. J. Hudleston, *Gentleman Johnny Burgoyne* (Indianapolis, 1927), p. 201.
39. Sir Henry Clinton Memo, 1785, Clinton Papers, William E. Clements Library, Ann Arbor, Michigan.
40. *Ibid.*, 1793.
41. "The Trial of Major General Schuyler, October, 1778," *Collections of the New York Historical Society for the Year 1879* (New York, 1880), p. 26.
42. *Ibid.*, p. 25.
43. Washington to Duane, May 14, 1780, Washington, *Writings*, XVIII, 356–57.
44. Schuyler to Washington, February 25, 1781, Sparks Transcripts, Houghton Library, Harvard University.
45. John Fitzpatrick, ed., *The Diaries of George Washington, 1748–99,* 4 vols. (Boston, 1925), II, 247.
46. *Ibid.*, II, 248.
47. Washington to Schuyler, January 8, 1782, Schuyler MSS, Huntington Library, San Marino, California.
48. *Albany Gazette*, November 22, 1804.

BIBLIOGRAPHY

Lossing, Benson J., *Life and Times of Philip Schuyler*, 2 vols. New York, 1872–73. The oldest but still the best biography of Schuyler.

Mayer, Brantz, ed., *Journal of Charles Carroll of Carrollton, during his Visit to Canada in 1776, as one of the Commissioners from Congress.* Baltimore, 1845. Contains important information for a study of the Canadian expedition of 1776.

New York Historical Society, "The Trial of Major General St. Clair, August, 1778," in *Collections*, 1880. New York, 1881. A valuable document about the surrender of Fort Ticonderoga in July, 1777.

New York Historical Society, "The Trial of Major General Schuyler, October, 1778," in *Collections*, 1879. New York, 1880. The equal of the St. Clair court-martial, as a source on the loss of Fort Ticonderoga in July, 1777.

Nickerson, Hoffman, *The Turning Point of the Revolution: or Burgoyne in America.* Boston & New York, 1928. This is one of the most useful and reliable works on the American Revolution and especially on the Burgoyne campaign of 1777.

Schuyler, George W., *Colonial New York: Philip Schuyler and His Family*, 2 vols. New York, 1885. It is more a work on the history of New York than on Philip Schuyler; has only a small section on him.

Sellers, Charles Coleman, *Benedict Arnold: The Proud Warrior.* New York, 1930. A well done popular biography. It contains good descriptions of the Quebec expedition, Saratoga, and Schuyler at St. Johns. The author is sympathetic toward Schuyler.

Tuckerman, Bayard, *Life of General Philip Schuyler.* New York, 1903. Contains information on Schuyler's military career that cannot be found elsewhere.

Horatio Gates:

PROFESSIONAL SOLDIER

———•———

GEORGE A. BILLIAS

Clark University

THE place of Horatio Gates in American history presents a paradox. By virtue of his victory in the most decisive battle of the war for independence, Gates deserves to be ranked among the founding fathers of the republic. His triumph at Saratoga, which is regarded rightly as one of the crucial battles in American and world history, marked the turning point of the Revolution. A professional soldier among generals who were mostly amateurs, Gates contributed much in molding the Continental army into an effective fighting force. But instead of being remembered with gratitude for his good deeds, Gates has gone down in history as "a weakling, a bungler, and a marplot." He remains a sinister figure in the minds of many Americans. In the words of Allan Nevins, Gates has been made "the whipping boy . . . of the Revolution." [1]

Two American generals, whose reputations lie poles apart, have prevented Gates from taking his proper place among the eminent men of his generation. One was the Revolution's greatest war hero, George Washington; the other, its most infamous traitor, Benedict Arnold. The so-called Conway Cabal—an alleged plot to oust Washington in favor of Gates as head of the Continental army—caused Gates to go down in history as a general who was disloyal to his commander-in-chief. Benedict

Arnold's daring attacks and dashing role at Saratoga led many historians to give Arnold, not Gates, the credit for that important victory. As a result, Gates remains the Revolution's most controversial military figure.

Gates hardly looked the part of a soldier. At the pinnacle of his career at Saratoga, he seemed much older than his fifty years. He was stooped in stature, ruddy-cheeked, had thinning gray hair, and wore spectacles perched precariously on the end of his long nose. Even his conversation was that of an old man, for he had a habit of using homely proverbs to illustrate his points. Little wonder that his men called him "granny Gates."

Appearances can be deceiving, however. This gray-haired, grandfatherly figure was a tough and experienced professional soldier. Military matters were his main concern throughout much of his adult life. He started soldiering at an early age and practiced his profession in two armies for almost a quarter of a century. Prior to accepting a commission in the Continental army, he could boast of fifteen years' service as an officer in the British regulars. When Congress appointed him a general in 1775, no other high-ranking officer, with the possible exception of Charles Lee, had seen more years of active military duty or knew as much about the business of warfare.

Horatio Gates was born the only child of Robert and Dorothea Gates, on July 26, 1727, probably at Maldon, England. Too much has been made of the fact that he sprang from humble origins. It is true that his mother was a housekeeper for the Duke of Leeds, but her occupation helped rather than hurt her son's career. Junior officers in the British army purchased their commissions and as a result such positions usually were acquired by those whose families possessed money and influence. Under ordinary circumstances, one of Gates's low birth would have had little chance of entering the officer class. Because of his mother's association with the Leeds household, however, Horace Walpole offered to become his godfather and namesake.[2] This connection with a prominent family probably helped Gates to gain his first army position. His father, a minor government official, assisted

Horatio's military career by providing the money to purchase
the commission.[3]

Gates left England for an overseas assignment at an early age.
He had barely turned twenty-two when he came to America as
a volunteer with Edward Cornwallis, governor of Nova Scotia.[4]
Stationed in this isolated northern outpost in 1749–50, the
young officer set about learning the ways of garrison life. Cornwallis soon appointed him captain lieutenant in Warburton's
regiment and in 1754 made it possible for him to purchase his
captain's commission.[5] By a strange quirk of fate, Cornwallis
helped to promote the very man who was destined to lead an
American army against the governor's own nephew, Lord
Charles Cornwallis, in the Revolutionary War.

During his stay in Nova Scotia, Gates took two steps that increased his chances for advancement. In 1754 he married Elizabeth Phillips, the eldest daughter of an army officer. Although
her father did not hold high rank, the Phillips family had proper
upper-class connections in England. Elizabeth, moreover, had
been left a little money of her own.[6] But in the long run, his
wife's ambitions may have hindered Horatio's career in the
American army. General Charles Lee once called her "that Me-
dusa . . . [who] governs with a rod of Scorpions." [7] Perhaps
even more damaging to her husband's future was the quarrel
Elizabeth Gates had with Martha Washington.

Gates cultivated also the friendship of General Robert Monckton, lieutenant governor of Annapolis Royal. This gallant and
generous soldier used every opportunity to promote the career of
his protégé. Gates for his part was genuinely fond of the bachelor
general, and named his first and only son, Robert, in Monckton's
honor.

When the French and Indian War broke out, Gates was sent
south to join General Braddock's army in Virginia as captain of
an independent company. He had little chance to gain combat
experience. On his first day under fire, Gates was badly wounded
when a musket ball tore through his body. Braddock's men had
been ambushed by a force of French and Indians who fought

frontier style from behind logs, thickets, and trees. As the red-coats huddled together, the enemy pouring a hail of arrows and lead into their ranks, a lowly private—one Francis Penfold—saved Gates from almost certain death by carrying him to safety from the battlefield. This incident may account for the warmth with which Gates always treated the common soldiers under his command. When he learned that Private Penfold needed help in later years, Gates offered him the hospitality of his home:

> Come and rest your firelock in my chimney corner, and partake with me; while I have my savior Penfold shall not want.[8]

The French and Indian War served as a kind of dress rehearsal in preparing Gates for his role in the Revolution. Fighting against the French afforded him an opportunity to test his talents for military leadership under combat conditions. He also encountered the tactics employed in frontier fighting, traversed some of the same terrain he was to battle upon in later years, saw the colonial militia in action, and gained valuable experience in dealing with the Indians. But his combat experience was limited because he commanded only small units on the lower echelons for the most part.

Gates mastered the details of military administration as well as leading troops into battle. He began serving as brigade major, or military secretary, to one British general—Stanwix—in 1759. When his old friend Monckton became Stanwix's successor in 1760, Gates served him in a similar capacity. The following year General Monckton was appointed governor of New York and brought along his young brigade major to do the desk work.

Toward the close of 1761, Gates sailed with Monckton on an expedition against the French-held island of Martinique in the West Indies. The conquest was carried off with great success. Although Gates took little part in the fighting, he served with such distinction that Monckton commended him to the attention of King George III as a "deserving officer." Selected for the honor of carrying the news of victory back to England, he was rewarded by being commissioned a major in 1762 at the age of thirty-four.[9]

When the war ended, he returned to England only to find that further advancement in the army was practically impossible. His low birth and limited resources, coupled with the fact that the British army was reverting to a peacetime footing, killed his chances for promotion. He became embittered and turned to "guzzling and gaming" for a time. By the mid-1760's, his military career seemed at an end. He was retired from active service in the Royal American Regiment and placed on half-pay. At about the same time, he underwent a religious conversion and began leading a quiet life in the English countryside.

During his years of retirement, Gates maintained an active interest in American political affairs. He had been linked with the Livingston-Whig faction while serving in New York and met many of the budding politicians who later led America down the road to revolution.[10] As the breach between the colonies and mother country widened, he showed his sympathies lay with the patriots.

Gates had acquired a reputation in England as a "red hot republican" by the year 1770.[11] His republicanism probably was motivated in large part by his frustrated ambitions in both social and military circles. As a servant's son living on a meager pension he found it difficult to rise in English society. He was often entertained by the nobility but such contacts only heightened his sense of frustration. He apparently felt that he had no future and that his friends either could not or would not help him.[12]

It was in this mood of dissatisfaction with English class barriers that Gates began to think of moving to the New World. In the spring of 1772, he wrote to George Washington, with whom he had served under Braddock almost twenty years before, to inquire about the possibility of buying an estate in the colonies. He sailed for America that same summer and in 1773 purchased a Virginia plantation which he called appropriately enough "Traveller's Rest." Gates seemed to take the name of his estate to heart; for the next two years he participated little in

public life beyond accepting an honorary commission as lieutenant colonel in the Virginia militia.

The outbreak of the Revolutionary War presented Gates with
a second chance for an active army career. He was too shrewd
an opportunist to pass up the possibilities that the military situation offered to someone with his background and experience.
Though it meant fighting against his former King and country,
he accepted a commission as brigadier general to become the first
adjutant general of the American army. His appointment as
general must have been a source of great satisfaction to Gates,
for it was a rank he could never have hoped to attain in the
British army.

He had a real flair for administration and quickly became
Washington's right-hand man in organizing the new American
army at Cambridge in July, 1775. By writing the first army regulations and maintaining military records, he brought some
semblance of order to the chaotic situation facing the new commander-in-chief. His professional experience enabled him to set
up procedures for recruiting new soldiers and for training older
ones. Efficient, hard-working, and loyal, he was able to relieve his
chief from many time-consuming clerical chores. Washington
was quick to recognize his merits as an administrator, and long
after Gates had left the post of adjutant general, the commander-
in-chief kept trying to persuade him to return.[13]

As a member of Washington's staff, Gates also had an opportunity to voice his views on strategy. The British army was
cooped up inside Boston during the last half of 1775 and hemmed
in on land by a semicircle of American troops. While other generals were suggesting an offensive to drive the besieged British
into the sea, Gates was in favor of remaining on the defensive.
Knowing how touchy the British government was to mounting
military expenses, he proposed to strike a blow at Parliament's
most sensitive spot—the pocketbook. "Boston Dirt will be a
Dollar a Bushell to the English Treasury," he argued. "The
Army, the Fleet, seventy Transports, and an Infinity of Cutters
&c in constant pay." [14] Like most military men in 1775, he

anticipated a short war and counted upon the costs of a stalemate to force Britain to abandon her policy of coercion.

When it became increasingly clear that a prolonged war was in prospect, Gates advocated a strategy based on caution. "Our Business," he wrote early in 1776, "is to Defend the main Chance; to Attack only by Detail; and when a precious advantage Offers." [15] In effect, this was the policy he was to follow during the early years of the war.

Caution was Gates's most outstanding characteristic in tactics as well as strategy. Throughout the siege of Boston, he opposed any rash moves. He voted against Washington's bold scheme for attacking the city across the ice. When a plan was proposed for seizing Dorchester Heights, Gates voted to postpone it.[16] But the majority of Washington's staff disagreed with him and approved the plan that finally resulted in driving the British out of Boston in March, 1776.

Cautious as he was on military matters, Gates found himself among the radicals on the political question of American independence. Few men, except the "brace of Adamses"—John and Sam—were more rabid for independence than this Englishman. Gates chided John Adams for failing to persuade Congress to break with Great Britain early in 1776. For those who wanted to steer a middle-of-the-road course, Gates quoted this couplet:

> The Midd[l]e way, the best, we sometimes call,
> But 'tis in Polliticks no way at all.[17]

Gates's politics had no adverse effects upon his military career, for he was promoted to major general in May, 1776. One month later, his first assignment to command American forces in the field came when he was ordered to take charge of the Northern army retreating from Canada into New York. By the time Gates reached his new command, the army at Crown Point was facing a major crisis.

Disease, desertion, and dissension had shattered the Northern army. Smallpox raged in the ranks and soldiers were dying in great numbers. The militia, discouraged by successive defeats, were melting away. There was a problem of divided command: General Philip Schuyler, a New York Dutch patroon-turned-patriot, claimed, with some justification, that Congress had made *him* head of the Northern army. To make matters worse, an Anglo-German army clad in scarlet and blue led by the capable Sir Guy Carleton was poised to sweep south down Lake Champlain upon the Americans.

Gates already had demonstrated his great gifts as a military organizer while helping Washington form the American army at Cambridge; he showed these same qualities in meeting the threat of this first major British invasion from the north. While Carleton busied himself building a fleet during the summer of 1776, Gates prepared to meet the enemy on both land and water. He began whipping his battered army back into shape and plunged into a shipbuilding race with the British.

Gates's primary success was in restoring the morale of the Northern army and instilling his troops with a fighting spirit. Within weeks after his arrival, one officer wrote: "Generalship is now dealt out . . . by our worthy and well-esteemed General Gates, who is putting the most disordered Army that ever bore the name into a state of regularity and defense." The new-found confidence of the troops was reflected in his next remark: "If our friends in *Canada* . . . will wait a few days, we will give them a very proper reception." [18] Gates himself reported two months later: "The army here are in good spirits and think only of victory." [19]

One way Gates helped to achieve this military miracle was by showing a deep concern for the physical welfare and well-being of his men. Realizing that smallpox posed a greater threat to his troops than the enemy, he bent all of his efforts to combat the disease. Sick soldiers were isolated immediately, the "pernicious practice" of inoculation was halted for fear it might spread the disease, and desperately needed medical supplies were procured.[20] By early September, he could report to the President of Congress: "Thank Heaven, the smallpox is totally eradicated from among us." [21] When the damp climate led to fever and the ague in the army, Gates won the affection of his men by ordering huge bon-fires built and by issuing extra rations of rum.

The army's morale improved also as bickering between the generals diminished. Gates showed admirable restraint in his initial dealings with the difficult Dutchman, Philip Schuyler. After Congress had confirmed Schuyler as head of the Northern Department, Gates took his defeat gracefully and served faith-fully under him for the remainder of the campaign. Although Schuyler was named over-all commander, Gates was put in charge of all the forces in the field at the foot of Lake Champlain.

In preparing his defenses on land, Gates decided with Schuyler that the Northern army should make its main stand at Fort Ticonderoga, the so-called "American Gibraltar." However, when Gates ordered the army to withdraw from the crumbling fortifications at Crown Point, Washington and General Israel Putnam wrote that they disapproved of his decision. Instead of resenting the criticism directed against him, Gates gently chided the proud Putnam, who had helped to build the fort, with this bit of good humor:

> Every fond mother dotes on her booby, be his imperfections
> ever so glaring, and his good qualities ever so few.
> *Crown-Point* was not indeed your immediate offspring,
> but you had a capital hand in rearing the baby . . .
> why should you not be fond of Crown Point? [22]

For all his good-natured bantering, he stoutly refused to order the army back to Crown Point.

Gates also played an important part in preparing the fleet that fought on the waters of Lake Champlain. He personally hand-picked fiery Benedict Arnold to serve as fleet commander.[23] The task of shipbuilding was placed primarily in Arnold's hands, but he could not have accomplished as much as he did without the assistance of his superior. Gates efficiently rounded up skilled ship carpenters to work on the makeshift fleet, sought out seafaring supplies, and recruited seasoned sailors to man some of the craft.

Gates not only helped to create the Champlain fleet—he directed its operations. The fleet operated as his naval arm and the general dictated naval strategy through his orders to Arnold. The cautious Gates conceived the role of his fleet to be a defensive one. In his eyes, it was to serve as a counterweight to the British naval force in opposing the invasion. Gates wrote to Arnold in August warning him to stay near the American end of the lake and to take "no wanton Risk" nor to make any "unnecessary Display of Power." [24]

His instructions went unheeded. Arnold, spoiling for a fight, took matters into his own hands by bringing on an engagement with the British fleet off Valcour Island on October 11–13. Despite a gallant running battle, the British smashed the Champlain fleet, swept the American ships off the lake, and Carleton's army moved down to occupy Crown Point.

Carleton may have won the naval battle, but it cost him the campaign. Valuable time had been lost while he halted his army to build a larger fleet than that of Gates. Even after defeating Arnold, Carleton still had to contend with the second line of American defense—the army inside Fort Ticonderoga. The British general probed the outer works of the rocky fortress but found them too strong to be stormed. His troops were not equipped for a winter campaign and it was too late in the season to begin a siege. There was little else for him to do but re-embark his army in early November and return to Canada.

Gates deserves much credit for turning back Carleton—though historians usually have given all the glory to Arnold. Because of Gates's rare abilities as a military organizer, the Americans were able to mount strong defenses on both land and water. He made a disciplined army out of what had once been a disorganized mob, took up a position at Ticonderoga where the fortifications were more formidable, and blocked the British advance until the approach of winter forced Carleton to retreat. Gates should share the honors with Arnold as builder of the

Champlain fleet and events were to show that his defensive naval strategy was sound. By halting this first British invasion, Gates not only saved the Northern army and Fort Ticonderoga—he also gave the patriots precious time to prepare for the second major British invasion from the north.

Gates remained at Ticonderoga until December, 1776, when he was ordered to march south with troops to reinforce Washington. Had he wished to be disloyal to his commander-in-chief, he had his opportunity at this time. The New York Committee of Safety urged him to disobey Washington's orders and to join his men with those of General Charles Lee. Their plan was to create a separate army independent of Washington's command to fight in the Hudson Highlands. Gates did not hesitate; he continued marching toward Washington and sent one of his aides to turn down the New York proposal.[25]

After a winter commanding troops in Philadelphia, Gates was ordered back to Ticonderoga in March, 1777, to take charge of the forces there. By this time his bitter controversy with Schuyler over the command of the Northern army had broken out into the open again. Both men had their champions in Congress. John and Sam Adams were Gates's strongest backers. Gates tried to lobby in his own behalf, but did his cause more harm than good by losing his temper with members of Congress. The Gates–Schuyler feud reflected little credit on either man, and it brought out the worst side of Gates's nature by showing him to be petty and vindictive where matters of rank and authority were concerned. After shuffling the two commanders back and forth, Congress finally removed Schuyler in favor of Gates in August, 1777.

The immediate cause for Schuyler's removal was the loss of Ticonderoga. While jealous American generals were contesting for command of the Northern army, "Gentleman Johnny" Burgoyne had started his southward drive down the Lake Champlain–Hudson River corridor with the aim of sealing off New England from the rest of the states. The British general scored a stunning surprise victory on July 6, 1777. He occupied a high peak known as Mount Defiance which overlooked Ticonderoga, and pointing his cannon downward, forced the Americans to withdraw from the fortress without a fight.

Gates, who had a keen eye for terrain, had long warned of this threat to Ticonderoga. In 1776, he tried without success to persuade his superior, Schuyler, to occupy the strategic summit. When Gates himself was in command of Ticonderoga the following year, he ordered his engineer, Thaddeus Kosciuszko, to reconnoiter the ground to determine if guns could be dragged to the top of Mount Defiance. Kosciuszko reported that such a move was a distinct possibility. Before Gates could do anything about the problem, however, he had been replaced by Schuyler. Even after he had gone south, Gates kept writing back to point out this flaw in the Ticonderoga defenses. But his warnings were ignored until it was too late.[26]

The Northern army was thoroughly demoralized by the time Gates returned to assume supreme command in mid-August. Spirit and discipline among the troops had deteriorated to the point where one officer described the army as "rabble." "Would to God Gates would arrive," he sighed. The army's mood changed from despair to confidence with startling suddenness once Gates came on the scene. "From this miserable state of despondency and terror," wrote the same officer, "Gates' arrival raised us, as if by magic. We began to hope and then to act." [27]

Gates had an electrifying effect upon the Northern army for a number of reasons. For one thing, he held a high opinion of the New England troops that formed the backbone of his army. Yankee soldiers responded by showing a great affection for this little gray-haired general who came to be known as "the darling of the New Englanders." [28] Gates also earned the respect of his men by sharing with them the rigors of camp life. As Sam Adams noted of Gates, "He . . . has the Art of *gaining the Love of his Soldiers* principally because he is *always present* with them in Fatigue and Danger." [29]

Schuyler, on the other hand, was as much loathed as Gates was loved. In part, this reaction was the result of the sectional

strife that existed between Yankees and Yorkers. But the Dutchman also earned the enmity of his men because he spent much
of his time at his upstate mansion, was haughty and rude to the
common soldier, and was suspected by some Yankees of having
secret dealings with the enemy.[30]

Besides gaining the confidence of his men, Gates restored the
army's effectiveness by insisting upon strict military discipline.
He had already achieved a reputation as an outstanding disciplinarian. While serving as adjutant general, he had introduced
stiff military regulations and was hailed in later years as "the
father of . . . discipline of the American army in 1775." [31] When
he was commander of the Northern army, both friend and foe
testified to Gates's ability in this regard. Benjamin Rush—who
admittedly was anti-Washington—claimed that Gates was a better disciplinarian than the commander-in-chief. "I have heard
several officers who have served under General Gates compare his
army to a well regulated family," he wrote. "These same gentlemen have compared General Washington's imitation of an army
to an unformed mob." [32] Less biased and more meaningful was
the praise from a fellow professional, General Burgoyne, who
inspected Gates's army after his capture at Saratoga and reported
back to his superiors in England: "The standing corps which I
have seen are disciplined. I do not hazard the term; but apply
it to the great fundamental points of military institution, sobriety, subordination, regularity and courage." [33]

Just about the time that Gates took command of the army,
the military situation began to swing slowly in favor of the
Americans. Burgoyne's invasion plans had suffered two serious
setbacks. To the west the British right wing, under veteran
Barry St. Leger, driving down the Mohawk Valley was checked
at Oriskany and eventually began falling back toward Canada.
In the east two lumbering German contingents conducting a
raid for supplies near Bennington were routed by scrappy John
Stark and Seth Warner. Despite these reverses and the slow progress Burgoyne was making because of Schuyler's delaying tactics,

the handsome British general confidently continued his thrust southward toward Albany.

In early September, Gates dealt Burgoyne's plans a sharp blow by a shrewd stroke of propaganda. Swarms of Indians accompanied the British and despite orders to the contrary carried out raids in which women and children were killed. Although the warriors had slain other victims, Gates deliberately chose the case of Jane McCrea to publicize these Indian atrocities. The circumstances surrounding her death could not have been more dramatic, for the comely young woman was killed while waiting to meet her lover. Gates did not allow the fact that she was a Tory sympathizer and her fiancé a Tory officer to stand in the way of making her a patriot martyr.

Weeks after her death, Gates sent a stinging letter of rebuke to Burgoyne filled with sweeping indictments of Indian atrocities with torch and tomahawk. He denounced the British general for hiring "the Savages of America to scalp Europeans and Descendants of Europeans," and accused him of paying "a Price for . . . each Scalp so barbarously taken." Dwelling at some length on the sad fate of Jane McCrea, Gates pictured her in glowing terms as a "young lady lovely to the sight," of "virtuous character" and "amicable disposition." He added a final touch of pathos by describing her as dressed in her bridal finery at the time of her death.[34] That Gates was resorting to propaganda was clear from his gleeful remark to a friend that he had given Burgoyne "a Tickler upon Scalping." [35] His letter proved to be most effective. By playing on the fears of the local inhabitants, Gates persuaded more militiamen to join his army.

More important than the McCrea incident in turning out the militia was Gates's effectiveness as a leader of such troops. Unlike most American generals, he had great confidence in short-term soldiers and showed a keen understanding of their temper. It was his announced policy never to call up the militia until almost the very moment they were needed.[36] Once they had finished their tour of duty, he was quick to thank them and to send them packing off to home.[37] For these reasons—plus the fact that

it was fall and most farmers had already harvested their crops—
he received unprecedented support from the militia during the
Saratoga campaign. "The farmers left their ploughs," reported
an enemy officer, "the smith his anvil, cobbler and tailor followed . . . [and] the militia came marching in from all the
provinces of New England." [38] By the close of the campaign,
the militia probably outnumbered the regulars in the Northern
army.

Gates showed the same sensitivity to terrain during the Saratoga campaign as he had at Ticonderoga. When he assumed command, the American camp was located on level ground at the
mouth of the Mohawk River. Had he remained on such terrain
it would have favored the British, because it allowed them to
employ their artillery and close-rank formations more effectively. In early September, however, Gates marched his army
north and eventually took up a position on Bemis Heights—a
strategic bottleneck located in one of the narrow passes which
lay across Burgoyne's path to Albany. [39] Here the terrain in
front of the American lines was rugged, rolling country, covered
with dense woods except for a few scattered farm clearings and
wagon trails. Gates improved on the natural defenses by having
Thaddeus Kosciuszko fortify the position with a series of batteries and breastworks. With the right wing of his army resting
on the Hudson River and his left on the high ground to the
west, Gates dug in and waited for the British to approach.

On the morning of September 19, Burgoyne, resplendent in
his bright scarlet and white uniform, stepped out to lead his
troops against Gates's prepared position. The battle that followed
has come to be known as the First Battle of Saratoga. Although
in sight of the American defenses for two days, the British general was forced to grope his way forward blindly. Indians and
British scouts who attempted to reconnoiter the ground were
driven back inside their lines by long-range fire from American
sharpshooters. Gates, on the other hand, knew from the reports
of the sentinels he had posted high in the treetops that Burgoyne's army was advancing in three widely separated columns.

Gates ordered two units to take up a position well in front of the American lines to meet the attackers gathering on his left flank. One outfit was the famous corps of light infantry dressed in faded brown hunting shirts and leggings, led by the burly rough-and-ready frontiersman, Colonel Daniel Morgan. Armed with their long rifles, these marksmen were not only deadly in their aim but equally adept at the hit-and-run tactics used in fighting Indian style. Gates was so impressed with the idea of a select corps that he soon created one of his own. Choosing 300 crack musketmen from his army to serve as light infantry, Gates equipped them with bayonets and ordered their commander, Major Henry Dearborn, to act in conjunction with Morgan's men. These two advance elements collided with Burgoyne's column of troops as they came crashing through the woods to enter the clearing at Isaac Freeman's farm.

Most of the fighting that day centered about the clearing at Freeman's farm and the surrounding woods. Morgan's men were in their element fighting in the forest, but Burgoyne was hampered in his efforts to employ the traditional British tactics that relied heavily on cannon and close-rank military formations. Both Burgoyne and Gates fed more troops into the battle as the fighting raged on into the afternoon. Gates, as was his custom, remained well to the rear, directing the battle from his headquarters. When night began to fall, he ordered the Americans to pull back inside their lines, leaving the British in possession of the battlefield.

Burgoyne claimed a technical victory because he held the disputed ground, but in reality the battle was a success for Gates. British losses were nearly twice those of the Americans—about 600 casualties as compared to 320. Much more important was the fact that Burgoyne's advance had definitely come to a halt. The following day the British went over to the defensive and began building a system of field fortifications hardly a mile from the American lines. Gates still stood between the British and Albany—the community where they hoped to find winter shelter and a food supply. As autumn turned the leaves from green to golden brown, time began running out for Burgoyne as it had for Carleton the year before.

There was no lull between battles. Gates kept putting pressure on the British. Each night raiding parties slipped out to attack enemy pickets and Burgoyne's men were forced to sleep with their weapons nearby. During daylight, American snipers posted in the treetops picked off officers and men who were so bold as to show themselves.

Burgoyne's predicament grew more and more desperate with each passing day. The morale of his men was deteriorating, his food supply of salt pork and flour was petering out, and desertions were reducing the size of his army. The Americans meanwhile were swelling their numbers as more militiamen kept coming into camp. A relief expedition under Sir Henry Clinton was pushing its way slowly up the Hudson toward the rear of Gates's army, but Burgoyne held little hope for immediate help. There was nothing left but to attack. When the British general personally led a reconnaissance-in-force against the left wing of the American army on October 7, 1777, it resulted in the Second Battle of Saratoga.

Gates had sized up his opponent well. Burgoyne was an "old gamester," he wrote just before the battle. "Perhaps his despair may dictate to him to risque all upon one throw." [40] Gates was ready, therefore, when Burgoyne emerged from his lines with 1,500 troops to probe the American position. Turning quietly to his military aide, he said, "Order on Morgan to begin the game." A three-pronged attack was developed to drive the British back inside their own lines.

While the American attack was proceeding according to plan, Benedict Arnold suddenly appeared upon the battlefield. Gates and Arnold had been friends earlier, but in the course of the Saratoga campaign ill-feeling sprang up between them. Arnold sulked because he felt he had not received the credit due him for his role in the First Battle of Saratoga. After a violent quarrel between the two men, Gates relieved his unruly subordinate of his command. Although he was acting without orders, the bold and dashing brigadier rode out to do battle. Rallying soldiers about him, he led a gallant charge against the Breymann redoubt—a key position in Burgoyne's fortifications. Lunging forward, Arnold carried the redoubt, and exposed the enemy's lines. When the battle came to a close, Burgoyne's position was no longer defensible.

The British army began retreating to the north and after a brief delay, Gates took up pursuit. He neatly cut off any possibility of escape, and by October 13, Burgoyne's army was virtually encircled. For several days the shooting war gave way to a war of words as the two generals negotiated. Burgoyne finally laid down his arms in accordance with a convention signed near the village of Saratoga on October 17. Gates, fearful of the threat to his rear posed by Clinton's relief expedition, did not insist upon an unconditional surrender. Even Washington was forced to confess that Gates's situation was so critical that he was in no position to demand a "more perfect Surrender." [41]

Many have given Arnold the glory for the Saratoga triumph as a result of his spectacular feat in turning the tide of the battle. The truth of the matter is, Gates had already set the stage for an American victory by his quiet organization and cautious strategy. Realizing that time and the terrain were in his favor, his strategy was to settle deep behind his fortifications, letting Burgoyne wear himself down in fruitless probes against the American position. He was determined to deny the British the opportunity of a pitched battle. Although both actions were fought in front of the American lines, Gates carefully kept a large part of the Northern army back inside his fortifications at all times. Arnold and Morgan should not be denied a share of the honors for their valiant fighting in the field and Schuyler should be given his due for the delaying tactics that slowed Burgoyne's advance to a crawl, but the primary credit for capturing the enemy's army belongs to Gates. He had fought the right kind of campaign at the right time and place. Gates's caution and Burgoyne's recklessness made inevitable an American military success.

The victory had world-shaking consequences. The British suf-

fered their greatest defeat of the war up to that time when
5,700 men, about one-fifth of the regular forces stationed in
America, laid down their arms. The Hudson River, lifeline of
the patriots, remained in American hands and the British campaign to cut off New England collapsed. Most important of all,
France was so heartened by the success at Saratoga that she
openly entered the war and began providing the foreign aid
which eventually made possible America's independence. As
John Adams so aptly noted in a letter from Paris, "General
Gates was the ablest negotiator you ever had in Europe." [42]

For a self-made man, Gates was exceedingly modest in this
most triumphant hour of his life. On the day of the Saratoga
surrender, he wrote to his wife:

> The voice of fame, ere this reached you, will tell you how greatly
> fortunate we have been in this department. Burgoyne and his great
> army have laid down their arms . . . to me and my Yankees. Thanks
> to the Giver of all victory for this triumphant success. . . . Tell my
> dear Bob not to be too elated at this great good fortune of his father.
> He and I have seen days adverse, as well as prosperous. Let us
> through life endeavor to bear both with an equal mind. [43]

In giving his son such philosophical advice, Gates seemed almost
to have a premonition of what lay in the future. His good fortune was soon overshadowed by misfortune.

Shortly after the Saratoga victory, a serious rift developed
between Gates and Washington. Relations between the two generals soured when Gates wrote directly to the Continental Congress to break the news of his success rather than writing to
Washington. Matters became more strained when the commander-in-chief complained that Gates was tardy in returning
reinforcements loaned to him for the campaign against Burgoyne.
The fact that most Americans were contrasting Gates's brilliant
victory at Saratoga with Washington's gloomy defeat at Germantown did not help the situation any. At this point, General
Thomas Conway, a veteran of the French army serving in the
American forces, wrote Gates a letter criticizing Washington as

a "weak General." News of the letter reached the commander-in-chief, who jumped to the conclusion that Gates was a member of a "Junto" engaged in "machinations" for "getting me out of the way." [44]

The Conway Cabal—or supposed plot to supplant Washington with Gates as supreme commander—seems to have little basis in fact. While it is true that Washington had critics both in Congress and the army, historians have been unable to uncover much evidence to indicate that there was such a conspiracy. No one ever dared to propose on the floor of Congress that Washington be removed. Gates certainly never committed himself on the matter. The key to the Conway Cabal, as one historian has suggested, may well lie in Washington's extreme sensitivity to criticism rather than in Gates's "machinations." [45]

The war's strain was beginning to tell on the health of the aging Gates. Among other things, he had been suffering from diarrhea.[46] Soon he was expressing the hope that the Saratoga campaign would be his last. Writing to his wife in September, 1777, he remarked, ". . . a General of an American army must be everything, and that is being more than one man can long sustain. This campaign must end my military labors." [47] But Congress would not let him go. In November he was appointed to the Board of War and spent the winter of 1777 reorganizing the American army.

As president of the Board of War, Gates was technically superior to Washington. It is clear that Congress had intended only to honor him for his Saratoga victory and not to humble or humiliate the commander-in-chief in any way. Gates, however, used his position to lord it over Washington and was both petty and rude. Without so much as consulting the commander-in-chief, he drew plans for an invasion of Canada. When the plans fell through, he vented his anger by squabbling with Washington over some negligible expenses that had been incurred in anticipation of the invasion. It was, according to Gates's biographer, the "pettiest thing he ever did." [48] Relations between the two generals as a result remained cool and distant.

Fortunately Gates and Washington were assigned to different commands during most of 1778 and 1779. The more miles between the two men the better both seemed to like it. In the spring of 1778, Gates expressed the desire to take to the field once more and was assigned to a post in the Hudson Highlands. Here he refuted the rumor that it was cowardice that kept him off the Saratoga battlefield by fighting a pistol duel with Colonel James Wilkinson. Gates thrice offered himself as a target without once trying to hit his opponent.

In the fall of 1778, he was sent to command the troops in Massachusetts—a sector where there was no fighting going on. When Washington offered him command of the expedition to be launched against the Indians in the Mohawk Valley in 1779, he turned it down on the grounds that he was neither young nor energetic enough for the task. He accepted instead the command at Providence, Rhode Island, where he spent more time fighting patriot profiteers than he did the enemy. After this tour of duty, Gates was given his choice of a command along the Hudson or a position in the main army. He asked, however, that he be given a furlough to see his family. His request was granted at the end of 1779 and he spent several months at Traveller's Rest.

Gates was called out from semi-retirement when Congress offered him command of the Southern army in June, 1780. The military situation in the South at the time was critical. The British had just won their greatest victory of the war by capturing Charleston and an American army numbering 5,500 men. Despite the sardonic remark supposedly made to him by Charles Lee—"Take care lest your Northern laurels turn to Southern willows"—Gates accepted the assignment. He joined his little army in Hillsboro, North Carolina, and immediately began laying plans for stopping the British invasion in the upper South.

He had few illusions about his chances of success. In the kindly letter written to Benjamin Lincoln whom he was replacing, Gates revealed his misgivings:

> The series of Misfortunes you have experienced, since you were
> doom'd to the Command of the Southern Department, has affected

Mount Prospect
Public Library

me exceedingly. I feel for you most sensibly.—I feel for myself who am to succeed to what? To the command of an Army without Strength—a Military Chest without Money. A department apparently deficient in public Spirit, and a Climate that encreases Despondency instead of animating the Soldiers Arm.[49]

Despite the apparent hopelessness of the situation, he set out upon a task which he had done so often and so well in the past— to organize an army into an effective fighting force.

Gates soon discovered that the South was a far different theater of operations than the North. Food and forage were hard to come by: there were no supply depots; the distances involved were vast; and the commissary services proved to be notoriously inefficient. Believing supply to be "the Mainspring of Military Motion," he urged that depots be established immediately. Without them, Gates warned, "our Army is like a dead whale upon the Sea Shore—a monstrous Carcass without Life or Motion."[50] But nothing was done. His troops were forced to live off the country while on the move and their marching rations soon were reduced to an unhealthy diet of green corn and unripe peaches.

There was also a great difference between the Southern militia forces and those of the North. Because of his striking success at Saratoga, Gates was inclined to place too much confidence in short-term troops. The Yankee and Yorker farmers, however, who turned out to fight Burgoyne's invasion were defending their own homes and families. In the South the theater of operations covered a much wider area and the militia were often forced to fight far from their firesides. When they did so, they frequently fought with less urgency. Although short-term troops in the South proved effective in guerrilla warfare and in certain battles such as the Cowpens, the militia under Gates turned out to be untrained, undisciplined, and thoroughly unreliable.

Within forty-eight hours after his arrival in late July, Gates broke camp and ordered his army to advance toward the British garrison at Camden, South Carolina. He has been severely criticized for his decision in taking the most direct route to his objective—one which passed through a desolate region filled with loyalists—rather than a more roundabout approach through more prosperous country controlled by patriots. He had two reasons for choosing the more difficult route: by moving quickly, he hoped to deny the British time to rush reinforcements to the Camden garrison; he was anxious also to reach General Richard Caswell, an unruly militia officer who was ignoring orders to join the main army. Despite dysentery, famine, the summer's heat, and threats of mutiny, Gates whipped his ragged, hungry soldiers forward to a junction with Caswell. Unbeknownst to Gates, however, Lord Cornwallis had arrived at Camden with reinforcements.

Driving deep into the enemy's territory, Gates appeared to be abandoning his cautious strategy at Saratoga for bolder measures. Ironically, he now found himself in the same situation in the South as Burgoyne at Saratoga. With supplies dangerously low, he felt compelled to strike a blow against the enemy before his army fell apart from sheer starvation. In early August, Gates wrote Governor Thomas Jefferson:

> I . . . hope your Excellency is doing all in Your power to supply your half Starved Fellow Citizens. Flour, Rum and Droves of Bullocks, should without Delay be forwarded to this Army or the Southern Department will soon want one to defend it.[51]

On a dark summer night outside the village of Camden, the two armies encountered one another unexpectedly. Gates found himself facing a fighting general in the bold and vigorous Cornwallis. The British commander had only 2,200 troops against Gates's 3,000. But two-thirds of Cornwallis' men were hardened veterans, including the famed and feared British legion of Banastre Tarleton. Only one-third of the Americans were soldiers from the Continental army, the rest were militia.

Gates could have avoided a battle by a withdrawal, but he decided to stand and fight. His position was a good one. His flanks were covered on both sides by swamps and there was cover for his men in the open pine forest to his front. Moreover, he had the concurrence of a council of war. Just before the battle, he called a meeting of his generals and asked: "Gentlemen, what is best to be done?" General Stevens, commanding the militia, answered, ". . . is it not too late *now* to do anything but fight?" [52] There was a brief moment of silence. Gates then ordered his generals to their stations.

The battle opened at daybreak on the morning of August 16. The British began advancing on the American right wing. When Gates's adjutant came riding up to report that the time was ripe for the Virginia militia on the left wing to attack, the general replied: "Sir, that's right—let it be done." [53] It was his last battle order of the day.

As the Virginians stepped out in ragged formation, Cornwallis sent his regulars forward on a charge. With a wild cheer, the British fired one volley and then rushed forward with their glittering bayonets. Frightened by this awesome sight, the Virginians dropped their guns and fled in sheer terror. They were soon joined by the North Carolina militia. As the entire American left wing collapsed, Gates rode into the midst of the panic-stricken men, trying in vain to rally them. "They ran like a Torrent," he reported, "and lost all before them." [54] Wheeling his horse into the milling throng, Gates tried a second time to stop their flight. It was all to no avail. While engaged in these efforts, Gates was spotted by British cavalrymen who sped after him in pursuit.[55] Spurring his horse, Gates galloped to safety, leaving the battlefield far in the rear. Cornwallis then turned most of his troops upon the Continentals and soon overwhelmed them.

Camden was one of the most crushing defeats of the entire war. Cornwallis, at the cost of only 320 British casualties, inflicted heavy losses of nearly 650 on the Continental veterans alone—to say nothing of the militia. The Southern army lay shattered, for most of the scattered militia never returned. When Gates gathered together the broken remnants of his force there were only 700 Continentals left. The road to North Carolina and Virginia lay open to Cornwallis.

Gates must bear much of the blame for the Camden debacle.

He made a grave tactical error by positioning his untrained militia face-to-face with the best British regiments. By putting too much faith in raw militia, Gates helped to bring about his own defeat. "His passion for Militia, I fancy will be cured," wrote Alexander Hamilton, "and he will cease to think them the bulwark of American liberty." [56]

Camden ruined Gates's military reputation. In addition to the humiliation of a disastrous defeat, he was accused of cowardice for leaving the battlefield. The fact that Gates galloped almost 200 miles from the battlefield in three days was used to taunt him. He explained that his purpose had been to reach the main base at Hillsboro where he could regroup his forces, but his critics interpreted his flight differently.[57] "[W]as there ever an instance of a General running away as Gates has done from his whole army?" asked Alexander Hamilton. Then, adding up the number of miles the fifty-three-year-old general had ridden, Hamilton added sarcastically, "It does admirable credit to the activity of a man at his time of life." [58] Because of Camden, Congress removed Gates from his command in October, 1780, and ordered a court of inquiry into his conduct of the battle.

Gates retired once more to Traveller's Rest. Besides his military misfortunes, he was grieving over the recent death of his son, Robert. He repeatedly insisted that a court be called to review the Camden battle. But Congress would not comply with his demands. In fact, in the summer of 1782, Congress repealed its resolve for an inquiry and reinstated Gates into the army. With his self-respect restored, he rode north to Washington's headquarters on the Hudson. Once there, he became the second ranking officer in the Continental army. Although his relations with Washington remained friendly on the surface, there is some evidence that he was involved in the Newburgh Address—a protest to the commander-in-chief by disgruntled army officers.[59]

Gates left the army for the last time in 1783 to hurry home to the bedside of his dying wife. After her death, he remained in retirement at his Virginia plantation. In 1786 Gates married Mary Vallance, an heiress with a fortune close to a half million dollars. His wife's fortune enabled him to live comfortably in his declining years. Though his own lot was easy, Gates did not forget his old comrades and spent large sums of money aiding less fortunate army veterans.

In 1790 he put Traveller's Rest up for sale and moved to New York City, where he purchased an estate called Rose Hill Farm. Upon selling his Virginia plantation, he called his slaves together and announced to them that they were free men. He became a Jeffersonian Republican, as might be expected of one with his liberal views, serving a single term in the New York legislature in 1800–01. He died at Rose Hill Farm on April 10, 1806, at the age of seventy-eight.

No honest appraisal of Gates's generalship can fail to concede that he had certain serious shortcomings. His conduct of the Camden battle reveals his limitations as a tactician. In his relations with Congress, he was too high-handed and demanding for his own good. His greatest defect, however, was his inability to work smoothly with his colleagues. Quarrels among American generals were quite common, but Gates seems to have been more contentious than most. Had he ever been made commander-in-chief, it is probable that his feuds with Washington, Schuyler, and Arnold would have wrecked the American army.

For all his shortcomings, Gates's virtues outweighed his vices. Few military men contributed more to the cause for independence. He was a key figure in halting two major British invasions and was largely responsible for winning the most decisive battle of the war. Although by no means a great general, he displayed considerable talent as an organizer and administrator. But the greatest secret of Gates's success lay in his qualities of leadership. He had few peers in the Continental army as a disciplinarian. By treating the common soldier with a kindness uncommon in that day, he inspired their confidence and was almost always able to rouse them to a fighting pitch. As a professional soldier he could view his career with pride; he had helped to create an army, defeat the enemy, and to secure the independence of his adopted country.

FOOTNOTES

1. Samuel W. Patterson, *Horatio Gates: Defender of American Liberties* (New York, 1941), p. vii.
2. Horace Walpole, *Journal of the Reign of King George the Third from year 1771 to 1783* (London, 1859), II, 200.
3. Robert Gates was Surveyor of Customs at Greenwich. George Sackville to Robert Gates, September 23, 1748, Gates Papers, New York Historical Society. Hereinafter the New York Historical Society will be cited as N.Y.H.S.
4. Edward Cornwallis to Robert Gates, March 18, 1749/50, Gates Papers, N.Y.H.S.
5. Commission as Captain, September 13, 1754, Gates Papers, N.Y.H.S.
6. Will of Thomas Parker, September 10, 1742, Gates Papers, N.Y.H.S.
7. Charles Lee to Robert Morris, June 16 1781, *New York Historical Society Collections*, VI, 458.
8. Hezekiah Niles, *Principles and Acts of the Revolution in America* (New York, 1876), p. 496.
9. Charles Townshend to Gates, April 26, 1762, Gates Papers, N.Y.H.S.
10. Milton M. Klein, "The American Whig: William Livingston of New York" (Columbia University, Unpublished Dissertation, 1954), pp. 506–07.
11. Thomas Hayes to Gates, May 16, 1770, Gates Papers, N.Y.H.S.
12. Elizabeth Gates to Lady Galway, August 1, 1772, Gates Papers, N.Y.H.S.
13. John C. Fitzpatrick, ed., *Writings of George Washington* (Washington, D.C., 1931–44), VII, 267.
14. Patterson, *op. cit.*, p. 53.
15. Massachusetts Historical Society, *Proceedings*, LXVII, 141.
16. Clifford K. Shipton, *Biographical Sketches of Those Who Attended Harvard College in the Classes 1746–1750, etc.* (Boston, 1962), XII, 372.
17. Massachusetts Historical Society, *Proceedings*, LXVII, 138.
18. Matthias Ogden to Aaron Burr, July 26, 1776, *American Archives*, 5th series (Washington, 1848), I, 603.
19. Gates to Schuyler, October 24, 1776, *ibid.*, II, 1257.
20. Gates to Jonathan Trumbull, August 11, 1776, Gates Papers, Houghton Library, Harvard University; General Orders, July 17, 1776, *American Archives*, 5th series, I, 654; Dr. John Morgan to Gates, September 1, 1776, *ibid.*, II, 106.
21. Gates to President of Congress, September 2, 1776, *ibid.*, I, 1268.

22. Gates to Putnam, August 11, 1776, *ibid.*, I, 900.

23. Gates to President of Congress, July 29, 1776, *ibid.*, I, 649.

24. General Gates' Orders and Instructions for the Honourable Benedict Arnold, Esq. etc. . . . August 7, 1776, Gates Papers, N.Y.H.S. Gates agreed to Arnold's move to the vicinity of Valcour Island, but his letter approving the shift to this position was sent on October 12, after the battle on Lake Champlain had been fought. See also *American Archives*, 5th series, II, 440–81, 591, 1015, for important instructions from Gates to Arnold.

25. Resolves of the Committee to Cooperate with General George Clinton, December 8, 1776, *ibid.*, III, 1126; Robert Livingston to Gates, December 8, 1776, *ibid.*, 1127; and William Duer to Gates, December 9, 1776, *ibid.*, 1128.

26. Gates to Arthur St. Clair [n. d.], cited in John Armstrong Memorial, December 4, 1831, Sparks MSS 49. 1 (7), Houghton Library, Harvard. John Trumbull also claimed to be the first to recognize that Ticonderoga was vulnerable from Mount Defiance.

27. Udney Hay to George Clinton, August 13, 1777, cited in John Armstrong Memorial, Sparks MSS, Houghton Library, Harvard; and H. A. Washington, ed., *Writings of Thomas Jefferson* (Washington, 1854), VIII, 496.

28. Ray W. Pettengill, ed., *Letters from America 1776–1779* (Boston, 1924), p. 98.

29. Edmund Burnett, *Letters of the Members of the Continental Congress* (Washington, 1923), II, 413.

30. James Thacher, *A Military Journal During the American Revolution* (Boston, 1827), p. 86.

31. Lyman H. Butterfield, ed., *Letters of Benjamin Rush* (Princeton, 1951), II, 767. Hereinafter *Benjamin Rush Letters*.

32. *Ibid.*, I, 159–60.

33. John Burgoyne, *State of the Expedition from Canada*, 2nd ed. (London, 1780), Appendix, pp. xcvi–xcviii.

34. Gates to Burgoyne, September 2, 1777. Gates Papers, N.Y.H.S.

35. Gates to Governor Trumbull, September 4, 1777, Gates Papers, N.Y.H.S.

36. *Ibid.*

37. See, for example, Gates to Colonel Hide, November 9, 1776, *American Archives*, 5th series, III, 623.

38. Pettengill, *op. cit.*, p. 98.

39. It is not clear whether Gates or Kosciuszko selected the site at Bemis Heights, but as supreme commander Gates had the ultimate authority on this matter.

40. Horatio Rogers, ed., *Hadden's Journal and Orderly Books* (Albany, 1884), p. lxxxiv.
41. Bernhard Knollenberg, *Washington and the Revolution* (New York, 1940), p. 29.
42. Francis Wharton, ed., *Revolutionary Diplomatic Correspondence of the United States* (Washington, D.C., 1889), II, 664.
43. Frank Moore, ed., *Diary of the American Revolution* (New York, 1860), I, 511.
44. Massachusetts Historical Society, *Proceedings*, LVIII, 317.
45. Knollenberg, *op. cit.*, pp. 65–77.
46. Benjamin Rush to Thomas Jefferson, *Benjamin Rush Letters*, II, 858.
47. Gates to Elizabeth Gates, September 22, 1777, Gates Papers, N.Y.H.S.
48. Patterson, *op. cit.*, p. 265.
49. *Magazine of American History*, V, 283.
50. *Ibid.*, pp. 281, 284.
51. Julian P. Boyd, ed., *Papers of Thomas Jefferson* (Princeton, 1951), III, 525.
52. Otho W. Williams, "A Narrative of the Campaign of 1780," in William Johnson, *Sketches of the Life and Correspondence of Nathanael Greene* (Charleston, 1882), I, 493.
53. *Ibid.*
54. Gates to Washington, August 20, 1780, Gates Papers, N.Y.H.S.
55. *Magazine of American History*, V, 277–78.
56. Hamilton to Duane, September 6, 1780, in Harold C. Syrett and Jacob E. Cooke, eds., *Papers of Alexander Hamilton* (New York, 1961), II, 420. Hereinafter *Hamilton Papers*.
57. Gates to Washington, August 20, 1780, Gates Papers, N.Y.H.S.
58. Hamilton to Duane, September 6, 1780, in *Hamilton Papers*, II, 421.
59. Douglas S. Freeman, *George Washington: A Biography* (New York, 1952), V, 437.

BIBLIOGRAPHY

Billias, George A., *General John Glover and His Marblehead Mariners.* New York, 1960. Shows the striking change in attitude that took place in the Northern army when Gates assumed command.
Emmett, Thomas A., ed., "The Southern Campaign 1780: Letters of Major General Gates from 21 June to 31 August." *Magazine of American History*, V (New York, 1880), 281–320. The letters of Gates covering the Camden campaign.

Knollenberg, Bernhard, *Washington and the Revolution*. New York, 1940. Contains the best brief appraisal of Gates's contribution to the American military cause. Gives a much less biased view of the relations between Gates and Washington.

Nickerson, Hoffman, *The Turning Point of the Revolution*. Boston, 1928. The standard work on the Saratoga campaign and quite fair on some points toward Gates.

Patterson, Samuel W., *Horatio Gates, Defender of American Liberties*. New York, 1941. The only full-scale biography of Gates, but far too uncritical and laudatory in approach to be of much value.

————, *Horatio Gates Reconsidered*. New York, 1941. A short address by Gates's biographer before the Saratoga Historical Society that contains some views not expressed in the longer work.

Shipton, Clifford K., "Horatio Gates," in *Biographical Sketches of Those Who Attended Harvard College in the Classes 1746–1750 with Bibliographical and Other Notes*, Vol. XII of *Sibley's Harvard Graduates*, 370–80. An informative sketch of Gates's life that catches the essence of the man.

Swiggert, Howard, *Forgotten Leaders of the Revolution*. New York, 1955. Contains a character sketch of Gates in one of the chapters.

Thacher, James, *A Military Journal during the American Revolutionary War*. Boston, 1827, pp. 437–44. Has one of the early biographical sketches of Gates by one of his contemporaries.

pendence National Historical Park Collection

GEORGE WASHINGTON

From a Private Collection

ANTHONY WAYNE

pendence National Historical Park Collection

HENRY KNOX

Independence National Historical Park Collection

NATHANAEL GREENE

pendence National Historical Park Collection

DANIEL MORGAN

Independence National Historical Park Collection

LE MARQUIS DE LAFAYETTE

ependence National Historical Park Collection

HORATIO GATES

American Antiquarian Society

BENEDICT ARNOLD

pendence National Historical Park Collection

JOHN SULLIVAN

Independence National Historical Park Collection

BENJAMIN LINCOLN

rican Antiquarian Society

PHILIP SCHUYLER

American Antiquarian Society

CHARLES LEE

Nathanael Greene:

REVOLUTIONARY WAR STRATEGIST

———•———

THEODORE THAYER

Rutgers University

GENERAL WASHINGTON was greatly impressed with Nathanael Greene the very first time the two men met. When the handsome and engaging Rhode Islander reported for duty with the army at Cambridge in the summer of 1775, Washington quickly sized him up as an "object of his confidence." [1] A keen judge of character, Washington became convinced within a year that if he were killed or captured Greene was the best qualified of all his generals to succeed him as commander-in-chief.

Time proved that Washington had taken the correct measure of his man. After fighting alongside Washington in the North for five years, Greene finally was given a command of his own in the South. Within the short space of a single year, he reorganized the Southern army, fought several bloody battles, and compelled Lord Cornwallis to relinquish most of the territory the British had conquered in South Carolina and Georgia. Greene somewhat humorously summed up the secret of his success in these words: "There are few generals," he wrote, "that have run oftener, or more lustily than I have done. But I have taken care not to run too far, and commonly have run as fast forward as backward, to convince the Enemy that we were like a Crab, that could run either way." [2] Greene's strategy and Cornwallis' impetuosity eventually sent his Lordship drumming down the road to Virginia and defeat at Yorktown.

Nathanael Greene literally appeared out of nowhere to become in the words of one soldier "the greatest military genius" of the war for independence. Many Revolutionary War generals had had previous military experience, but he had none. Greene was, moreover, a Quaker opposed to war for religious reasons. But when England's colonial policies became unbearable, he discarded his pacifism, joined a military association, and threw himself wholeheartedly into the struggle for liberty and independence.

As a boy, Greene had little formal education. It was not because his family lacked the means, for his father along with some of his uncles owned a forge that produced iron anchors and chains for sailing ships. Rather, it was because his father was "a man of industry" who brought up his children "to business." "Early, very early," wrote Greene, "when I should have been in the pursuit of Knowledge, I was digging into the Bowels of the Earth after Wealth." [3] But a precocious youth, he soon discovered the world of books and learning. In time he accumulated a fine library of more than two hundred books on history, religion, law, philosophy, and most important of all, military science. One of the first volumes he acquired was a copy of Euclid, which he kept by his side at the forge, sweating over every theorem until he had mastered the whole book.

This self-taught, awkward anchorsmith from Coventry, Rhode Island, reported to Washington at the age of thirty-three as brigadier general at the head of his colony's three Continental regiments. Why was this unsophisticated youth chosen when others appeared to be better educated or more experienced for the command? The answer lay in Greene's rare qualities of leadership and his sound grasp of military affairs. From the time of the Boston Tea Party, he spent his spare moments reading military manuals, studying the lives of great generals, and drilling the local Kentish Guards. He put his newly-acquired knowledge to use as a member of the legislative committee charged with the responsibility of preparing Rhode Island's defenses in 1775. Con-

sequently, when the General Assembly cast about for an officer
to lead its "Army of Observation," Greene was a logical choice.
He went from the rank of private in the Kentish Guards to that
of brigadier general in the Continental army in less than two
months.

When Greene first reported to Washington, the commander-
in-chief saw before him a rather stocky, good-looking man, five
feet ten inches tall with sparkling blue-gray eyes. Like Washington, Greene cut a fine athletic figure, despite a slight limp caused
by an accident during his youth. The commander-in-chief immediately was impressed by the young man's astute comments
concerning certain problems then confronting the army. He was
amused, too, by the way the Rhode Islander seasoned his remarks
with homespun witticisms. Greene's sunny disposition and winning ways soon offset the lack of polish he had shown upon entering the military service. Henry Knox, Washington's artillery
commander, noted that Greene "came to us, the rawest, the most
untutored being" he ever saw, but in less than a year, he was the
equal in military knowledge "to any General Officer in the army,
and very superior to most of them."

One year prior to his entry into the army, Greene had married
pretty Catherine Littlefield, of Block Island. Kitty, as she was
called, was the life of any party she attended. Washington, who
had an eye for feminine charm, was naturally attracted to her
and at one social affair he is said to have danced with her all of
three hours without stopping. During the war, Kitty became a
frequent visitor to Nathanael's headquarters and her presence
helped to brighten the drabness of army life. When Cornwallis
surrendered, she made a long and arduous trip to South Carolina
to be with her husband until the war ended.

After serving through the long and sometimes boring Boston
siege, Greene accompanied the Continental army to New York
in the spring of 1776. Washington by this time regarded the
Rhode Islander as one of his best divisional commanders and put
him in charge of the Brooklyn defenses where the first British
blow was expected to fall. But when General Howe did arrive in

the early summer of 1776, Greene, who had just received his promotion to rank of major general, was sick abed with a fever. He
was removed to New York City to recover and was not on hand
when his comrades-in-arms were whipped soundly in the Battle
of Long Island. Henry Knox was of the opinion that if Greene
had been there "matters would have worn a very different appearance. . . ." Greene, on the other hand, modestly observed,
"I have not the vanity to think the event would have been otherwise had I been there, yet I think I could have given the commanding general a good deal of necessary information. Great
events, sometimes depend upon very little causes. . . ." [5]

Recovering from his illness, Greene was placed in charge of the
forces guarding the shores of New Jersey. Within his jurisdiction was Fort Washington, a strategic bastion high on the rocky
heights at the northern end of Manhattan Island. Fort Washington was destined to be Greene's most costly mistake of the entire
war. After the British had landed and occupied the lower end of
Manhattan, enemy ships sailed safely past the guns of Fort Washington to the wide waters of the Hudson farther north. When
Washington removed the major part of his army from New
York's Westchester County into New Jersey in mid-November,
the peril to the fortress increased. Greene, however, strongly advised Washington to hold on to the post.

Then Greene compounded his error by reinforcing the garrison so that more troops poured into the impending trap. If Howe
attacked, Greene was convinced, the Americans, fighting behind
breastworks, could give the British a bloodbath similar to the one
at Bunker Hill. In any event, he argued, the fort could be evacuated at any time by small boats from the Jersey shore. Until
such a move seemed necessary, the Rhode Islander was for holding Fort Washington, since it might prevent the British from
launching a drive into New Jersey or posing a threat to General
Charles Lee's division in Westchester County. Most of the other
generals, including Israel Putnam and Hugh Mercer, agreed with
the young strategist. Indeed, Greene's views were regarded so
highly that Washington was persuaded to hold the seemingly

impregnable fortress for a little while longer. "His Excellency, General Washington, has been with me several days," reported Greene. "The evacuation of Fort Washington was under consideration but finally nothing concluded on." [6]

General Howe suddenly appeared before the fort on November 15 and demanded that the garrison surrender. In answer to the British ultimatum Greene ordered Colonel Robert Magaw, commander of the fort, to stand fast. That evening while crossing the Hudson, Washington met Greene and Putnam as they were returning from a last-minute inspection. Both generals, Washington discovered, were convinced that the fortress could withstand the threatened attack. Although apprehensive of the outcome, the commander-in-chief let Greene's orders stand and returned to spend the night in New Jersey. Early the next morning Washington, Greene, and several other officers recrossed the Hudson to Fort Washington and arrived just as Howe opened up his attack with about 10,000 soldiers. Although the Americans numbered less than 3,000, Greene was still confident that all would go well.

Magaw's men fought valiantly, but the overwhelming odds soon began to tell. As the fort's outer defenses started to crumble, Washington boarded a boat and was rowed to safety. Greene begged to remain behind to direct the battle, but Washington would not hear of it for fear of losing his pugnacious young general.

The stunning news that Magaw had surrendered reached Greene as he returned to his headquarters. With the fall of Fort Washington, some 3,000 soldiers and quantities of badly needed military supplies were lost. Greatly chagrined, Greene sat down and poured out his anguish in a letter to his good friend Henry Knox: "I feel mad, vexed, sick, and sorry; Never did I need the consoling voice of a friend more than now." [7]

Greene's military reputation took a plunge as a result of the Fort Washington fiasco. Men began inquiring if he were really the "Heaven born genius" he had been called. Washington entertained some doubts as to whether or not he had overrated

Greene. Although Washington never openly charged Greene with the loss of Fort Washington, his failure to come to the Rhode Islander's support caused the blame to fall squarely on the shoulders of his subordinate. As commander-in-chief and superior officer at the scene of action, Washington was, in fact, the one primarily responsible for the costly mistake.

Greene's prestige suffered, but the setback was only temporary. Washington apparently charged off the loss to the fortunes of war and before long was again relying on the quick-thinking Greene for advice and counsel. But the fall of Fort Washington had the effect of making both generals more cautious. Washington and Greene henceforth placed more emphasis upon tactics calculated to wear down the enemy to a point where the patriots could assume the offensive.

After playing a prominent role in conducting the masterly retreat of the ragged American army as it fled across New Jersey, Greene participated in the Battle of Trenton. He commanded one wing of Washington's task force which launched a surprise attack on the Hessian garrison during the early hours of the morning after Christmas day. The triumph of American arms which followed lifted the sagging hopes of the patriots. During the battle, Greene wrote his wife that he went "thirty hours in all the Storm without the least refreshment." [8]

Heady with victory, Greene with some other officers tried to persuade Washington to "push on" to attack the neighboring German garrison at Burlington. But Washington could not be swayed and refused to risk his precious gains for higher stakes. In retrospect, it appears that the commander-in-chief made a mistake by not acting on Greene's advice, for the Germans at Burlington were so stunned and demoralized by the Trenton defeat they might have made an easy mark. Washington, himself, is said to have regretted later that he had not seized "the golden opportunity." [9]

Fortune smiled again upon American arms with the victory at Princeton early in January, 1777. Riding his spirited dark horse, Greene once more was in the thick of the battle. Besides the victory, Greene was particularly pleased that the commander-in-chief was depending upon him for advice. Writing to Kitty, Greene noted he was enjoying "the full confidence of his Excellency General Washington." Indeed, he added, "the more difficult and distressing our affairs grew," the more Washington had relied upon him.[10]

After the army had gone into winter quarters at Morristown, Washington sent Greene off to Congress in March, 1777, to acquaint the politicians with the pressing needs of the Continental army. Among other things, the commander-in-chief was hoping that Congress would create three new positions for the rank of lieutenant general and that Greene would be nominated as one of the high-ranking officers. But Congress failed to act on Washington's recommendation. Despite the fact that he had not been promoted, Greene was not unhappy about leaving Philadelphia, for he was convinced that Congress was little more than a useless debating society. "The Congress have so many of those talking gentlemen among them," he observed "that they tire themselves and everybody else with their long labored speeching that is calculated more to display their own talents than to promote the public interest." [11]

Upon his return to the army at Morristown, Greene was given a series of important assignments. With Henry Knox, the portly artillery commander, he was sent in May to view the defenses along the strategic Hudson Highlands. He had no sooner completed his inspection than Washington sent him to Middlebrook, New Jersey, to select a safe position from which the army might launch its summer campaign. Greene chose a spot high up on the first range of the Watchung Mountains. Here the Continental army took up a position and defied all attempts by General Howe to bring on an engagement. Finding that Washington could not be dislodged or lured from his eagle's nest, Howe finally pulled his troops out of New Jersey.

Howe next sought to capture the American capital, Philadelphia. After landing at the head of the Chesapeake Bay, the British general outmaneuvered Washington on a warm day in early

September at the Brandywine River. While his forces made a feint at the American center at Chad's Ford, Howe sent the major part of his army on a wide end sweep to outflank the American left wing under General John Sullivan. Although he had been anticipating a flank attack, Sullivan was caught by surprise and his line soon collapsed under the superior weight of the enemy. When word reached Washington at Chad's Ford of the impending disaster, he ordered Greene to hasten to the rescue. Greene's division, made up of many Virginians, raced four miles through broken country in less than fifty minutes. Reaching a strategic spot called Sandy Hollow, Greene set up a defensive line and opened his ranks to allow Sullivan's battered division to scramble through to safety. Then he closed his lines and confronted the enemy, holding the British at bay until darkness fell. Under this protection, the whole American army was able to pull back without further harassment and to lick its wounds from the more than 1,000 casualties suffered.

Despite the fact that he had saved part of the American army, Washington failed to mention Greene's division in his report of the Brandywine battle to Congress. Unhappy at the omission, the Rhode Islander mentioned the matter to the commander-in-chief. Washington is said to have answered: "You Sir, are considered my favorite officer: Weedon's brigade, like myself, are Virginians: should I applaud them for their achievement under your command, I shall be charged with partiality, jealousy will be excited, and the service injured." [12] Washington's policy was to bend over backward so that he would not be charged with favoritism to his own state and Greene was forced to suffer in consequence.

Early in October, after Howe had succeeded in taking Philadelphia, Washington attempted a surprise attack upon the main body of the enemy encamped at Germantown. Greene led the left wing of the army into the attack. Unfortunately his men lost their way in the darkness and fog and arrived forty-five minutes late at their appointed place. Washington's initial advantage began to ebb as a heavy fog rolled in during the early

morning and allowed the enemy time to recover and get reinforcements. With the tide of battle running against him, Washington prudently ordered a retreat. Once more a battle with a
promising beginning had come to a disappointing end. Washington was asked after the battle if the failure was caused by
Greene's tardy arrival. "Not at all," replied the commander-in-
chief, "the fault lay with ourselves." [13] The fog had been so intense that even General Howe's dog lost his way in the mist and
Washington returned him to his owner under a flag of truce.

Both Washington and Greene came under severe criticism as
the defeats in Pennsylvania were compared with Gates's glowing
victory at Saratoga. The grumbling grew more ominous with
each passing day. James Lovell, the Massachusetts congressman,
warned that "the list of our disgusted patriots is long and formidable and their Resentments keen against the reigning Cabal."
By the "reigning Cabal," he meant the officers upon whom
Washington leaned for advice—Greene, Knox, Lafayette, and
Joseph Reed. Greene was generally considered to be the one
closest to the commander-in-chief and consequently he was
blamed for influencing Washington in the wrong direction. Despite the fact that Greene was under fire in Congress at the
time, Washington took the opportunity to state once again that
he desired the Rhode Islander to succeed him as commander-in-
chief in the event he were killed or captured.[14]

No matter how highly Washington regarded Greene, the latter never would have been made commander-in-chief if Lovell
and like-minded congressmen had had their way. Greene, according to Lovell, was the "languid Counsellor" whose strategy
had brought about the loss of Philadelphia. Because of the
mounting attacks upon himself and Washington, Greene finally
felt compelled to take up his pen to answer his detractors. Comparisons between the Philadelphia and Saratoga campaigns were
unfair, he noted. Howe's army had been far more powerful than
Burgoyne's and Washington had performed a great feat in maintaining a force in the field capable of opposing the British near
Philadelphia. As for Gates, he was "a child of good fortune"

according to Greene, and one whose success "was laid long before his arrival there." [15]

Criticism of both Washington and Greene soon died down as the result of the so-called "Conway Cabal." This supposed plot to replace Washington with Gates as commander-in-chief of the Continental army revealed the extent of Washington's popularity, and his detractors quickly changed their tune and halted their attacks upon him. One congressman wrote to Greene "that the Junto [in Congress] are alarmed at their unpopularity on account of their malevolent machinations, & now deny all their Practices." [16]

While the army was in winter quarters at Valley Forge, Washington decided to seek a replacement for Thomas Mifflin, the quartermaster general. Affairs in that department had fallen into such a sorry state that only a person with unusual administrative abilities could set matters right again. In desperation, he turned to Greene, who had been gathering provisions for the army. Although the Rhode Islander did not relish the thought of leaving behind a battlefield command, he accepted the post out of deference to Washington's wishes. After one year on the job, Greene had some second thoughts about his decision. "There is a great difference between being raised to an office, and descending to one," he wrote. "Had I been an inferior officer I might have thought myself honored by the appointment. But as I was high in rank in the army, I have ever considered it derogatory to serve in this office." [17]

Despite his dissatisfaction with the position, Greene quickly proved his worth. Through his efforts, the Continental army was ready when it came time to begin campaigning again in the summer of 1778. Greene's preparations, declared Washington, "enabled us, with great facility, to make a sudden move with the whole Army and baggage from Valley Forge in pursuit of the Enemy." [18] Considering the obstacles that beset him, Greene's achievements were little less than miraculous. Laboring long hours, he managed to keep the army going from season to season despite shortages of funds, supplies, and means of transportation.

If he gained little glory as quartermaster general, Greene did pocket some rather handsome profits. He was allowed, according to practice of the day, a commission of 3 per cent on all funds expended by his department. These profits he divided equally with his two assistants. Critics were soon charging that Greene and his associates were making a fortune at the expense of their country. Greene admitted the financial compensation was attractive, but declared the recompense was small considering that he had been deprived of his command in the field. All in all, he earned a total of $170,000 measured in terms of specie.

Large as this amount was, Greene cannot be accused of padding the army's accounts or buying overpriced goods. It is true that he issued some army contracts to his relatives in Rhode Island, but he saw nothing wrong with nepotism so long as the army received its supplies in good condition and at the going market price. At the close of the war, Greene was under suspicion of having speculated with army funds, but the charges were never proved.[19]

While serving as quartermaster general, Greene tried also to assert that he had a right to command troops in battle. Such was the understanding, he maintained, when he took the administrative post. Much to his displeasure, however, Washington failed to support his claim when the question became an issue in 1779. Greene, in reality, had little to complain about on the question of command. He was always consulted by Washington on strategy and tactics and participated in all the councils of war. During the Battle of Monmouth, he fell heir to Lee's command when Washington summarily ordered Lee from the field. Because of Greene's intimate knowledge of his state, he served under Sullivan during the Rhode Island campaign of 1778. Washington also gave him a command at Springfield, New Jersey, in June, 1780.

Greene's opportunity to resign as quartermaster general and to return to a full-time command in the field came in the summer of 1780. Having run out of funds, Congress decided supplies and money could only be procured by requisitions drawn from the states. Greene was convinced such a system would not work and tendered his resignation. Some members of Congress reacted bitterly to his stubbornness and wanted to discharge him from the service altogether. Washington came to Greene's defense and warned Congress that dire consequences would follow if he were dismissed. The commander-in-chief worked out a compromise and persuaded the disgruntled Greene to continue as quartermaster until a suitable replacement was found.

While Greene was having his set-to with Congress, the country was shocked to learn of the crushing defeat of General Gates by Lord Cornwallis at Camden, South Carolina, in August, 1780. With the British in almost undisputed possession of South Carolina and Georgia, the way seemed clear for Cornwallis to sweep north into North Carolina and Virginia. The patriot cause south of the Potomac looked hopeless.

Fortunately, Congress left the choice of the new commander to replace Gates as head of the Southern army to Washington. It was a foregone conclusion that he would pick Greene and once the appointment was announced, there was universal acclamation within the army. The sentiment of most military men was succinctly summed up by one officer up North who wrote: "If anything is to be expected from the abilities and exertions of a single person, I think no one will be more likely to answer every reasonable expectation than this amiable officer. There can be no better proof of his worth than the universal regret all ranks among us feel at the idea of parting with him." [20]

Greene decided to go south at once. He left his headquarters at West Point in October, 1780, in such a hurry that he missed seeing his wife who was coming over from Rhode Island to be with him. "My dear Angel," he wrote hastily to Kitty. "What I have been dreading has come to pass. His Excellency General Washington by order of Congress has appointed me to the command of the Southern army." Greene made one last desperate effort to contact his wife at Fishkill, New York. "But alas," he wrote, "I was obliged to return with bitter disappointment. My longing eyes looked for you in all directions, and I felt my heart leap with joy at the sound of every carriage." [21]

Upon reaching Philadelphia, Greene did everything in his power to procure supplies for his new command. Because he was convinced that cavalry units would prove of great value in the southern theater of operations where hit-and-run tactics were employed, he made a special effort to raise more horsemen. By a happy coincidence, "Light-Horse Harry" Lee and his famed legion of 150 dragoons was available and the unit was assigned to him. The legion would strengthen the company of horse under Lieutenant Colonel William Washington already serving in the South. Besides these two veteran outfits, Greene was counting upon using mounted militia—provided he could get such irregulars to co-ordinate their moves with those of the main army.

Throughout the rest of his trip, Greene stopped at all the leading towns in Maryland and Virginia to urge local authorities to raise both troops and arms. The prospects, however, looked bleak. The farther south he traveled, the more apparent it became that except for food his supplies would have to come mainly from the North. Greene wrote letter after letter to the Congress spelling out his needs in great detail. But his attention was not always directed toward military problems. Sometimes trotting down the dusty roads, the conversation turned to other subjects and an aide-de-camp recalled years later how on one occasion Greene had led a brilliant discussion of great Latin poets.

One of Greene's primary concerns was to gather a staff of experienced officers to assist him. He lost his most valuable subordinate when he was forced to leave Baron von Steuben behind in Virginia to supervise recruiting and the procurement of supplies. He gained another, however, when Colonel Edward Carrington, a first-rate officer, agreed to serve as his quartermaster general. At Hillsboro, North Carolina, he encountered the Polish engineer, Thaddeus Kosciuszko, and promptly put him to work improving transportation facilities and building supply magazines. Another excellent addition to his staff was Colonel William R. Davie, a famed cavalryman and expert swordsman who became Greene's commissary general. Davie was reluctant to accept the post, claiming he knew nothing about keeping money or accounts, but Greene told him he could take the job with a clear conscience because there were no funds in the military chest to manage.

Upon his arrival at Charlotte, North Carolina, Greene found what remained of the shattered Southern army. All that was left after the Camden battle were 2,000 ragged and famished creatures who resembled scarecrows more than soldiers. Discouraging as the outlook appeared, Greene decided not to retreat or to abandon North Carolina. Instead, he hoped to keep Cornwallis at arm's length while he rebuilt his army with the help of local leaders. Greene sized up the situation so quickly that within twenty-four hours, according to one officer, he understood the problems confronting him better than Gates ever had.[22]

The military picture in the South brightened a bit for the Americans about the time Greene arrived on the scene. In October, 1780, a small band of mountaineer militia had met and defeated a British force made up mainly of loyalists atop King's Mountain in South Carolina. Unknown to all, King's Mountain was to be the turning point of the war in the South. Cornwallis still had an army that was far superior in numbers to any force Greene could put in the field, but the British soldiers were scattered throughout South Carolina and Georgia in numerous small forts and garrisons. After the British defeat at King's Mountain, these occupied states grew restless, and Cornwallis did not dare to enlarge his main force at the expense of the garrisons. Consequently he was forced to fall back to Winnsboro, South Carolina, where he waited for reinforcements from Virginia. Once they arrived, he hoped to crush Greene as he had Gates at Camden.

Greene was fully aware of the dangers facing him. If Cornwallis were left unmolested at Winnsboro, he would be able to strengthen his force by enlisting local loyalists and could overwhelm the Southern army once reinforcements arrived. Something had to be done to distract Cornwallis and prevent a British buildup. Greene decided to take a bold move. He would split his

little army in the face of an enemy who was superior in size and
fighting ability—a dangerous tactic that, if not successful, could
result in complete disaster. To assist him in his plan Greene called
upon Brigadier General Daniel Morgan, a tough old frontier
fighter who had served brilliantly in the Canadian and Saratoga
campaigns earlier in the war. Greene ordered Morgan to take 700
light troops plus some cavalry and to circle to the north of the
British at Winnsboro. From his position above the British, Morgan could harass the enemy and discourage any loyalists who
might think of enlisting under Cornwallis. Greene in the meantime would be free to move to a more favorable location and to
rebuild his army unmolested.

Once Morgan had departed, Greene marched the rest of the
Southern army to Cheraw Hill, South Carolina, 75 miles east
of the British at Winnsboro and over 100 miles away from Morgan. Despite the fact that his army was divided, Greene was
satisfied with his moves. He summed up his strategy in these
words:

> I am here in my camp of repose, improving the discipline and spir-
> its of my men, and the opportunity for looking about me. I am well
> satisfied with the movement, for it has answered thus far all the
> purposes for which I intended it. It makes the most of my inferior
> force, for it compels my adversary to divide his, and holds him in
> doubt as to his own line of conduct. He cannot leave Morgan be-
> hind him to come at me, or his posts of Ninety-Six and Augusta
> would be exposed. And he cannot chase Morgan far, or prosecute
> his views upon Virginia, while I am here with the whole country
> open before me. I am as near Charleston as he is, and as near Hills-
> borough as I was at Charlotte; so that I am in no danger of being
> cut off from my reinforcements.[23]

While Greene was working hard to whip his army into shape,
his lieutenants in the field kept the enemy off balance by scoring
a series of minor victories in South Carolina. Operating in the
region of Ninety-Six to the west of Winnsboro, William Washington's horsemen swept down upon a sizable force of loyalist
militia and wiped them out. Other victories over loyalist bands in

the area further disenchanted any recruits who might have thought of joining the British. General Francis Marion, the famed "Swamp Fox," following Greene's orders, pounced upon British supply trains in the lowlands. Henry Lee's dragoons meanwhile were carrying on guerrilla warfare in the region between Winnsboro and Orangeburg.

Greene gained even more precious time when the British reinforcements under General Alexander Leslie were tardy in reaching South Carolina. Tossed by winds and gales at sea, the transports with 2,500 men aboard did not reach Charleston until mid-December. After disembarking, Leslie's march into the interior was delayed for lack of wagons. It was the middle of January, 1781, before the British reinforcements arrived near the scene of action.

With Leslie's men drawing near, Cornwallis decided it was time to march against Morgan's force. Once it was destroyed, he could turn upon Greene for a showdown. To smash Morgan's men, Cornwallis picked Colonel Banastre Tarleton, the cavalry leader known as the "Green Dragoon." Tarleton's force was made up of crack troops—350 dragoons and 800 trained infantry. Morgan had about the same number of soldiers, but many of his men were untrained militia. In one of the most remarkable engagements of the Revolution, Morgan scored a stunning victory over Tarleton at the Battle of Cowpens on January 17.

As soon as Cornwallis learned the news of Tarleton's defeat, he fairly panted for revenge. He tried to intercept Morgan, hoping to recapture the British prisoners taken at Cowpens. But the wily old frontiersman raced for the Catawba River at the best speed he could make and crossed the stream two days ahead of the pursuing British. By the time Cornwallis reached the Catawba, the winter rains had swollen the stream to a point where it was unfordable.

Temporarily safe from pursuit, Morgan rested his men and reported his position to Greene. In a daring ride through a country infested with Tories, Greene galloped 125 miles with a small escort to join Morgan and to direct his march. In Morgan's camp, the two generals sat down to discuss strategy. Morgan wanted to take to the mountains where his troops would be safe from pursuit. Greene turned down the idea. Instead, he ordered Morgan to march for Salisbury, North Carolina, where the rest of the Southern army was headed. Morgan, disagreeing with this dangerous strategy, declared he would not be answerable for what might happen if he had to retreat through North Carolina. "Neither will you," Greene is said to have replied, "for I shall take the measure upon myself." [24]

If the North Carolina militia turned out in sufficient force, Greene planned to fight it out with Cornwallis. But if they did not respond, he would retreat all the way to Virginia, if necessary. Greene's plan was bold and daring but not foolhardy in its conception. He was well aware of the risks involved and warned, "Our prospects are gloomy notwithstanding these flashes of success." [25]

Realizing that Cornwallis would cross the Catawba as soon as the river subsided, Greene sent riders through the countryside to rouse the patriot militia. He was hoping that a sufficient number of men would turn out to delay Cornwallis' crossing temporarily. The delay would allow Morgan time to reach Salisbury and to cross over the next river, the Yadkin. But the militia failed to respond. In fact, rather than gaining strength, Greene lost some of his best troops. Just twelve hours before Cornwallis began crossing the Catawba, the Virginia militia whose enlistments had expired cut out of the army and headed for home.

Greene waited in vain at the rendezvous where the militia were supposed to gather. When it became clear that none were coming, he set out for Salisbury in a driving rain. By the time the British reached the river crossing, the only troops there to oppose them were a handful of North Carolina militiamen who had been with Morgan since the beginning of the campaign. Even these troops fled in confusion after exchanging a few shots with the enemy and the British pressed on their pursuit.

Determined to catch his prey, Cornwallis burned his baggage and mounted two men on each horse in order that he might move more rapidly. Morgan, however, had too much of a head start. The Americans reached Salisbury safely and crossed the Yadkin easily, for Greene had had the foresight to collect numerous small craft at one spot on the river. Cornwallis, on the other hand, had no means of getting his army across the stream.

Angered by his failure to trap his quarry, Cornwallis ordered a furious bombardment on the American camp across the Yadkin, but because of the river's high banks the cannonade did little more than amuse the patriots. During the bombardment, one British gunner concentrated his fire on the roof of a certain building unaware that it was Greene's headquarters. Shingles and boards went flying as the gunner found his mark. Greene, who was inside, went right on writing his reports. "His pen," reported one officer, "never rested but when a new visitor arrived, and then the answer was given with calmness and precision, and the pen immediately resumed." [26] From Salisbury, Greene carried away 1,700 muskets he had found stored for use by the militia. The sight of the muskets and the failure of the militia to respond stirred Greene to cry out in anguish in one letter: "O that we had in the field as Henry the Fifth said, some few of the merry thousands that are idle at home!" [27]

Leading Morgan's men, Greene finally reached Guilford Court House, North Carolina, where he linked up with the main army that had arrived from Cheraw Hill. Despite repeated calls for more militia, few men came into camp to offer their services. Feeling that his army was still too small to risk a battle, Greene decided to continue his retreat to the Dan River and to cross over into Virginia. Cornwallis by this time was drawing near with the hope of pinning Greene's army up against one of the rivers.

Greene at this point came up with another of his stratagems. He detached a sizable force under Colonel Otho H. Williams and ordered him to march toward the upper fords of the Dan, making it appear that he intended to cross the river at that point. Greene's intent was to draw Cornwallis away from the main army which would take the road leading in the opposite direc-

tion toward Irwin's Ferry lower down on the Dan. There Kosciuszko was waiting with boats to take the army over.

Back at the Yadkin, Cornwallis had been forced to march
miles upstream before he found a suitable place to ford. When
he learned the Americans were heading for the upper fords of
the Dan, he felt he had Greene at his mercy. Pointing his march
toward the upper fords, Cornwallis hurried out to head off his
foe. To his astonishment, the force under Williams which he
was following suddenly wheeled about and started back toward
Irwin's Ferry. Greene, by that time, had gained a whole day's
march and was well on his way to the crossing.

The race to the Dan, some seventy miles away, was on. Greene's
little army trudged along clay roads that turned into slippery
mud as the rains began to fall. His men suffered terribly. Hundreds of soldiers were without shoes and left bloodstains behind
to mark the army's route. Without tents the ill-clad troops were
forced to huddle by campfires or inside makeshift bough shelters
to keep from freezing at night. Greene suffered along with the
men. One evening he and John Rutledge, the South Carolina
governor, found shelter against the cold rain in an abandoned
hovel. During the night, they awoke and accused one another
of kicking. When the kicking continued, they examined their
bed of straw and discovered that a hog had joined them in the
night to get out of the cold.

While the main army was heading for the Dan, Colonel Williams followed them keeping just a step ahead of Cornwallis. To
prevent the enemy from circling around his camp, Williams kept
half his men patrolling at night while the rest snatched a few
hours of sleep. He often began marching as early as three in the
morning. When his men were far enough ahead of Cornwallis,
Williams permitted them to stop and cook rations to last through
the next twenty-four hours.

Although they were often in sight of Williams' task force, the
British were never able to overtake the Americans and to force
them into a battle. Tarleton's dragoons sometimes attempted to
rush the light troops while crossing streams, but such brushes

usually ended up with British losses because the horsemen under "Light-Horse Harry" Lee and William Washington were more than a match for Tarleton's troopers. Most of the time the British were content to trudge along in the footsteps of their retreating foe. "The demeanor of the hostile troops," wrote Lee, "became so pacific in appearance, that a spectator would have been led to consider them members of the same army." [28]

At long last, Colonel Williams and his exhausted men received the welcome news that Greene had crossed the Dan. The report spread rapidly through the line and with one voice the men gave a shout of joy. General Charles O'Hara, leading Cornwallis' advanced corps, heard the cry and guessed its meaning. By the time O'Hara reached the Dan, he glimpsed the last of Washington's cavalry swimming across the river to the opposite shore. Greene's army had reached sanctuary at last.

Greene summed up his historic retreat in a letter to Thomas Jefferson. He was "almost fatigued to death," he wrote, "having had a retreat to conduct for upwards of two hundred miles, maneuvering constantly in the face of the enemy, to give time for the militia to turn out and get off our stores." [29] The British were as high in their praise of Greene's exploit as were his own countrymen. Tarleton wrote that "Every measure of the Americans during their march from the Catawba to Virginia, was judiciously designed and vigorously executed." [30]

Cornwallis longed to pursue Greene further, but he dared not. His men were tired and sick and his supplies were dangerously low. There was little else to do but to turn back. Cornwallis retreated to Hillsboro, North Carolina, hoping to replenish his supplies and to enlist more loyalists. Only a handful of loyalists joined his force, however, and he found few supplies.

The initiative now passed to Greene. Determined to give Cornwallis as little time as possible to build up his army, Greene recrossed the Dan into North Carolina late in February, 1781. Lee's legion and Washington's cavalry were sent on ahead to harass the enemy and to frighten the loyalists from joining the British. Pressed by Greene, Cornwallis fell back slowly. At

Guilford Court House in mid-March, Greene decided it was time
to fight. It was a sound strategic move. As Tarleton so aptly
noted, "A defeat of the British would have been attended with
the total destruction of Earl Cornwallis's infantry, whilst a victory at this juncture could produce no very decisive consequences
against the Americans!" [31]

Greene's ranks were swelled by this time with new units from
the Continental army and fresh bodies of militia. His force was
nearly twice the size of the British; Greene had 4,200 men and
Cornwallis about 2,000. But the armies were more evenly
matched because more of Cornwallis' troops were veterans. Both
generals joined in battle confident of victory.

Greene rose early on the morning of March 15 and mounting
his horse, gave last-minute instructions to his officers. While riding about he often paused to rub his upper lip as was his habit
when thinking out a problem. His battle formation according to
Tarleton was "unexceptionable," and his choice of ground excellent. He stationed his troops in three lines at the crest of a
long rise with some open ground on their front. Despite these
well-laid plans, however, the opening encounter was nearly disastrous. Greene's front line, made up of North Carolina militiamen, ran from the field after delivering but one volley. His
second line, composed mainly of Virginia militia, stood their
ground for a time. But they too were slowly pushed back
through some woods and finally retired in confusion. Now it
was up to Greene's third line of Continentals from Maryland,
Delaware, and Virginia. Fortunately, his third line held firm.

The fighting grew desperate and bloody and the battle hung
in the balance. Cornwallis' force on occasion was threatened
with complete destruction. To prevent an American break-
through at one point, Cornwallis ordered his gunners to fire
grapeshot into the thick of the fighting even though it meant
killing some of his own men. For an instant Greene himself
was in grave danger of being killed or captured when he rode
through the din and smoke to get a better view of the battle.
He had almost reached the British line before one of his aides

shouted at him to turn back. After a bitter two-hour struggle, Greene ordered a retreat. His ammunition was running low and the enemy had broken through the Maryland regiment to threaten his whole line.

Cornwallis won a technical victory at Guilford Court House, but it was a costly one. Tarleton marked the battle as a great disaster for British arms. Fully one-quarter of Cornwallis' fine army had been knocked out of action. Too weak to continue the campaign, Cornwallis retreated to Wilmington on the coast, where he could be supplied by sea. His withdrawal left Greene the master of North Carolina.

More significant, perhaps, than the retaking of North Carolina, was the effect the campaign had on Cornwallis' thinking. Convinced that British control could not be sustained in the Carolinas as long as Virginia remained an American supply base, Cornwallis made a fateful decision. He would march into Virginia and join the British forces already there. Greene, he was quite sure, would follow him and the combined sections of the British army would make short work of destroying the Southern army. After Greene was crushed, organized resistance in the South would cease and the states below the Potomac would become conquered provinces once more.

But Cornwallis miscalculated. As soon as he was well on his way to Wilmington, Greene broke off his pursuit and turned south to swoop down upon the British forts and garrisons in South Carolina and Georgia. With the help of local partisans like Francis Marion, Thomas Sumter, and Andrew Pickens, he hoped to take all the enemy posts except Savannah and Charleston. After driving the enemy from the interior, Greene planned to leave behind some local forces to contain the British at the two southern cities while he marched his army northward to confront Cornwallis once again.

When Greene's strategy to move into South Carolina became known in the North, it evoked high praise. Lafayette thought Greene's decision was "a great piece of generalship." Richard Henry Lee declared that "like Scipio" Greene had "left Corn-

wallis in N. Carolina and pushed into S. Carolina intending no
doubt to compel the British general to relinquish his prospects
this way, or find his southern conquests wrested from him, if he
does not return to defend them." In Virginia, Jefferson saw the
wisdom of Greene's move and wrote: "North as well as South
Carolina being once in the Hands of the Enemy may become
the Instruments of our Subjugation and effect what the Enemy
themselves cannot. The British may harass and distress us greatly
but the Carolinas alone can subdue us." [32]

Marching into South Carolina in the spring of 1781, Greene
suffered a repulse at the hands of Lord Rawdon at Hobkirk's
Hill, near Camden. This battle only served to arouse his fighting
spirit and he wrote doggedly, "We fight, get beat, rise, and fight
again." [33] He ran into trouble once more at Ninety-Six when reinforcements led by Rawdon arrived on the scene to lift the
siege Greene had imposed on the strong British garrison there.
But while he was keeping Rawdon occupied, Greene's subordinates captured all of the small forts in South Carolina except
those in the vicinity of Charleston. With the coming of summer
and the stifling heat, Greene withdrew his tired troops to the
High Hills of the Santee to rest. Rawdon evacuated Ninety-Six
and all but the lower part of South Carolina was now back in
American hands.

Greene kept himself informed on developments in the North
while conducting his Southern campaign. Upon learning that a
powerful French fleet was expected in American waters that
summer, he sensed the opportunity this would have afforded
him had he been able to dash back into Virginia. With the co-
operation of the French fleet, he might cut off the British army
in Virginia from outside help and Cornwallis' fate would be
sealed. This was to be the future course of events at Yorktown,
but it was Washington and Rochambeau, not Greene, who were
destined to trap Cornwallis.

While the Yorktown campaign was beginning to take shape,
Greene marched down from the High Hills of the Santee. The
British forces in South Carolina and Georgia were still formi-

dable. If Cornwallis managed to break free from Lafayette in
Virginia before Washington and Rochambeau arrived and retreated south, there was a possibility that Greene might be
crushed between two British armies. To prevent this, Greene
sought to destroy the enemy in South Carolina by a full-scale
attack on the British army at Eutaw Springs on September 8,
1781. Before the battle, he was joined by Marion, Pickens, and
other local militia leaders itching for a fight. During the bloody
struggle that followed, both sides suffered heavily. The British
claimed a technical victory because they were in possession of
the field when the fighting was over. But, as in all Greene's battles in the South, the results were decisively in favor of the
Americans. British losses were so heavy that the enemy were
forced to relinquish all territory in the state outside of Charleston.

Praise for Greene again ran high after the Eutaw Springs battle. Henry Knox wrote, "The exalted talents of General Greene
have been amply displayed in North and South Carolina—without an army, without Means, without anything he has performed
wonders." From Holland, John Adams wrote that Eutaw
Springs was "quite as glorious for the American arms as the
capture of Cornwallis." [34]

Although Cornwallis surrendered at Yorktown in October,
1781, fighting continued in the deep South. The British were
bottled up inside Charleston but they were so well entrenched
that Greene could do no more than clamp a tight siege on the
city by land. If Admiral de Grasse had sailed for Charleston
with the French fleet after the Yorktown victory, Greene was
convinced the city would have fallen. But the French admiral
had orders to return immediately to the West Indies. It was not
until December, 1782, that the British finally evacuated Charleston. Fearing the British might resume hostilities, Greene kept a
small force together despite the gradual disintegration of his
army. After the peace treaty was formally ratified, he disbanded
what remained of his army and prepared to leave for home. With
his faithful soldiers gone, Greene said he felt "like Sampson
after Delilah cut his locks." [35]

When Greene rode northward, he was greeted everywhere as a conquering hero. All along his route, he was honored by banquets, meetings, and celebrations. At Alexandria, while Greene lay ill with a fever, a public gathering was held in his behalf. The principal speaker voiced the sentiment of all when he declared that Greene had "the honor of proving to the World that circumstances of the greatest distress . . . can be nobly surmounted by brave men . . . under the command of wise, virtuous, and persevering Leaders." [36]

Upon reaching Philadelphia, Greene found himself as famous in the North as the South. As much as possible, however, he avoided public demonstrations, preferring as he did the company of old friends like Clement Biddle, Charles Pettit, and Robert Morris. At Trenton, a spot that brought back many memories, Greene met General Washington. Together they rode to Princeton, where Congress was sitting. From Congress, Greene received permission to return home as a civilian. As a symbol of its appreciation of his services in the Carolinas, Congress presented him with two brass cannon captured in the South. When he arrived at Newport, Rhode Island, the town turned out to greet him. "In this mighty Revolution," declared the principal speaker, "Which regard the Rights of Humanity for its Base, we feel a Pride . . . that a Citizen of this State had brightened the Paths of Glory. . . ." [37]

In the postwar period, Greene returned south to live at Mulberry Grove, the beautiful plantation near Savannah given to him by the state of Georgia for his military services. He struggled for a few years to get his plantation in operation and to find relief from a ruinous debt contracted while he was still in the army. Worn out by the strains of war and worried by debts, he succumbed to an infection and died at the age of forty-four in June, 1786.

Thomas Jefferson acknowledged long afterward that Greene was second to none among the Revolutionary War generals. Francis Kinloch, a congressman who fought in the war, declared the Rhode Islander was "the greatest military genius produced by the War for Independence." [38] With the passing of years, such appraisals of Greene by his contemporaries seem justified. In the North he gave Washington sound advice, his mistake at Fort Washington notwithstanding, and he performed brilliantly at Brandywine and other battles. In the South, Greene's strategy and daring played a major role in the final undoing of British power in that region. Carrying on a warfare of attrition, Greene harassed Cornwallis to the point that he decided to abandon North Carolina for Virginia. After marching away from Cornwallis, Greene carried out a whirlwind campaign that enabled him to free much of the deep South from complete subjugation. Always a great leader and a deadly strategist, he deserves to be remembered as the logical successor to the commander-in-chief had anything ever happened to Washington in the course of the war.

FOOTNOTES

1. George Washington Greene, *Life of Nathanael Greene, Major General in the Army of the Revolution* (New York, 1867–71), II, 417. Hereinafter G. W. Greene.
2. Greene to Henry Knox, July 18, 1781, Greene Papers, Connecticut Historical Society.
3. Greene to Samuel Ward, Jr., September 26, 1771, Greene Papers, Rhode Island Historical Society.
4. Alexander Garden, *Anecdotes of the American Revolution* (Brooklyn, 1865), I, 65.
5. Knox to John Adams, September 25, 1776, *Proceedings of the American Antiquarian Society*, V, 56, 217; G. W. Greene, *op. cit.*, I, 207.
6. Theodore Thayer, *Nathanael Greene: Strategist of the American Revolution* (New York, 1960), p. 118.
7. Henry P. Johnston, *The Campaign of 1776 around New York and Brooklyn* (Brooklyn, 1878), p. 284.
8. Greene to his wife, January 10, 1777, Greene Collection, V, 88, William Clements Library.
9. William Gordon, *History of the Rise, Progress and Establishment of the Independence of the United States of America* (London, 1788), II, 296.
10. G. W. Greene, *op. cit.*, I, 310–11.

11. Greene's letter, May 20, 1777, Greene Papers, Rhode Island Historical Society.
12. G. W. Greene, *op. cit.*, I, 457.
13. *Ibid.*, II, 483–85, 500–02.
14. John Clark to Greene, January 10, 1778, Greene Collection, II, William Clements Library; G. W. Greene, *op. cit.*, II, 1–40.
15. Douglas Southall Freeman, *George Washington: A Biography* (New York, 1952), IV, 592–611; G. W. Greene, *ob. cit.*, II, 2.
16. George Lux to Greene, May 26, 1778, Greene Collection, II, William Clements Library.
17. G. W. Greene, *op. cit.*, II, 466, 505–06.
18. *Ibid.*, II, 86, 512; John C. Fitzpatrick, ed., *The Writings of George Washington* (Washington, D.C., 1934), XII, 277.
19. Thayer, *op. cit.*, pp. 229–38, 413–20.
20. Samuel Shaw, *The Journals of Major Samuel Shaw* (Boston, 1847), pp. 82–83; G. W. Greene, *op. cit.*, II, 374–75, 377–78.
21. G. W. Greene, *op. cit.*, II, 381–94; Greene to wife, October 14, 1780, Greene Collection, X, William Clements Library; Thayer, *op. cit.*, p. 280.
22. Henry Lee, *Memoirs of the War in the Southern Department of the United States* (Philadelphia, 1812), I, 244–45; Elkanah Watson, *Men and Times of the Revolution* (New York, 1856), p. 259.
23. G. W. Greene, *op. cit.*, III, 131–32.
24. Gordon, *op. cit.*, IV, 39.
25. Greene to John Mathews, January 23, 1781, Greene Papers, Bancroft Collection, New York Public Library.
26. G. W. Greene, *op. cit.*, III, 161.
27. Greene to Steuben, February 3, 1781, Greene Papers, XVIII, William Clements Library.
28. Lee, *op. cit.*, I, 289–90.
29. G. W. Greene, *op. cit.*, III, 174.
30. Banastre Tarleton, *History of the Campaign of 1780 and 1781 in the Southern Provinces of North America* (London, 1787), p. 229; Greene to Jefferson, December 15, 1781, Greene Papers, Bancroft Collection, New York Public Library.
31. *Ibid.*, p. 277.
32. *Letters of Richard Henry Lee* (New York, 1912–14), II, 218–19; Julian Boyd, *The Papers of Thomas Jefferson* (Princeton, 1952), V, 541; Greene to Joseph Reed, March 18, 1781, Reed Papers, IX, New York Historical Society.
33. Greene to Luzerne, June 22, 1781, Greene Collection, XXXI, William Clements Library; Greene to Lafayette, May 23, 1781, Greene Papers, Library of Congress.

34. Knox to John Adams, October 21, 1781, *Proceedings of the American Antiquarian Society*, XVI, 225; Charles Francis Adams, *The Works of John Adams* (Boston, 1852), VII, 487.
35. Greene to Charles Pettit, July 29, 1783, Reed Papers, X, New York Historical Society.
36. Greene Papers, VII, 330, Library of Congress.
37. Greene to Malgine, Channing, and Goodwin, November 29, 1783, Greene Collection, LXXXIX, William Clements Library.
38. Paul Leicester Ford, *The Works of Thomas Jefferson* (New York, 1905), XII, 246; Francis Kinloch, *Letters from Geneva and France* (Boston, 1819), II, 142.

BIBLIOGRAPHY

Alden, John R., *The South in the Revolution 1763–1789*. Baton Rouge, 1957. Contains a brief but accurate account of Greene's campaigns in the South.
Caldwell, Charles, *Memoirs of the Life and Campaigns of the Hon. Nathanael Greene*. Philadelphia, 1819. An older work that is very inaccurate.
Freeman, Douglas S., *George Washington: A Biography*, 6 vols. New York, 1954. Volumes III and IV contain excellent accounts of Greene's contributions to the campaigns in the North.
Greene, Francis V., *General Greene*. New York, 1893. An old and incomplete account of Greene's life, but one that is especially good on military analysis.
Greene, George W., *Life of Nathanael Greene*, 3 vols. New York, 1867–71. The most comprehensive biography of Greene and written by his grandson. A mine of information on Greene's life, but lacks critical analysis of both the men and events of the Revolution.
Johnson, William, *Sketches of the Life and Correspondence of Nathanael Greene*. Charleston, 1822. A useful biography for a detailed account of Greene's southern campaigns.
Pratt, Fletcher, "Nathanael Greene: The Quaker Turenne," in *Eleven Generals: Studies in American Command*. New York, 1949. A brief and illuminating sketch.
Thayer, Theodore, *Nathanael Greene: Strategist of the Revolution*. New York, 1960. The most recent biography of Greene.

John Sullivan:

LUCKLESS IRISHMAN

———•———

CHARLES P. WHITTEMORE

South Kent School

OF ALL Washington's generals, John Sullivan deserves the reputation of a fighter, whether in the field or in the halls of Congress; for when this fiery Irishman was not busy warring with the British, he found time to take on Congress or his colleagues. But throughout his entire career, battling either friend or foe, Sullivan was dogged by bad luck. His failure to succeed against the British might be explained by his not having battle experience—though he was no worse off in this respect than many of his fellow officers. Because he had been a small town country lawyer, one might expect John Sullivan to have acquired the knack of getting along well with people, but he was a contentious soul and had no trouble finding ways to irritate those about him. Like so many men who complain of ill-luck, Sullivan helped to bring on many of his own misfortunes. The same driving ambition that caused him to make errors on the field of battle, also caused him to alienate politicians in Congress. He strained for success with every fiber of his being, sought the plaudits of the crowd, and strove without letup to advance his own welfare. In the end it was Sullivan's ambition that brought him down and ended his military career before the Revolutionary War was concluded.

John Sullivan came from a humble background. His parents

arrived from Ireland as redemptionists, or indentured servants, in the 1730's and settled in Somersworth, New Hampshire, where John was born on February 17, 1740. His father, a schoolteacher, gave his son a far better education than most boys could expect in those years. For a time the family lived in Berwick, Maine, a frontier community across the border from New Hampshire. When he was eighteen, Sullivan read law with Samuel Livermore, and shortly afterward launched out on a practice of his own. After his marriage to Lydia Worster in 1760, he moved from Berwick to Durham, New Hampshire, which was to be his residence for the rest of his life.

Even at this early stage in his career, his contentious streak became evident. Overly zealous in suing for debts owed him, he once antagonized some of his neighbors to the point where they formed an armed mob to storm the house at which he was staying. He became a passionate hater of Great Britain, and soon advocated independence. His driving ambition made him a talented politician in spite of his tendency to irk people, and New Hampshire chose to send him to the First Continental Congress. Upon his return in November, 1774, he urged his fellow townsmen to co-operate in economic coercion against the mother country, organized a raid upon the British fortress in the Portsmouth harbor, and found himself on the road to Philadelphia to attend the Second Congress in May, 1775. He was now ready for any eventuality, and brought much fire and zeal to the task facing him.

In June, 1775, Sullivan left Congress to go to Boston to assume his duties as a brigadier general. His appointment to so high a rank came as no surprise. As a former major in the militia and spokesman of the patriot forces in New Hampshire, Sullivan was a logical choice.[1] His striking appearance lent dignity to his new command, for although he was of middling stature, he stood erect. His black, piercing eyes and his ruddy complexion helped give him the look of a daring leader. And time would show that he had the qualities needed for combat—courage, energy, and enthusiasm.

General Sullivan's military career may be considered as having three phases. At first he was completely cocky, absolutely convinced of his own ability, and daring almost to the point of being foolhardy. During the siege of Boston, for example, he wrote that the Americans would "take possession of the town, or perish in the attempt." [2] When Washington sent him to take command of the pathetic little army in Canada, Sullivan still was confident, and only after he knew for sure that he faced quick disaster did he reluctantly order a retreat. His clumsy performance and capture at Long Island were somewhat redeemed by his part in the successes at Trenton and Princeton, after he had been exchanged as a prisoner of war. Thus ended the first phase: he was still cocksure despite his setbacks.

The second phase of Sullivan's career came in the last half of 1777, when he suffered successive defeats at Staten Island, Brandywine, and Germantown. With severe criticism buzzing about his head, Sullivan seemed unnerved. Confidence began giving way to caution as he entered the third phase. Thanks to the caution that came with experience, Sullivan performed competently from this point on. He proved a sound commander during the Rhode Island campaign in the summer of 1778, although his handling of the French allies left much to be desired. His final contribution was his march into the Indian country in the Finger Lakes district of New York in 1779. Sullivan had come into his own by this time. He was now the careful tactician stalking an elusive prey. His scorched-earth policy dealt the Indians a blow from which they never fully recovered.

Sullivan's role in the early stages of the war was a relatively minor one. After joining the new American army in Cambridge in July, 1775, he commanded a brigade in the force that kept the British penned up inside Boston. Whenever Washington's staff met to discuss strategy, Sullivan joined those who advised against any attempts to attack the enemy during the summer or fall. He preferred to wait, he said, until winter. True to his word, Sullivan led an abortive assault to seize outbuildings and barracks on Bunker Hill, late in December. The attempt failed and with it went Sullivan's first chance to gain military glory.

The British remained in Boston until the following spring, and the two armies did little else but glower at one another. The military stalemate came to an end when Washington captured Dorchester Heights in March, 1776, and the British decided they must evacuate the city. As the enemy prepared to embark, the energetic Sullivan galloped down to where he could have a good look at Bunker Hill. There he saw sentries with shouldered firelocks standing guard, but they stood suspiciously motionless. Putting his spyglass to his eye, Sullivan saw that the "sentries" were effigies left by the departing redcoats. Convinced that the siege was over, he moved forward with a small party and "bravely took a fortress Defended by Lifeless Sentries." [3]

The joy of outlasting the British was dampened by Sullivan's controversy with the New Hampshire legislature regarding his right to appoint militia officers. When the militia was threatening to leave at the end of 1775, Sullivan set out to re-enlist as many of the men as would listen to his pleas. He even took the liberty of making some of the men officers, a prerogative which the legislators at home claimed for themselves. Displeased by Sullivan's actions, they criticized him for highhandedness. Always a touchy man, Sullivan did not take the reproach lightly. Soon he would be off to New York, he wrote, then "those persons will . . . have no more fear of the Destruction of their Liberties from a person who has spent more money undergone more Fatigue and oftener Risqued his Life than any other person in your Province. . . ." [4]

His ego bruised, Sullivan set off for New York City in March with the rest of Washington's army. He did not linger there for long, for he was soon on his way upstate to take reinforcements to the Northern army invading Canada. No sooner had he arrived than he learned he must assume command in place of John Thomas who was dying of smallpox. The Canadian campaign was crumbling, and Sullivan should have had enough sense to order an immediate retreat. But he wanted to fight, and this seemed to him to be the time to show Washington and Congress that here was an Irishman eager to strike blows at the British. Glory was just around the corner and to retreat seemed ridiculous in his eyes. He stubbornly insisted upon a raid at Trois Rivières. Even after his men were defeated there, he still would not consider pulling back. "I now think only of a glorious Death or a victory obtained against Superiour numbers," he wrote.[5] But an army riddled with smallpox cannot fight, and even Sullivan was finally forced to face the inevitable. As Sullivan told the story, however, it was not the certainty of defeat that caused him to withdraw. Instead he blamed his dispirited army, the desire of some officers to resign, and the possibility that his men might not stand up to the British as his reasons for turning back to New York. The retreat, surprisingly enough, was orderly and efficient, although the agony of pain and illness which his unhappy men had to endure was a nightmare. On July 1, 1776, the shabby remnants of a once confident army reached Crown Point, thereby bringing to an end America's attempt to win the "fourteenth colony."

Shortly after his return, Sullivan learned that Congress was sending on Horatio Gates to supersede him as commander in the Northern Department. He smarted at the setback. Sullivan was not the type of man to stand idly by and let Gates move in without opposition. Unbeknownst to Sullivan, however, Washington had assessed his candidacy at the time Congress was considering the matter, in these frank words:

[Sullivan] . . . is aiming at the Command in Canada. . . . Whether he merits it or not, is a matter to be considered; and that it may be considered with propriety I think it my duty to observe . . . that he is active, spirited, and Zealously attach'd to the Cause; that he does not want Abilities, many Members of Congress, as well as myself, can testify. But he has his wants, and he has his foibles. The latter are manifested in a little tincture of vanity, and in an over desire of being popular, which now and then leads him into some embarrassments. His wants are common to us all; the want of experience to move upon a large Scale; for the limited, and contracted knowledge which any of us have in Military Matters stands in very little Stead; and is greatly over balanced by sound judgment, and some knowledge of Men and Books; especially when accompanied by an enterprizing genius, which I must do Genl. Sullivan the justice to say, I think he possesses. . . .[6]

Washington's appraisal confirmed the congressmen in their opinion that a more experienced man was needed in the Northern Department. But Sullivan had no intention of settling for second place and in a fit of pique he requested leave to go to Philadelphia so that he might submit his resignation. This episode was but the first of many temperamental blasts from the constantly irate Irishman.

In Philadelphia, some of his friends soothed him and sought to dissuade him from handing in his resignation. Sullivan eventually acceded to their request. It is just as well he did. Congress had been prepared to give him a "rap on the knuckles," to use Thomas Jefferson's words.[7] Sullivan, however, never saw it that way, and remained quite unaware that he had antagonized anyone. In fact, he felt he had been quite shabbily treated.

It was in such a truculent frame of mind that Sullivan faced his next military assignment on Long Island. He still was full of confidence, convinced that he was one of Washington's better officers. He had just been promoted to major general, and was most eager to show his talents. The Battle of Long Island, fought August 27, 1776, would be the proving ground. To protect New York City, Washington had scattered his army in three separate locations: Manhattan Island, Long Island, and along the New Jersey shore. The force on the western tip of Long Island guarding the entry into New York's inner harbor was commanded by Nathanael Greene. When Greene became ill in August, his command was given to Sullivan. Joseph Reed, Washington's adjutant, thought little of the choice, claiming that Sullivan "was wholly unacquainted with the ground or country." [8] Israel Putnam was likewise disgruntled because he wanted the assignment for himself.

The patriot forces on Long Island took up a position behind the breastworks on Brooklyn Heights controlling the East River and New York City. In front of the redoubts and entrenchments, about a mile and a half away, ran a ridge of hills. In these hills some American units stood guard at the passes, for this would have to be the British route of entry to the American position at Brooklyn—unless the British chose to swing far to the right to enter the pass that opened on Jamaica Road behind the ridge. But who in Washington's army expected the enemy to make such a detour?

On August 22, 1776, the British ferried troops from Staten Island to Long Island. A battle was obviously in the offing, but Washington was not sure what to do next. At this point he apparently had second thoughts about placing Sullivan in charge on Long Island. He sent Putnam over to take command instead. But the tough old Connecticut farmer, although brave and vigorous, was no tactician and was incapable of handling the large command of about 9,000 troops.

Historians, unfortunately, have never been able to determine the definite scope of Putnam's command. Consequently it is hard to pin down just who was responsible for the American defeat that followed.[9] Most likely Sullivan had command of the forces outside the Brooklyn breastworks, although he denied this later, claiming that another American general—Lord Stirling—had this honor. Yet Sullivan certainly acted as though he had authority to protect the approaches to Brooklyn Heights. On August 23, he ordered regiments to all the passes except the one which opened upon the Jamaica Road. There he sent only a patrol of five men. This was a fantastic piece of misjudgment on his part. The total inadequacy of the weak forces at the passes and puny guard at the Jamaica Pass should have been obvious to any competent military commander. Yet Washington toured the lines on the eve of the battle and seemed satisfied with the disposition of the troops. The commander-in-chief was far from keen on this occasion; his better days still lay ahead.

Sullivan, who was commanding the center of the American

lines, had little inkling of the masterful attack which the British were about to unfold. While General James Grant and the Hessians under Von Heister assaulted the passes on the morning of the twenty-seventh, General Howe along with Lord Percy was circling the American left for a flanking attack. The British had moved out on the previous evening and soon learned of the small patrol at the Jamaica Pass. They hoped to reach Sullivan's rear before the Americans even knew of their whereabouts.

Howe's plan succeeded brilliantly. When dawn came, Sullivan found himself hotly committed along his front in the middle of the American lines. But he was able to hold his own. Suddenly firing broke out behind him as Howe completed his encirclement. Fighting furiously, Sullivan tried to break through to the lines at Brooklyn Heights, but with no success. His men were overrun and the general himself was forced to surrender to three Hessian soldiers in a cornfield. After his dreams of military glory, Sullivan's surrender seemed ludicrous.

The Battle of Long Island ended with a serious defeat of the American forces. The patriots found themselves driven into a tight little defense perimeter on Brooklyn Heights, barely two miles wide and one mile deep. At this time the British undoubtedly could have overwhelmed them and pushed them into the sea. Fortunately, however, Howe chose not to press his advantage and Washington escaped by an amphibious midnight evacuation back to the island of Manhattan. This safe withdrawal was the only bright spot in the American efforts.

Was Sullivan responsible for the turning of the American left and the defeat that followed? The question is not easy to answer, as it hinges upon the issue of who was in command of the lines in front of the Brooklyn defenses. Sullivan certainly must share some of the blame for the poor watch kept at the Jamaica Pass. Washington also must assume some blame for failing to spell out more clearly the duties of his subordinates and for the poor deployment of troops in front of the Brooklyn breastworks. But what really had happened was that a professional, William Howe, had won by outsmarting the American amateurs. Sullivan summed up the battle best by saying: "General Howe was too old for us." [10]

Sullivan, now a captive aboard the ship of Lord Richard Howe, William Howe's brother, found the admiral likewise "too old" for him. The captured American received the polite treatment so typical of eighteenth-century warfare. He soon fell under the influence of Lord Howe, who was most anxious to serve as conciliator between England and her rebellious colonies and kept telling Sullivan why the Americans should come to terms. At first Sullivan paid little attention to Howe's persuasive efforts, but gradually he gave way and consented to carry a message to Congress seeking reconciliation.

It is not easy to explain Sullivan's willingness to serve as Howe's errand boy. Certainly no one in Washington's army was more anxious to whip the British than the New Hampshire Irishman. But apparently Lord Howe had convinced Sullivan that the British were ready to make major concessions in giving up taxation and the control of internal policy. Sullivan, at least, thought Howe had gone that far, but the British admiral later denied it. Allowed to leave on his parole, Sullivan went off to Philadelphia to talk with the delegates in Congress.

The members of Congress, still displeased over Sullivan's petulance earlier in the summer, were not so gullible as the captured general. John Adams, for example, was not the least bit impressed by Sullivan's stories of British change of heart. Leaning over toward Benjamin Rush, Adams whispered that he wished "the first ball that had been fired on the day of the defeat of our Army had gone through his [Sullivan's] head." In Adams' mind Sullivan was no less than a "decoy duck whom Lord Howe has sent among us to seduce us into a renunciation of our independence." [11] In his summary of the episode, John Adams, who was thoroughly annoyed, had nothing to say that would credit Sullivan. He wrote:

> The conduct of General Sullivan, in consenting to come to Philadelphia, upon so confused an errand from Lord Howe, though his

situation, as a prisoner, was a temptation, and may be considered as
some apology for it, appeared to me to betray such want of pene-
tration and fortitude, and there was so little precision in the information he communicated, that I felt much resentment, and more
contempt, upon the occasion, than was perhaps just. The time was
extremely critical. The attention of Congress, the army, the States,
and the people, ought to have been wholly directed to the defense
of the country. To have it diverted and relaxed, by such a poor
artifice and confused tale, appeared very reprehensible.[12]

Nothing came of the British peace overtures. The delegates
were wary of taking the bait, and after an inconclusive conference between the two sides, the matter came to a close. Sullivan,
however, gained his exchange and by the end of September had
rejoined Washington's army in New York.

Despite the many reverses he had suffered, Sullivan was not
downhearted. Fortunately for his morale and for the patriot
cause, the Battles of Trenton and Princeton around the turn of
the year allowed the patriot army to demonstrate to the British
that it had some fight left. In the Trenton battle, Sullivan crossed
the Delaware with Washington's main task force, took half of
the men and cannon, and marched along the road close to the
river to strike at the southern end of town. The result was a
quick victory and a bag of prisoners. At Princeton, Sullivan's
column was not positioned to be in the main fight, but his men
took part in the pursuit that followed. These two surprising victories gave Washington the time he needed and he settled in
Morristown for the winter. Sullivan had proved to be a tireless
and brave fighter, whether in the heartbreaking defeats suffered
earlier or in the victories at Trenton and Princeton. The first
phase of his military career had come to a close.

Sullivan entered 1777 with high hopes that better days lay
ahead now that the Americans had had some success. But he was
doomed to be disappointed. During the winter he fell ill from
a digestive disorder, most likely a peptic ulcer.[13] That a man of
such a mercurial and excitable nature had an ulcer is understandable. Nor did he help matters by drinking heavily. Doctors

warned him to stop, but to no avail. "Spirits I must never again use but with the Greatest Caution (if at all)," was the way Sullivan casually stated the matter. But throughout the rest of his life, John Sullivan remained a heavy drinker.[14]

The general's ulcer was not soothed by the report that Arthur St. Clair had been given the command at Ticonderoga, a post that Sullivan had wanted for himself. The news caused another of Sullivan's outbursts. He sent a whining letter to Washington in March complaining that he had been passed over for a separate command and offered to resign since the commander-in-chief had shown such little confidence in him. Washington's stinging reply was abrupt and to the point:

> Do not, my dear General Sullivan, torment yourself any longer with imaginary Slights, and involve others in the perplexities you feel on that Score. No other officer of rank, in the whole army, has so often conceived himself neglected, Slighted, and ill treated, as you have done, and none I am sure has had less cause than yourself to entertain such Ideas. Mere accidents, things which have occurred in the common course of Service, have been considered by you as designed affronts.[15]

These caustic words silenced Sullivan, but not for long. In June when he learned that a French officer, Philippe du Coudray, had been granted a major general's commission to command the artillery and engineers and to be responsible only to Washington and Congress, Sullivan burst forth again. This time he had some support. Nathanael Greene and Henry Knox were also furious that Du Coudray was outranking them. There was a mild storm when the three generals threatened to resign. But Congress refused to give way and expected an apology from the American generals. No apology was forthcoming. Fortunately for the patriot cause, Du Coudray foolishly rode his horse across the deck of a ferry and drowned in the Schuylkill. The Frenchman's drowning brought an end, for the time being, to the promotion problem.

Irked by his failures and anxious to win a victory of his own,

Sullivan planned an independent raid on Staten Island from the New Jersey shore in the summer of 1777. On the morning of August 22, Sullivan moved his men across to Staten Island and at first met with some success. But as the hours went by, he ran into trouble. His officers could not maintain strict discipline and the men began to straggle and plunder. As though the unruly men were not enough trouble, chaos and confusion arose from a misunderstanding about the rendezvous whence the men were to recross to New Jersey. Although Sullivan had taken some prisoners, he also had lost some men so that his neat *"coup"* was somewhat of a failure. Congress was beginning to have some doubts about Sullivan's ability and a crisis approached, both for the American army and the Irishman's future.

When Howe invaded Pennsylvania in late August to capture Philadelphia, Sullivan faced the most bitter controversy of his career. Washington marched his men to face Howe southwest of Philadelphia and took up his position along the Brandywine in September to halt the Britisher's advance. The most likely place for the enemy to cross was at Chad's Ford and there Washington placed several brigades. To Sullivan he gave the key assignment of guarding the right flank at Brinton's Ford, just above Chad's Ford. The American lines were not unlike those at Long Island, except this time Washington was determined not to allow the British to march around him as they had a year before.

Sullivan did not assume his post at Brinton's Ford until the eve of the Battle of Brandywine on September 11. Before taking command, he visited Washington's headquarters on the night of September 10, for a briefing, and at that time he was told to have men reconnoiter as far north as Buffington's Ford, the fork at which two branches of the Brandywine joined. Washington assured him he need not worry about the fords beyond Buffington's because there were no likely crossing places for at least twelve miles to the north and there were light-horse units scouting in that direction to warn of any surprise flanking move. Lulled into a false sense of security, Sullivan reported to his command and made no move to check Washington's information that there were no places to cross immediately north of Buffington's Ford. He had little time to study the terrain, for the battle was soon joined.

Early that morning, Howe moved some of his forces to Chad's Ford, giving the impression that he was about to attack the American center. At the same time, he sent Lord Cornwallis on a wide sweeping march north to cross the Brandywine well above Buffington's Ford and to fall upon the American right wing under the hapless Sullivan. Once again Howe was using the tactics of Long Island, and the inept Americans were to be an easy prey.

Yet Sullivan could not get Long Island out of his mind, and as a result he was wary of a flank attack. He expected such a move, at least he claimed so later, but unfortunately he failed to take proper initiative to check on possible crossing places. On two separate occasions during the morning, he sent word to Washington that some flanking move was coming. Washington, who had received other reports of a flanking march, thought it would take the enemy some time to make such a move and to be in position to attack. If Howe chose to divide his army, a tactic frowned upon by many, Washington thought the time had come to take advantage of the daring British move. It seemed as though he had a perfect opportunity to strike at the British stationary force at Chad's Ford. After attacking the force in front of him, Washington thought he would have plenty of time to regroup his forces to meet the reported movement on his flank. Making his decision, the commander-in-chief ordered Sullivan to cross the Brandywine to assist him in attacking the enemy's stationary unit.[16]

Just as Sullivan was getting ready to move, Major Joseph Spear of the Pennsylvania militia rode up to report that there was no sign of the enemy in the branches of the Brandywine. Sullivan was in a quandary; the facts seemed to run counter to his own opinion of a flanking attack. He quickly relayed Spear's report, with his own conclusion that his earlier information about a flanking march was "wrong," to Washington.[17] The confused Washington hesitated momentarily, for he dared not order an assault if there were any possibility that the enemy facing him was at full strength across Chad's Ford.

The lull continued until about two o'clock in the afternoon, when another messenger rode up to General Sullivan, bringing an intelligence report from Colonel Theodorick Bland, who was scouting for Washington. Bland's message was short and alarming. The enemy were at Sullivan's rear barely two miles away! What Sullivan had been expecting all along, until fooled by Spear's account, had actually come to pass. Although not quite sure of the location of the enemy, Sullivan began to deploy his troops. He hardly had time to do so. Within an hour and a half about 7,000 British troops were pressing upon him, and by four o'clock the attack had become general. Some of Sullivan's men were still not in place. The enemy's rapid approach threw his division into a panic and soon the whole line was giving way. Fortunately, Nathanael Greene arrived on the scene and with Sullivan's help managed to turn the rout into an orderly, if hard-pressed, retreat. It had been a bad day for the Americans, who suffered 1,000 casualties and were forced to move in the direction of Philadelphia. The capital could not be saved much longer.

The next few weeks following the defeat at Brandywine were bitter ones for John Sullivan. Members of Congress demanded his removal for what appeared to be poor performance at both Staten Island and Brandywine. Sullivan's most outspoken critic was Thomas Burke, of North Carolina, whose charges carried extra weight because he had been on hand and witnessed parts of the battle. Burke levied two major complaints against Sullivan—faulty intelligence and incompetent deployment of troops: he censured Sullivan for passing on Spear's inaccurate information to Washington and claimed the New Hampshire general had handled his troops badly in the battle. Both charges were unfair. Washington said that Sullivan was correct in relaying Spear's message, although possibly Sullivan should have attempted to evaluate the information for the commander-in-chief. There is a good chance, though, that the faulty information saved Washington from an embarrassing beating had he chosen to cross Chad's Ford to attack the British stationary force, for the British were far stronger than he had estimated. Burke's second complaint that Sullivan brought his men into action by a circuitous rather than a direct route had some basis of fact. But it may be said in Sullivan's defense that he did not know where the adjoining patriot forces were located at the time or the exact position of the attacking enemy. His reaction to events as they unfolded was logical and reasonable, but he lacked brilliance.

Congress, however, was more interested in finding a scapegoat on whom to blame the battle than in explanations. To the members, Sullivan looked like the logical man to be sacrificed. He had been consistently unlucky, had failed as yet to win a major victory, and had never endeared himself to the delegates in his earlier relations. Congress voted to recall the unhappy general until an inquiry could be made into his conduct, not of the Brandywine battle, but of the ill-fated Staten Island raid. Washington, fearful of losing one of his top officers, persuaded the politicians to delay Sullivan's recall until the military crisis in Pennsylvania had passed.

Washington's gesture on Sullivan's behalf brought the Irishman small consolation. Faced with an inquiry on Staten Island and with criticism for incompetence at Brandywine, Sullivan was thoroughly angered. He hoped Washington would speak favorably of his actions at Brandywine, and asked the commander-in-chief to come to his defense, but Washington demurred on the grounds that he had not been in Sullivan's sector. All he could say to comfort the irate subordinate was, "Some have condemn'd your disposition [at Brandywine] tho' time perhaps wd. not allow a better but none have accused you of want of bravery, and exertion, that I have heard of." [18] Sullivan's own reaction to the attack on his reputation was a pathetic whine: "I am the butt against which all the darts are levelled." [19]

In the midst of all this bickering came another battle, this time at Germantown, the site of Howe's main encampment.

Washington's army moved out on the night of October 3, 1777, and in four widely separated columns headed toward the enemy. Once again Sullivan had a major assignment, command of the right wing, but this time Washington accompanied him, probably to shield the unfortunate New Hampshire man from any further criticism. As the morning of October 4 opened, the Americans had some initial success, but then a variety of factors —fog, confusion, and lack of co-ordination—deprived them of the victory they desired so ardently. Instead of achieving the triumph which had been close at hand, the patriots had to tumble backward from the field of battle, and Sullivan's men retreated with the rest. Although the retreat in no way was Sullivan's fault, some insinuated that his division had been the first to quit the battle. This time, however, Washington was quick in coming to his subordinate's assistance and he silenced the critics.

While the repercussions over Germantown were still in the air, the inquiry on Staten Island was held. Sullivan was quickly cleared of any blame, and the members of the court unanimously agreed that the expedition had been well-planned and with better luck would have been a stunning success. With this favorable decision given some publicity, Sullivan found that criticism of his conduct at Brandywine began to abate. Now exonerated of any negligence, Sullivan joined Washington's men as they prepared for the harsh winter at Valley Forge during the remainder of 1777 and the early part of 1778. The second phase of Sullivan's military career had concluded. Although he continued to be somewhat cocky, his defeats had had a sobering effect. He was no longer what Benjamin Rush called him—"in the field a madman." [20] The third phase lay ahead, and it would be his best and most productive one, thanks to the caution Sullivan had learned from bitter experience. He was to gain the independent command that he had so eagerly sought. With this new responsibility would come a more able performance.

Although he changed his tactics on the battlefield, Sullivan remained as peevish as ever. At Valley Forge, he constantly pestered Washington for leave to go home to recoup his financial losses. When told he could not be spared, he complained that he still was hoping for an independent command. It was an unhappy John Sullivan who wrote to Washington:

> I Reallize my Command as high in The Army at the Same time Consider it as arising from mere Fortuitous Circumstances & not from any notice that has been taken of my Constant & faithful Services—In fact I have never yet had a post assigned me where there was Even a probability of Acquiring Honor Those posts are Either Reserved for older or for younger officers (more in favor Than myself) I have often Sensibly felt The Degrading prefference given to others & have Suffered it So far to operate upon me: That I am now unhappy in the Service—I am willing as heretofore to Live upon my own fortune in the Service a Campaign or Two Longer provided I can have an opportunity of putting my affairs in Such a Situation as will afford me the necessary Subsistance but if I might have my Choice it would be that Some more Suitable person Should fill my place in the Army & I be permitted to Retire.[21]

Washington finally had all he could take of Sullivan's complaints and gave way to the Irishman's pleas for a better post. From his commander-in-chief Sullivan got a choice assignment—command over the forces in Rhode Island in the spring of 1778. It was his first independent command since the debacle in Canada two years earlier. Soon Sullivan became the envy of the rest of the military, for he was destined to be the first American general to conduct joint operations with the new foreign allies, the French. "You are the most happy man in the World. What a child of fortune," wrote Nathanael Greene.[22]

Sullivan busily prepared for battle, writing frantic letters to the New England governors requesting troops and supplies. In gathering munitions for his expedition, he became so greedy that he roused the anger of General William Heath, commander of the Eastern Department at Boston. But Sullivan was determined to let nothing stand in his way. With the French in the fight, he had every intention of launching a devastating attack upon the

British in Newport. Visions of glory danced in front of him. The Comte d'Estaing's fleet, which had given up operations in New York waters, arrived off Newport on July 29 for action, but it was not until August 8 that Sullivan's forces were sufficient in number to begin the assault. Considering the short time at his disposal for building an army, Sullivan had done a commendable job. Now fortune seemed to be in his camp, for Washington had sent on veteran regiments under Greene, and the New England states had forwarded militia. To this land force were to be added D'Estaing's sixteen ships with 4,000 troops aboard. With all this military might converging on the Newport garrison that was cut off from help, Sullivan seemed assured of success.

Sullivan and D'Estaing had agreed upon a plan calling for the French to force the entrance to Narragansett Bay and to land north of Newport—a spot from which they could co-operate with the American forces. On August 8, 1778, the French moved into the channel between Conanicut and the island of Rhode Island, today called Aquidneck. Sullivan was supposed to cross from the mainland at Tiverton on August 10, the day the French were told to land. But when Sullivan discovered that the British had left their fortifications at the northern part of the island to pull back to Newport, he impatiently moved across a day earlier than planned, much to the annoyance of the French leader. D'Estaing, however, managed to keep up with the Irishman and landed some troops on the opposite side of the island on the same day. It looked as though the British were about to be caught in a vise.

Suddenly the customary Sullivan ill-luck occurred and brought a quick change to the scene. A British fleet appeared off the coast and D'Estaing, after hastily re-embarking his troops, put out to engage the enemy. Despite Sullivan's pleas that he wipe out the British garrison immediately, D'Estaing was adamant that the enemy fleet be disposed of first. On August 11, no sooner had the French dipped over the horizon in pursuit of the British than a storm lashed forth from the northeast, whipping not only the ships at sea but also Sullivan's tattered forces standing on Rhode Island. Once the storm had abated, word came that the French would sail for Boston to repair the damage to their ships rather than assist in the attack upon Newport.

Frustrated by the near victory that had eluded him, Sullivan lashed out at the new allies. He wrote a stinging letter to D'Estaing spelling out the ruinous consequences that would ensue if the French persisted in going on to Boston. Then after D'Estaing's ships did sail, Sullivan and his officers prepared a remonstrance accusing the French of not living up to their agreement to attack Newport. These foolish words may have soothed the frantic Sullivan, but they failed to bring back the French and did little to start the alliance off on a satisfactory course. Lafayette was irate because of the slanders against his fellow countrymen; Sullivan, however, was oblivious to the fact that he had been indiscreet.

Convinced at last that the French fleet was not going to return immediately, Sullivan gave his full attention to the campaign on land. His army had marched to Newport and placed the town under siege. He then had three alternatives: continue the siege, attack, or retreat. After talking the matter over with his officers, he decided to retreat from Newport and to continue the siege from a greater distance. There he would wait for D'Estaing's return.

Without the French, Sullivan seemed to have small hope of taking Newport; his retreat made sense. But he did not take into account one crucial factor: he failed to foresee what the enemy might do. The British had no intention of remaining bottled up. As Sullivan fell back to take up a new position at Butt's Hill, British redcoats and Germans clad in blue and yellow came out of their lines and advanced down two roads toward him. For the first time in his military career, Sullivan was to have over-all direction of a battle. At Long Island, Trenton, Princeton, Brandywine, and Germantown some senior officer had been present. Now he was on his own. In the fight that followed on August 29, Sullivan managed to repulse the enemy. But although

Sullivan bombastically claimed a complete victory, the losses on both sides were equal.

The stalemate could not last. When Sullivan learned that British reinforcements were sailing toward Newport, he wisely ordered an amphibious retreat. The withdrawal was beautifully executed and was completed under the cover of darkness without the loss of a single man, or any guns or supplies. He had not moved a moment too soon, for British reinforcements appeared on the scene the very next day. The new troops and the naval forces that accompanied them would have trapped Sullivan's men.

In the days that followed, Sullivan was at his worst. He sniped at the French, whom he felt had let him down. He also accused his suppliers of providing him with inadequate service and vented his wrath upon the commissary department under Jeremiah Wadsworth. Sullivan never hesitated to fight his own comrades when no British were about.

When spring of 1779 approached, however, Sullivan found that he had a new assignment to challenge his energies. Washington asked him to undertake a punitive expedition against the Indians in the Finger Lakes district of New York. Too often the savages had devastated the frontier settlements of Pennsylvania and New York, and the Wyoming and Cherry Valley massacres were fresh in the minds of many Americans. Retaliation became a necessity and the commander-in-chief decided to send some of his troops against the marauding Indians.

Washington's plan called for a two-pronged invasion of the land of the Six Nations. Sullivan, with three brigades and a regiment of artillery with small cannon, was to enter the redman's country from the south by way of the Susquehanna River and to march north. General James Clinton was to march along the Mohawk River and to turn south to meet Sullivan. Once joined, the two men would jointly carry out their assignment against the enemy. Washington's instructions to Sullivan were brief but to the point: destroy the Indian settlements and capture as many prisoners as possible. If any Indians sued for peace they were to be told to attack Fort Niagara, the British stronghold to the north, as proof of their loyalty to the American cause.

In May, Sullivan arrived in Easton, Pennsylvania, the starting point for his expedition. This time he had every intention of succeeding and caution dictated his every move. Unfortunately he placed his needs too high. He wanted to have 3,000 men with him, in addition to the guards and boatmen, although it was estimated that the enemy numbered no more than 1,400 men. His demands for men and matériel were insatiable, causing Alexander Hamilton to write: "General Sullivan appears to be very anxious to have his supplies of every kind forwarded to him, that he may begin his career—He is in his usual pother; but dispatch is certainly very desirable." [23] In mid-June, Sullivan was ready at last and marched toward Wyoming (Wilkes-Barre, Pennsylvania), whence he planned to march into the territory of the Senecas.

Some had hoped that the expedition would not tarry at Wyoming, but the careful Sullivan still felt his supplies were not adequate. He refused to move on until he got what he wanted. His long delay is hard to excuse. He should have started toward the Seneca land long before he did, but instead he carped at his suppliers and at the Board of War for insufficient support. Someone had to crack down on Sullivan, and Washington curtly told him that his demands for more men were unreasonable.

It was the end of July before Sullivan finally moved out for Tioga (Athens, Pennsylvania). With him were 2,000 men, 1,200 packhorses and 700 beef cattle. His numbers were to swell to 4,000 men when Clinton joined him. Certainly this was no light expeditionary force trying to move swiftly through Indian country; it was a fully equipped army starting upon an invasion of alien land.

At Tioga, Sullivan built a fort and waited for Clinton to arrive. Once Clinton had joined him on August 22, Sullivan set out for one of the largest Indian settlements in the region at Newtown—a site near present-day Elmira, New York. It was here that the Indians, with loyalist support, decided to make their stand on August 29. The fight at Newtown showed that Sullivan was no longer the "madman" Benjamin Rush had dubbed him. Although he had overwhelming numerical superiority, he showed extreme caution and fought the unorganized redmen as though he were battling a formidable foe on a grand scale. The Indians offered resistance at first, but then thought better of it and fled. After entering Newtown, Sullivan razed huts, destroyed crops, and burned fields to deny the Indians food and shelter in the future.

The rest of the story is much the same: the story of a moving army, burning and destroying as it marched against no resistance. His army had one slight mishap when a small scouting party was ambushed and the two survivors were tortured by the Indians. Sullivan gained revenge by putting to the torch the Indian stronghold at Genesee (near Cuylerville, New York). Although he was now only fifty miles from the Niagara River, Sullivan did not push on toward Fort Niagara. Instead, he turned his army toward Tioga and began a long march back. On October 8, he reached Wyoming, where he took leave of his troops to report to Washington that his mission was finished.

Sullivan's campaign had accomplished much. His soldiers had destroyed more than forty Indian villages with their orchards and food plots, and he had seized more than 160,000 bushels of beans and corn. He had met and defeated the enemy once in pitched battle. If Sullivan had failed to take any Indians captive, or had caused few to sue for peace, he had significantly reduced their military strength for the time being. That winter the Indians were to suffer for lack of supplies, and not until 1780 were they able to resume their sporadic raids.

Ironically, Sullivan's most successful venture led to his retirement. He had complained and criticized once too often. His barbed remarks aimed at the Board of War during the Indian campaign had created powerful enemies. Members of the Board told Congress that the general's criticisms were unjustified. When Sullivan offered his resignation in November, 1779, citing poor health as his principal reason, he expected Congress to respond by giving him temporary leave. Instead, Congress accepted his resignation and Sullivan's military career came to a close.

He returned to Durham hoping to settle down to a quiet domestic life. But after his four-year stint in the army, he found it hard to sit still for long. In September, 1780, he entered the Continental Congress to serve as representative from New Hampshire for one year. All of his energy went into the war effort and the approaching problem of peace negotiations. His career as a legislator, however, was marred by the same mistakes he had exhibited as a military man. He showed bad judgment, for example, in accepting a loan from the French minister in Philadelphia, the Chevalier de la Luzerne. There is no evidence that the loan was ever repaid, or that it was intended to be. The French certainly looked upon the loan as an investment in gaining a voice in Congress. Although Sullivan never subordinated America's interests in legislation, he did show a marked partiality toward French policy. During this same time the British made an effort to woo Sullivan over to their side, using his captive brother, Daniel, as bait. Sullivan's behavior may have been somewhat strange with regard to these British moves, but in no way did he compromise the American position.[24] Nothing ever came of the British overtures.

In August, 1781, Sullivan headed back for New Hampshire bringing to an end his years on the national scene. He became an important figure in New Hampshire politics, acting as attorney general and holding three terms as president of the state in the late 1780's. Always a nationalist in his outlook, he helped put down New Hampshire's counterpart to Shays' Rebellion and gave his full support to the ratification of the Federal Constitution. Washington appointed him a Federal district judge in 1789, but he was unable to sit upon the bench beyond the spring session of 1792.

The few remaining years of his life were tragic ones. He rapidly deteriorated into senility either as a result of a nervous disease that grew progressively worse, or from excessive drinking, or both. He died at the age of fifty-five on January 23, 1795, and was buried in the little family cemetery on the knoll behind his home.

Sullivan's reputation as one of Washington's generals has paled with the passing of years partly because he never had a brilliant victory. Yet Washington always held a good opinion of this battling Irishman, and found him to be a loyal, albeit a difficult, officer. Sullivan never shirked his duty or sought an easy assignment. When given a mission he fought hard and gave his best. But too often his best was not good enough. Luck, which must accompany any successful military man, did not choose to march with John Sullivan.

FOOTNOTES

1. There were some, however, who argued that John Stark or Nathaniel Folsom would have been a better choice. See George W. Nesmith, "Services of General Sullivan," *Granite Monthly,* I, No. 11 (April, 1878), 325–30; Howard P. Moore, *A Life of General John Stark of New Hampshire* (Boston, 1949), p. 209.
2. Sullivan to John Adams, December 21, 1775, in Otis G. Hammond, ed., *The Letters and Papers of Major-General John Sullivan* (1930–39), I, 152.
3. Sullivan to John Adams, March 19, 1776, *Massachusetts Historical Society Proceedings,* XIV (1876), 284.
4. Sullivan to New Hampshire Committee of Safety, March 14, 1776, Hammond, *op. cit.,* I, 187.
5. Sullivan to Philip Schuyler, June 12, 1776, *ibid.,* 234.
6. Washington to President of Congress, June 17, 1776, in John C. Fitzpatrick, ed., *The Writings of George Washington* (1931–44), V, 152; hereinafter Washington's *Writings.*
7. Thomas Jefferson to R. H. Lee, July 29, 1776, in Edmund C. Burnett, ed., *Letters of Members of the Continental Congress* (1921–36), II, 28.
8. Joseph Reed to William Livingston, August 30, 1776, in Thomas W. Field, "Battle of Long Island," *Long Island Historical Society Memoirs* (Brooklyn, 1869), II, 397.
9. Since no records have been found limiting Putnam's command, Douglas Freeman assumes it "was real, and not merely titular." Douglas S. Freeman, *George Washington,* 6 vols. (New York, 1948–54), IV, 155n. Henry Knox wrote somewhat ambiguously that Putnam commanded on Long Island with a number of other

generals. Knox to Lucy Knox, August 26, 1776, Knox Papers, III, 28, Massachusetts Historical Society.

10. Edward H. Tatum, Jr., ed., *The American Journal of Ambrose Serle* (San Marino, California, 1940), p. 84.
11. Burnett, *op. cit.*, II, 70n.
12. C. F. Adams, ed., *The Works of John Adams* (Boston, 1856), III, 80–81.
13. Sullivan to Washington, February 9, 1777, Hammond, *op. cit.*, I, 315.
14. Sullivan to Washington, August 7, 1777, *ibid.*, 424; see also William Plumer, "John Sullivan," *New Hampshire State Papers*, XXI, 825.
15. Washington to Sullivan, March 15, 1777, in Washington, *Writings*, VII, 290–91.
16. Sullivan to John Hancock, October 6, 1777, in Hammond, *op. cit.*, I, 475–76; Freeman, *op. cit.*, IV, 476.
17. Freeman, *op. cit.*, IV, 476.
18. Washington to Sullivan, September 20, 1777, in Washington, *Writings*, IX, 242.
19. Sullivan to John Adams, September 23, 1777, in Hammond, *op. cit.*, I, 471.
20. Benjamin Rush, "Historical Notes of Dr. Benjamin Rush, 1777," *Pennsylvania Magazine of History and Biography*, XXVII, No. 2 (1903), 147.
21. Sullivan to Washington, February [?], 1778, in Hammond, *op. cit.*, II, 21.
22. Greene to Sullivan, July 23, 1778, *ibid.*, II, 103–04.
23. Hamilton to Nathanael Greene, May 22, 1779, Nathanael Greene Papers, V, No. 59, American Philosophical Library.
24. See Bibliography.

BIBLIOGRAPHY

Amory, Thomas C., *Daniel Sullivan's Visits . . . to General John Sullivan in Philadelphia*. Cambridge, Mass., 1884. Contains interesting information on the British attempt to win Sullivan over when he was in Congress in 1781.

———, *General Sullivan Not a Pensioner of Luzerne*. Boston, 1875. Argues that Sullivan was not in the pay of the French while in Congress.

———, *The Military Services and Public Life of Major-General John Sullivan*. Boston, 1868. This is the first biography and is of value for information on the family and for anecdotal material.

Cook, Frederick, ed., *Journals of the Military Expedition of Major General John Sullivan*. Auburn, N.Y., 1887. Contains many diarists' accounts of the march against the Six Nations. Should be supplemented by the Flick material listed below.

Flick, Alexander C., ed., "New Sources on the Sullivan–Clinton Campaign." New York Historical Association, *Quarterly Journal*, X, July and October, 1929.

————, *The Sullivan–Clinton Campaign in 1779*. Albany, 1929. Both of the Flick entries contain many valuable diaries and letters on the march against the Six Nations.

Hammond, Otis G., ed., "Letters and Papers of Major-General John Sullivan," 3 vols. *New Hampshire Historical Society Collections*, XIII to XV, 1930–39. This collection contains most of the Sullivan letters in existence, and is essential reading for understanding of the man.

New Hampshire Provincial and State Papers, 40 vols. Concord and Manchester, N.H., 1867–1943. This is an invaluable collection of source material for the history of New Hampshire in the early years.

Scott, Kenneth, "Major General Sullivan and Colonel Stephen Holland." *New England Quarterly*, XVIII, September, 1945. An interesting treatment of the British overtures to Sullivan in 1781, which suggests that Sullivan may have considered these overtures—a supposition which this author does not accept.

Whittemore, Charles P., *A General of the Revolution: John Sullivan of New Hampshire*. New York, 1961. A recent treatment of the general and contains a full bibliography.

Benedict Arnold:

TRAITOROUS PATRIOT

————•◆•————

WILLARD M. WALLACE

Wesleyan University

FEW generals in the Continental army demonstrated greater qualities of leadership than Benedict Arnold, but not one proved, in the end, so disloyal. Arnold was an extremist in his actions, and his behavior has usually evoked a vehement response. Until his act of treason, men were always divided in their opinions of him; after it, his countrymen were unanimous in condemning him. Because of the disgrace into which he fell, his contributions to the patriot cause have often been forgotten or ignored. That the most perfidious traitor in American history should have rendered heroic service to the country he subsequently betrayed, has seemed incredible to many. Treason itself was a most shocking act to the Revolutionary generation. To none was this more so than to General Washington, who had given his trusted lieutenant command of West Point. Washington never recovered his former good opinion of Arnold, but the passing of time and the work of numerous scholars have now enabled people to appreciate the value of Arnold when he was loyal and to comprehend a little more clearly his defection, without condoning it.

Arnold was born on January 14, 1741, in Norwich, Connecticut. Descended from an early governor of Rhode Island bearing the same name, Arnold spent a lively boyhood, but one not unmixed with sadness and disaster. His father, likewise called Bene-

163

dict, had married a wealthy widow, Hannah Waterman King, whose family was among the local colonial aristocracy. All went well for a time with the Arnold fortunes. Then the elder Benedict Arnold overextended his mercantile ventures, lost heavily, and consoled himself at the local taverns, from which his young son often had to lead him home. While Arnold was attending school in Canterbury, yellow fever struck at his family. His mother, now deprived of all but two of her six children, and with her husband a heavy charge on her, bade Arnold constantly to keep in mind his duty to himself and his Maker.

With the family's fortunes declining, his mother was forced to withdraw him from school. Once home, the spirited boy frequently broke loose from parental control. His feats of strength, agility, and daring earned him a position of leadership among his peers. One Thanksgiving, Arnold and a number of other boys undertook to roll barrels from a nearby shipyard to the village green for a bonfire as a boyish prank. When the local constable interrupted the fun, Arnold offered to fight him on the spot. Instead of arresting him, the officer dragged the angry boy home to his mother.

Unable to handle the rebellious youth, his mother turned for assistance to her cousins, Daniel and Joshua Lathrop, graduates of Yale College. They ran one of the largest and most prosperous drug stores in eastern Connecticut and agreed to take the boy on as an apprentice. He remained with them for years, leaving on at least two occasions, however, to enter the army for brief terms of service during the French and Indian War. Arnold's mother died in 1759 and his father, two years later. Once his apprenticeship was completed, he sailed for Europe, bought large stocks of supplies, and set up an apothecary's shop in New Haven. He kept in close contact with the only surviving member of his immediate family, his sister Hannah, who became his able assistant.

But Arnold was not satisfied to remain a simple apothecary. Buying shares in a number of ships, he soon developed a lively trade with Canada, the West Indies, and Central America, and

sailed as one of his own shipmasters. Like many merchants of
the period, he resorted to smuggling in defiance of British customs laws and became a leader of the more radical political element in New Haven.

At the same time Arnold had a keen eye for respectability.
He built a fine house, kept a small stable of horses, and dressed
in the style befitting a gentleman. In appearance he was short
but powerfully built, with black hair, dark skin, and light blue
eyes. Before long he caught the eye of Margaret Mansfield,
daughter of the sheriff in New Haven, and they were married
in 1767. His wife soon bore him three sons—Benedict, Richard,
and Henry.

Just prior to the Revolution, the Governor's Second Company
of Guards was formed, a militia organization consisting of sixty-
five New Haven "gentlemen of influence and high respectability." A vigorous man with a fiery and commanding presence,
Arnold was a logical and successful candidate for the commission
as captain. He made it clear from the outset that his company
would not stand idly by should hostilities commence between
the colonies and the Crown.

When news of the fighting at Lexington and Concord reached
New Haven, Arnold started his company marching toward Cambridge within twenty-four hours. The selectmen at first refused
his request for powder, but when he told David Wooster, who
sought to intercede, that he would break open the powder magazine by force, the town fathers handed him the keys. "None but
Almighty God shall prevent my marching!" Arnold had exclaimed when defied. As it happened, none did, nor Providence
either.[1]

Arnold was eager for action while the American army lay
inactive in the siege lines around Boston. He proposed to the
Massachusetts Committee of Safety, in April, 1775, that he be
empowered to capture Fort Ticonderoga, a strategic post rich in
artillery and other military supplies. After several days of pon-
dering, the Committee finally assented; the need of the army
for siege guns and fieldpieces was too compelling. Arnold

promptly left Cambridge for Ticonderoga, raising recruits as he went, largely from Massachusetts.

Unfortunately for his high hopes of accomplishing the feat alone, Arnold had revealed information about the war matériel at Ticonderoga to Colonel Samuel Parsons, another Connecticut officer. Parsons, upon his return to the Hartford area, discussed plans with several important politicians for a swift raid north, and soon Connecticut had its own expedition underway. Agents were sent into Vermont to mobilize more men, and Ethan Allen, leader of the Green Mountain Boys, was approached with the idea of commanding Connecticut's force.

Passing through western Massachusetts, the Connecticut group was joined by forty men with two officers who were to haunt Arnold for years to come. One was Major John Brown, an agile-minded, fast-talking lawyer who had recently been in Montreal and who also entertained the notion of capturing Ticonderoga. He was married to the sister of Arnold's cousin, Oliver Arnold, attorney general of Rhode Island, a man whom Arnold disliked intensely. The other nemesis was Colonel James Easton, a tavern-keeper who was neither gentle nor genteel.

At the Catamount Tavern in Bennington, where the Green Mountain Boys held forth with shouts and rum, both the Connecticut force and the small Massachusetts force under Arnold were surprised to find Ethan Allen raring to go against Ticonderoga. He, too, had an eye on the fortress, knowing that it was garrisoned by only a small detail of the 27th Foot under Captain William Delaplace. Apparently all Allen had been waiting for was some kind of authorization beyond his own impulse. He accepted the Connecticut commission, sent word out to the Boys, and presently led the Connecticut force and his own hard-drinking, quarrelsome fighters in the direction of the fort at the foot of Lake Champlain.

Arnold discovered to his chagrin that his authorization from the Massachusetts Committee of Safety meant nothing to Allen and that unless he could persuade Allen to relinquish command, the glory of the capture would be denied him. But arguing with the Vermonter was like arguing with the north wind. The best Arnold could do was to win an agreement from Allen that he might accompany, but not command, the force. On May 10, the Americans surprised the small British garrison, which yielded, according to Allen, upon his demand "in the name of the great Jehovah and the Continental Congress." Arnold was completely ignored by the raucous Green Mountain Boys, who celebrated their bloodless seizure of the fort by breaking open the garrison's rum kegs and getting roaring drunk; or, as Allen euphemistically wrote, his Boys "tossed about the flowing bowl."

Frustrated, Arnold presently encountered further humiliation. In camp the Boys jeered him and even shot at him. When a report was prepared for the Massachusetts authorities, informing them of the Ticonderoga conquest, Arnold engaged in a violent quarrel with Colonel Easton who was to deliver the message. Small wonder that Arnold found two captured British officers better company than his own countrymen.

At length, however, more of Arnold's recruits arrived aboard a schooner seized by Allen's men from a Tory proprietor. Because Arnold was an experienced seaman, Allen sent him to raid St. Johns at the northern end of the lake and to seize a sloop moored there. Arnold brought her back to Ticonderoga and armed her. With the Green Mountain Boys disbanding, he was gradually gaining control over the situation both at Ticonderoga and Crown Point, which had also been taken. Allen was still around to dispute the command, however, and the only point on which the two men saw eye-to-eye was the necessity of invading Canada.

While Arnold and Allen were in the midst of planning a Canadian invasion, Colonel Easton returned from his mission to Massachusetts. Almost at once Arnold had another quarrel with him because he felt Easton had done his best to diminish Arnold's reputation while delivering the report. When Easton refused to accept Arnold's challenge to a duel, the fiery Connecticut captain used the toe of his boot on the man. Presently Arnold was gratified to see both Allen and Easton leave. Thereafter he proceeded with his plans for a Canadian invasion, specifying that there should be no Green Mountain Boys involved.

His period of gratification was limited. Colonel Benjamin Hinman arrived from Connecticut with a thousand men. Though Arnold refused to turn over his command, a Massachusetts committee arrived on the scene and ordered Arnold to place himself at Hinman's service. Arnold resigned and, in a fit of pique, discharged his men. His temper scarcely improved when many of his men were recruited by Easton, who had popped up again, with John Brown as his second in command. Arnold went off in a huff to Albany, where at the suggestion of General Philip Schuyler he dashed off a letter to the Continental Congress regarding the situation at Ticonderoga. He also began an accounting of his expenses for the Massachusetts Congress.

His experience in the Champlain area had been a bitter one. Granted that he was a hot-tempered person, impatient and restless, and that his behavior toward Easton was inexcusable, Arnold still had grounds for being angry at the shabby treatment he had received. Most of the men with whom he dealt had neither the legal authority nor the military insight he possessed. Some had cut his reputation to shreds behind his back in their presentations to the Massachusetts authorities and the Continental Congress. Barnabas Deane, who was on the scene, declared that Arnold had been "greatly abused and misrepresented by designing persons." Arnold, moreover, had been the unhappy victim of the rivalries between Massachusetts and Connecticut, both of whom were contending for the military honors of taking Ticonderoga. When Massachusetts acknowledged Connecticut's claims of supremacy on Lake Champlain, it is not difficult to understand Arnold's conclusion that the Bay Colony had renounced both him and its own authority. Since it was a humiliation he could not endure, he left. That it might have been even more honorable to remain than to depart seems not to have occurred to him.[2]

Arnold's stay in Albany was cut short by news of his wife's sickness. Hastening home, he found her already in her grave and his three boys in his sister's care. Hannah, in fact, had become a second mother to them. She had taken charge of Arnold's business affairs as well as his family, and when, on returning from Albany, he fell ill with a serious attack of the gout, Hannah nursed him through that, too.

Though not wholly recovered, Arnold rode up to Cambridge to settle his accounts with the Massachusetts Congress. Once again, he received questionable treatment. The authorities expressed dissatisfaction with a number of items, including Arnold's difficulty in accounting for sums he claimed to have expended from his own funds. They were willing to give him only about half of what he said he had spent. This amount was so far short of what Arnold expected that he turned his accounts over to Silas Deane, who reported them to the Continental Congress. After a careful scrutiny, the Congress refunded the balance to Arnold.

During the summer of 1775, Congress began planning a Canadian invasion. The main effort would be made by an army under General Schuyler, of New York, who was to seize St. Johns, Chambly, and Montreal, then move down the St. Lawrence to Quebec. When illness prevented Schuyler's participation, General Richard Montgomery assumed command and captured the three towns by early November.

But this drive was only one arm of a pincers movement; the other was a march through the rugged Maine wilderness to Quebec. Arnold, among other men, had drawn up a plan for such an expedition, and Washington proposed his name to Congress for the command. He was commissioned a colonel in the Continental army and began busily making preparations. His plan was to follow the network of waterways consisting of three rivers, the Kennebec, Dead, and Chaudière. Washington wrote Schuyler that Arnold would compel the British commander, General Carleton, to withdraw to Quebec, thus facilitating Schuyler's advance. If, on the other hand, Carleton remained at Montreal, Quebec would fall an easy mark for Arnold. To the delight of Arnold, who always did his best work in an independent capacity, Schuyler agreed to give him a free hand.

The wilderness march has been celebrated in historical narrative and fiction.[3] The march was a remarkable feat under incredibly difficult conditions largely occasioned by nature but complicated by the faulty construction of the wrong kind of craft for river navigation. In the annals of American military history, it still stands as a classic.

Arnold rose magnificently to the great trust Washington placed in him. Notwithstanding their dissimilarities in physical size, social background, experience, and disciplined character, both were energetic men capable of superb leadership. But even Washington's faith in Arnold could not compensate for the lateness of the season. Arnold went into a flurry of conferences, ordering bateaux built on the Kennebec, mustering guides and supplies, organizing a force of about a thousand men, and assembling ships to transport them from Newburyport to the Kennebec. The expedition, consisting of three rifle companies from Pennsylvania and Virginia and ten companies with muskets from New England, finally sailed. Arnold reached Gardiner on September 22, where he ordered a number of the green-lumbered bateaux rebuilt, and then went on to Fort Western. Once there, he divided his little army into four divisions, the leading division under the harsh but able frontiersman from Virginia, Captain Daniel Morgan, who was to make a road across the Great Carrying Place between the Kennebec and the Dead, and the rearguard under Lieutenant Colonel Roger Enos, of Vermont. By the twenty-ninth, all divisions had shoved off from Fort Western.

With cold weather coming early in Maine, Arnold pushed his men along. It was not easy, for the river was often shallow and rocky, and the bateaux, weighing 400 pounds apiece, had to be carried around numerous falls. Arnold retained his cheerfulness despite the shocking discovery that the bateaux were falling apart and many of the provisions were already ruined. At the Great Carrying Place, with the men's shoulders raw and blistered, downpours turned the portage into a sea of yellow mud. Some men drank the water and came down almost at once with nausea and diarrhea. Still resolute, Arnold lent a helping hand here and an encouraging word there. At the same time he wrote Washington, expressing the hope that the commander-in-chief would not be too critical of the slow progress made thus far. He wrote also to Schuyler, informing the New Yorker that they might be meeting soon at Quebec.[4] The Schuyler letter was given to an Indian named Eneas, who was presumed trustworthy; but the Indian delivered the letter to the British instead.

Although Arnold had sounded a note of optimism, subsequent developments proved his hopes for a swift trip were unfounded. The Dead River overflowed its banks in a torrential rain lasting three days. Bateaux foundered, units marching by land lost their way in the morass, and rations began running out. Arnold called his officers together to inform them he intended to push ahead to the Canadian settlements and bring back supplies. It is possible that had he remained, he might have prevented the desertion of Colonel Enos, who carried back most of what was left of the food with his rear division. As it was, if Arnold had not rushed across the Height of Land and down the roaring, rock-strewn Chaudière to send back bullocks and flour, the rest of the army would have starved to death. With game driven away by the weather and the passage of so large a body of troops, the exhausted, half-frozen, famished men were down to meals of boiled moccasins and a gruel of shaving soap. Many, in fact, were dying in the snow when food supplies arrived from Arnold in the nick of time. He personally saved the life of one young man, who, despite Arnold's infamy, testified later to the regard with which the soldiers held their leader. Another soldier spoke of the troops being "inspired . . . with resolution" by their commander's "firmness and zeal." [5]

Washington's gratitude was profound when he learned that Arnold had finally reached the St. Lawrence with more than 600 men. "It is not in the power of any man to command success; but you have done more—you have deserved it," he wrote Arnold. "My thanks are due, and sincerely offered to you," he continued, "for your enterprizing and persevering spirit." He wrote Schuyler that Arnold's "merit" was "great." [6]

Warm as this praise was, Arnold would have been deserving of more commendations had he been able to take Quebec. When Eneas handed his letter to the British, however, reinforcements came racing from Montreal in an effort to protect Quebec. Though Arnold assembled canoes to cross the St. Lawrence, a wild storm arose to prevent his crossing for three days. By the time the river waters had calmed, reinforcements reached Quebec to strengthen the shaky garrison. Eluding two men-of-war and their patrol boats, Arnold finally slipped his men into Wolfe's Cove, paraded them before the walls, but could not persuade the British to come out and fight as Wolfe had done with Montcalm sixteen years before.

Presently Arnold retired to Pointe aux Trembles, where he waited for Montgomery. After having taken Montreal, Montgomery was deeply embarrassed by the departure of a large part of his army for home because enlistments had expired. He brought only 300 men to add to the Kennebec column, which he admired for "a style of discipline . . . much superior to what I have been used to see in this campaign." [7]

Though the combined columns moved back to Quebec, what to do next became a troublesome problem. Carleton had reached the city by ship, and his garrison was twice as large as the American force. Smallpox had broken out among the Americans, and the enlistments of many of Arnold's soldiers were to expire on the last day of the year. The two leaders decided, therefore, to attack the city on the first stormy night. To their relief snow started to fall late in the afternoon of December 30, and in the dark and stormy night that followed, the Americans launched their attack. Montgomery was to lead a force against the lower town from Wolfe's Cove and Arnold against the lower town from St. Roque.

From the very start things went wrong. A deserter alerted the British to the impending attack. Montgomery fell almost at once, and his second in command refused to press the attack and turned back. Arnold drove furiously against the British but went down with a bullet in the leg. Though burly Daniel Morgan took over and fought with great gallantry, he and hundreds of the troops, lacking the knowledge of the Quebec streets that Arnold possessed, were trapped and forced to surrender.

Now in sole command, Arnold refused to give up the siege. From his hospital bed he issued orders to keep the city under harassment. He dashed off letters to Washington and the Continental Congress, and appealed for assistance to his fellow Connecticut officer, General David Wooster, commanding the troops at Montreal. "I have no thought of leaving this proud town," he wrote his sister Hannah, "until I first enter it in triumph." [8]

It was not to be. True, he received recognition that delighted him. Wooster praised him, Washington sent congratulations and appointed him commander of a new regiment being raised, and Congress unanimously promoted him to brigadier general. But meager reinforcements, smallpox, and the lukewarm reception from the Canadians prevented him from doing anything decisive at Quebec.

When Wooster arrived on the first of April to take over the command, Arnold faced the humiliating prospect of again resuming a lieutenant's role. His horse solved the problem for him by slipping on the ice and mauling Arnold's game leg so painfully that he asked permission to withdraw to Montreal. Later he explained to Schuyler that had Wooster chosen to consult him about plans, he might have remained. [9]

At Montreal, Arnold was kept busy. He received a delegation from Congress whose aim was to bring the Canadians into an official alliance. This effort at diplomacy failed. Then Arnold plunged again into military affairs. When Wooster was succeeded by General John Thomas, who was subsequently forced to withdraw from Quebec, Arnold checked an attack on Montreal from the west by British and Indians. He carried out the evacuation of Montreal as the defeated and smallpox-stricken army began its retreat toward Lake Champlain. Ordered by the Congressional delegation to seize from the Montreal merchants whatever was needed to sustain the army, Arnold plundered thoroughly, though on a legal basis. He remained in the city until Carleton's fleet was sighted. Then, accompanied by young Captain James Wilkinson, he joined the new commander of the Northern army, General John Sullivan, at St. Johns. When the army subsequently withdrew in mid-June to Ile-aux-Noix, Arnold was the last to leave the Canadian shore. He accompanied the remnants of the shattered invading army as they retreated southward to Crown Point.

During the summer of 1776, as the British were preparing their thrust down the Lake Champlain corridor, Arnold was fighting legal, not military, battles. He was deeply involved in a court case rising over the plundering of the Montreal merchants for provisions and supplies. Many of these goods were ruined and stolen during the retreat from Chambly, where they had been sent, and Arnold was the officer held responsible. Colonel Moses Hazen, a Canadian who had wavered between the British and the Americans and finally chose the latter, had refused to take charge of the goods. At least this was the story given by one witness, Major Scott, who claimed that Arnold then had been forced to accept the responsibility. Charges and countercharges flew back and forth; Arnold accused Hazen of laxness in allowing the goods to be stolen and Hazen charged Arnold with stealing from the Montreal merchants. Hazen ultimately insisted upon a court-martial to clear his name.

When the trial got underway, Arnold found himself in more difficulty than the defendant. The court refused to admit Scott, Arnold's principal witness, on the grounds that he was prejudiced. Arnold's hot temper boiled over. He protested the refusal as unprecedented and unjust, and dressed down the court members in scathing language. The court retaliated by demanding an apology, and Arnold refused, offering, instead, to give "any gentleman of the court the satisfaction his nice honor may require." [10] Court members responded by demanding Arnold's arrest.

The quarrel went through channels to the newly appointed

commander of the Northern army, General Horatio Gates, who
sent the trial record on to the Continental Congress. In May,
1777, the Board of War, ruling on a charge that Arnold had
plundered the Montreal merchants for his own gain, exonerated
him. As to the demand for Arnold's arrest, Gates responded by
dismissing the court. He explained to Congress, "The United
States must not be deprived of that excellent officer's service at
this important moment." [11]

The "important moment" to which Gates alluded, pertained
to desperate American efforts to counter the British threat gathering in the north. With no roads the length of Lake Champlain,
Carleton was putting together a fleet at the northern end to be
manned by the Royal Navy. Arnold at an earlier date had stressed
to Washington the need for building an American fleet on the
lake. Washington approved, and appeals went throughout New
England for woodsmen, carpenters, armorers, and crewmen.
Gates placed Arnold in charge of the construction of the row-
galleys and gondolas at Skenesborough, and a flotilla put together
with green lumber and armed with swivel guns and small cannon
rapidly took shape.

Once the fleet was built and ready for action, Gates summoned
Arnold to Ticonderoga to take command of it. The Connecticut
general was ordered to sail down the lake, but he was given instructions to retire if the British appeared with a greater force.
Arnold made an initial cruise in August and kept the British
under surveillance during September. Discovery that the British
not only matched his fleet but possessed heavier vessels with superior firepower was disturbing, though not dismaying, intelligence. As he appraised the situation, it appeared that a defensive
effort would be his best course and that the most defensible position was not near Ticonderoga but between high, thickly
wooded Valcour Island and the western shore. In several letters
to Gates he explained the situation and his choice of the Valcour
Island position, offering to return if Gates did not approve. Gates
replied that he was gratified to learn that Arnold and the fleet
"ride in Valcour Bay, in defiance of our foes in Canada." [12] By

a stroke of irony Gates's letter was dated October 12, when Arnold's fleet had already suffered heavy casualties and was desperately trying to get back to Ticonderoga.

Carleton's fleet sailed south and engaged Arnold on October 11. Though Arnold's position was strong, the major British vessels, superior in every way except fighting heart, were too powerful for the Americans. Arnold fought a furious seven-hour battle, losing the schooner *Royal Savage* and the gondola *Philadelphia* and many casualties. In operating their guns, the Americans were exposed not only to the enemy fleet but also to the galling musketry of hundreds of Indians whom the British had landed on Valcour Island and the mainland.

That night, after the British drew off to refit and fog settled down over the lake, Arnold held a council of war and listened grimly to his captains' reports. Capture appeared inevitable. But Arnold was resourceful. He proposed to move southward that night between the British ships and the shore, each vessel showing a hooded lantern in the stern. Silently, like gray ghosts, the crippled American ships slipped through the dark waters. From out in the lake came the sound of hammers and saws as carpenters repaired the damage to the British fleet, while ashore the glow of campfires was visible and the Americans could hear the howling of the Indians as they anticipated the morrow's fight and the scalps they would lift.

Fortunately Arnold's maneuver proved successful, and, with morning, his squadron was clear of the enemy and on its way to Ticonderoga, which a number of ships reached safely. The breeze was light, however, and a few of the shattered vessels wallowed along in a half-sinking condition. Carleton caught up with them on the thirteenth off Split Rock. Lingering behind in his own row-galley, the *Congress*, to cover the retreat, Arnold fought a bloody rearguard action and ran his ship ashore rather than surrender. After setting fire to the *Congress*, he and the blood-stained survivors of his crew slipped through an Indian ambush and soon arrived at Crown Point.

Critics leaped on Arnold at once. He had lost the fleet, or at

least eleven of the sixteen ships, and his action failed to prevent
Carleton from seizing Crown Point and moving on toward Ticonderoga. But the great naval historian, Alfred Thayer Mahan,
has pointed out that Arnold recognized that the purpose of a
fleet is to contest control of the waters and to impose delay even
if victory is impossible. Admiral Mahan, therefore, has defended
Arnold's choice of the Valcour position. True, the British naval
victory had been complete, but the sheer construction of the
American fleet had long delayed Carleton's advance. Moreover,
Arnold's fight had given some indication of the fierceness of the
resistance Carleton might meet on land, resistance that might
frustrate him until the snows arrived to put an end to campaigning. Carleton approached Ticonderoga, but declined to lay siege
owing to the lateness of the season. He retired to Canada, confident that nothing could prevent the capture of Ticonderoga in
the spring. It was a happy decision for the Americans because it
may well have saved the young republic whose main army under
Washington was suffering humiliating reverses in the New York
campaign.[13]

The winter that followed was a stormy one professionally and
emotionally for Arnold. John Brown, his old nemesis, dragged
up a series of charges against him, claiming that Arnold had been
guilty of "great misconduct" on the march through Maine, had
attempted treason at Ticonderoga, and had lost the Lake Champlain fleet because of incompetence. Gates refused to countenance
the charges, but he was obliged by regulations to send them on
to Congress. Arnold's other enemy, Colonel Hazen, hauled him
before a military court on a charge of slander and won a decision. Undoubtedly, however, the event that troubled Arnold
most of all was the fact that he was on a mission in Rhode Island
when the Battle of Trenton took place. Arnold hated missing
the spirited attack. His personal life suffered as well. He sought
the hand of Elizabeth Deblois of Boston, daughter of a Tory,
and, to his chagrin, the girl rejected him.

His rebuffs were far from ended. Congress dealt his pride the
greatest blow by promoting five brigadier generals, every one

junior to him, to the rank of major general in February, 1777. Arnold, who was the oldest brigadier by date of commission in the Continental army, was passed over. Congressmen explained that in their voting they gave "due regard . . . to the line of succession, the merit of the persons proposed, and the quota of troops raised, and to be raised, by each state." [14] Once again political considerations had robbed him of military rewards due him.

Washington was disturbed when he learned what had happened; he had not even been consulted. He wrote Arnold, bidding him do nothing hasty and acknowledging that the refusal of Congress to promote him revealed "a strange mode of reasoning." [15] The commander-in-chief was in a delicate position in view of his high regard for civil authority and his need of good officers. A number of the latter were likewise so indignant at having been passed over by Congress that they threatened to resign. Arnold's case was so flagrant, however, that Washington sought, on the one hand, to appease his scrappy little general and, on the other, to find out from friends in Congress whether the action was the result of accident or design.[16] He was no more successful in getting a satisfactory answer to his inquiry than he was in calming Arnold. The Connecticut officer considered the action of Congress "an implied impeachment" on his character, and was convinced that he had enemies in Philadelphia who had worked against him. Hence he requested and received permission to go to the capital to plead his case.[17]

How successful he might have been without additional considerations to support his cause is a matter of speculation. Many congressmen undoubtedly shared the feelings of John Adams who wrote his Abigail that he was "wearied to death with the wrangles between military officers . . . scrambling for rank and pay like apes for nuts." [18] But on the way to Philadelphia, Arnold had the good fortune to perform a distinctive service. While he was visiting his family in New Haven, the British landed near Norwalk and raided Danbury, leaving it in flames. When Arnold heard the news, he helped raise the countryside and harassed the enemy's withdrawal. He lost one horse, had another wounded, and was nearly captured and killed. This valiant fight persuaded Congress to appoint him a major general on May 2. For some unexplained reason, however, his seniority was not restored.

Arnold was still indignant about the tardiness of Congress in settling his accounts for the Canadian campaign. The records were in wretched condition owing to the lack of finance officers, to the exigencies of the military situations, and to the loss of many of Arnold's papers on the lake. Brown, of course, had long been busy alleging that the discrepancies were explicable; "Money is this man's god," he said in a handbill published in Pittsfield on April 12, "and to get enough of it he would sacrifice his country." [19] Although Brown's crystal ball was working well for the future, it was evidently less revealing for the past. The Board of War cleared Arnold's character and conduct, and even John Adams confessed that the Connecticut man had been "basely slandered and libeled." [20]

However cordial Congress might appear, that body persisted in its refusal to restore his seniority. Arnold chafed mightily. Washington supported him loyally, pointing out to Congress that "he has always distinguished himself, as a judicious, brave officer, of great activity, enterprize and perseverance." [21] These kind words had no effect on Congress, and Arnold angrily resigned his commission in July, 1777.

But the very day he wrote his letter of resignation, Washington recommended Arnold as the logical officer to help General Schuyler in stopping the alarming advance of Burgoyne's invading army that had just captured Ticonderoga. This was too attractive an opportunity to miss. Arnold sought a suspension of his resignation, then hurried northward to assist Schuyler. After he was gone, Congress voted down a motion to restore his seniority. Some members of Congress questioned the propriety of a military man like Arnold having challenged the authority of the ruling civilian body.[22] For his part, Arnold never forgot or forgave the slights dealt him by the Continental Congress.

Upon his arrival at the Northern army headquarters, Arnold

had the misfortune once again to step into the middle of another rivalry between states. The army was composed mostly of New Englanders and New Yorkers, who mixed about as well as oil and water. There had been antagonism between the two in peacetime over conflicting land claims, and during the war the antipathy manifested itself in military circles by the Schuyler–Gates feud. Most New Englanders despised Schuyler and wanted Horatio Gates to be named commander. New Yorkers, on the other hand, backed Schuyler and wanted no part of Gates. Arnold had occasion to be grateful to both generals, but perhaps his recent experiences with Congress made him particularly sympathetic toward Schuyler, who was having similar difficulties.

From his initial task of slowing Burgoyne's progress through the woods toward the Hudson and Albany, Arnold presently left on a mission to the Mohawk Valley. As Burgoyne pushed southward, another force, composed of Tory regiments and Indians under Colonel Barry St. Leger, drove eastward from Fort Oswego on Lake Ontario and laid siege to Fort Schuyler. If the fort fell, the way would be open to Albany, where a junction with Burgoyne was to be effected. The post held out valiantly under Colonel Peter Gansevoort. An attempt by old General Nicholas Herkimer to relieve the fort ended when his Tryon County militia were ambushed in a thickly wooded ravine at Oriskany. Conditions soon becoming desperate at Fort Schuyler, Gansevoort slipped an officer through the enemy lines at night with an urgent plea to General Schuyler for help. When Schuyler called for a volunteer from among his officers to lead a rescuing expedition, none, least of all any of the New Englanders, offered to go— with one exception, Benedict Arnold.

The hazardous situation was one that Arnold met with a skillful blend of force and guile. He had fewer than a thousand men in his relief column, and there was no prospect of aid from the Tryon County militia, who had been thoroughly intimidated by their experience at Oriskany. On approaching the fort, Arnold halted. Among his prisoners was a man named Hon-Yost Schuyler, a distant relative of General Philip Schuyler, who was due to hang for his part in planning a Tory uprising. But Hon-Yost, besides being a Tory, was also a half-wit and well known to the Indians, who regarded him as being under the protection of the Great Spirit. When Hon-Yost's mother and brother pleaded with Arnold for Hon-Yost's life, Arnold said that he would spare him provided he went into the Indian camp and told the Indians that Arnold was coming with an enormous army. The Schuyler family agreeing, Arnold kept the brother as hostage and sent out Hon-Yost. First, however, he had the half-wit's coat shot full of bullet holes. To confirm Hon-Yost's information, and also to keep an eye on him, a friendly Oneida runner was dispatched behind him.

True to his word, Hon-Yost burst among the British Indians with his terrifying tale of near-capture by Arnold's overwhelming numbers. When the Indians asked just how many troops were coming with the dreaded American general, Hon-Yost pointed to the leaves on the trees. Staggered by the news, the Indians had scant chance to recover before the Oneida appeared with similar information, and then still another runner behind him. With whoops of dismay the Indians dashed for the woods, pausing only to drink up the British liquor and scalp a few Tory soldiers who straggled in the rush for safety. When Arnold, marching hard, came up to Fort Schuyler, he found the besiegers gone and the garrison as incredulous as it was joyful.[23]

Once back with the main army, Arnold discovered that Burgoyne's German troops had lost at Bennington and that Gates, who had replaced Schuyler, was a less congenial commander than the New Yorker. In fact, trouble between Gates and Arnold was not long in developing. During the first battle between Burgoyne's army and that of Gates at Freeman's Farm on September 19, the two American generals had a difference of opinion over the kind of battle that should be fought. Gates, who had fortified his lines, was content for the most part to wait behind a protected position for the British to approach. The impetuous Arnold favored an attack upon the enemy in front of the American lines. In the initial stages of the battle that followed, Gates allowed Arnold to lead some troops on the left wing against the British and to engage the enemy considerably ahead of the American breastworks. But as the battle progressed, Gates grew cautious, refused reinforcements, and restrained Arnold by ordering him to remain in the rear at main headquarters. Arnold was furious because he was confident that if he had received reinforcements, he could have delivered a decisive victory.[24]

Arnold's indignation, already simmering, really boiled over as a result of two other incidents. He learned that a number of troops had been removed from his command without his knowledge and he was apprised of the fact that Gates had not given credit to his division in the battle report on Freeman's Farm that was sent to Congress. Arnold at once bulled his way into Gates's headquarters, and a bitter argument ensued. When the Connecticut general, unable to contain his anger and disgust, requested permission to leave the area, Gates deprived him of his command for insubordination.[25]

Arnold, on sober second thought, was reluctant to leave with the showdown with Burgoyne imminent. Instead, he hung around camp, sulking in his tent and complaining to his aides, who were former aides to Schuyler. When Burgoyne made his last effort against Gates at Bemis Heights, on October 7, Arnold was thus without a command. Though the Americans had such superiority of numbers and fought so valiantly that there was little likelihood of a British victory, the outcome was still in doubt as the late afternoon wore to a close. Gates, whose headquarters was two miles from the scene, had little actual control over what was happening in the field.

The situation was too much for Arnold. Striding restlessly back and forth in front of his tent, the frustrated officer listened to the roar of the battle and fired impatient questions at his aides, who were trying to keep him informed of the progress of the fighting. News of the indecisive nature of the contest suddenly infuriated him. Forgetting his pique as well as the fact that he had no official command, he ordered his horse saddled and galloped to the sound of the guns.

His appearance at first startled, then exhilarated the troops. Regiment after regiment broke into cheers as the bay mare with its blue-coated rider dashed to the front. Seeing a Connecticut brigade moving up, Arnold waved his sword in response to their cheers and shouted, "God bless you! Now, come on boys, if the day is long enough, we'll have them all in hell before night!" He led them in two furious assaults, and the second momentarily broke the enemy's center. When the British rallied, Arnold slid to the right, picked up two more brigades, and stormed the enemy's line again. Reinforced, the redcoats held fast.

Arnold now swung his horse to the left and spurred between the two armies under a hail of British lead. Finding the Connecticut brigade again, he swept a force of Canadians and Indians out of a number of cabins in front of a powerful German redoubt guarding Burgoyne's right flank. If this redoubt could be taken, the flank would be uncovered and Burgoyne would have to withdraw from the field. Fortunately a force was at hand, Daniel Morgan's crack riflemen and two regiments in support. Dashing up to them, Arnold pointed his sword at the redoubt. The men greeted him with a shout and followed him in a fierce charge against the position. Though the Germans fought hard, the American pressure was so severe that the defense finally crumbled. Arnold, a torrent of troops behind him, burst into the entrenchments.

But at the very moment of victory, the mare went down before a storm of bullets, and a German soldier fired point-blank at Arnold. The little general fell, severely wounded in the same leg that had been hit at Quebec. "I wish it had been my heart," he said bitterly to the stretcher party that quickly reached him. Perhaps more than any single officer he had been responsible for the decisive American success that day. Ten days later, without further action, Burgoyne capitulated; and the triumph brought France to the side of the young republic.[26]

From this point on, Arnold's career with his countrymen ran downhill, and at a steadily accelerating pace. Though Congress restored his seniority in grade shortly after Burgoyne's capitulation, the action came too late to save his pride. Furthermore, he was crippled for life, one leg shorter than the other, a sharp blow indeed for a man who was a remarkable athlete and gloried in physical prowess. With Arnold's wound only partially healed, Washington appointed him commandant of the city of Philadelphia, which the British had evacuated in June, 1778.

All of Arnold's vanity and pride came to the fore in his new command. It was not simply the duties of the assignment that were responsible, it was also because of his marriage to Peggy Shippen. Margaret Shippen was the youngest of the three vivacious, fun-loving daughters of Edward Shippen, a prominent jurist whose cousin, William Shippen, was surgeon general of the Continental army. Like many of the Philadelphia girls, Peggy had greatly enjoyed the dances and parties that had enlivened the British occupation. When Sir Henry Clinton took the British army back to New York, Philadelphia became something of a social desert for these girls. Peggy especially missed Captain John André, a handsome young staff officer, who had paid her a good deal of attention. Arnold met the restless Peggy at a party during the summer and lost his heart to her. She, in turn, was impressed by the virile charm of the wounded hero, yet neither she nor Judge Shippen was enthusiastic when Arnold sought her hand in marriage. Arnold was so persistent in his wooing, however, that Peggy finally succumbed; and the judge assented, somewhat hesitantly, to the marriage. The wedding took place in early April of 1779, with Arnold's leg still so weak that he had to be supported by a soldier during the ceremony. At the time he was thirty-eight years old; Peggy, eighteen.

Though marriage into one of Philadelphia's leading families brought Arnold great social status, in his pursuit of Peggy and his attempts to keep her in the style to which she was accustomed, he was forced to live far beyond his means. Hard-pressed, he developed a number of money-making schemes, most of them of a dubious character. These included speculating in real estate, trying to get hold of property belonging to Tories who had fled from the city, issuing a pass to a ship in which he subsequently invested contrary to a regulation of the Pennsylvania authorities, and using government wagons to save his own property from capture. Arnold's enemies were not slow in pointing to the impropriety of his actions. Of enemies, moreover, he had no lack, particularly within the Council of Pennsylvania, which as a civilian political body deeply resented any military authority. The radical patriots within both the Council and the Continental Congress criticized him likewise for his lavish entertaining and his association with Tories. Finally the Council preferred charges, and Arnold, on Washington's advice, demanded a court-martial. Though Arnold defended himself vigorously, the court-martial refused to clear him of two charges, issuing the pass and using government wagons, and it sentenced him to receive a reprimand from Washington. The commander-in-chief, in April, 1780, accordingly pronounced Arnold's conduct with respect to the pass "peculiarly reprehensible" and with respect to the wagons, "Imprudent and improper." [27]

Stung though he was by the reprimand, Arnold already had been sufficiently hurt and angered by the spring of 1779 that in May he had opened negotiations with the British. Why he should have committed treason must remain a matter of speculation. That the financial reward was an inducement is beyond doubt; Brown had been at least partially correct in his prediction that money meant much to Arnold. But there were other motivations. He was deeply humiliated, affronted, and angered by the treatment he had received at the hands of the Massachusetts Congress, the Continental Congress, and the Council of Pennsylvania. There is no doubt, moreover, that he considered himself unappreciated and deserted by his own countrymen, in whose service he had been crippled. A man of greater moral stature might have been able to take this treatment in stride, but not Arnold. For that matter, few generals had escaped criticism—even Washington was subjected to caustic comments from officers and politicians concerning his military capacity. But though there were hot words, grumbling, some resignations, and a few dismissals, outright treason of a gross nature was the exception among higher officers.[28] It is possible, too, that Arnold mistrusted the French alliance; certainly after the treason he said this was so. Even if one grants this possibility earlier, it is difficult to be certain how potent an influence it was in his decision. A conviction of betrayal by his countrymen, injured pride, and avarice were probably the principal motivations for his treason.

One is on surer ground in conjecturing about his wife's involvement and influence. For years Peggy's innocence was freely conceded by Arnold's worst enemies. Recent research, however, has revealed that she both knew of his negotiations and aided him with them.[29] She may have merely confirmed his will, but the admiration she acquired for the British during the occupation and the friendships she developed were not likely to lead her to discourage her husband's disgust with his own compatriots.

The story of Arnold's betrayal of the American cause is a fascinating one.[30] Through a number of intermediaries, a long correspondence ensued with John André, who remembered Peggy from the British occupation of Philadelphia. Now serving as adjutant general of the British army and Sir Henry Clinton's intelligence chief, André understood the value of a defection as important as Arnold's. Yet if Arnold was cautious, so was Clinton. As a pledge of Arnold's sincerity, Clinton wished the Connecticut general to bring about the surrender of a sizable force. Arnold saw his chance to do so by securing command of West Point, which he proposed to surrender for £10,000. Washington temporarily disconcerted him by offering him the left wing of the army—an opportunity for fame and action that would have delighted him in earlier years. Hastening to plead his physical incapacity, he was given the West Point command instead.

To complete the details of the surrender of West Point, André left New York on September 20, 1780, for his clandestine meeting with Arnold. General Clinton, in the meantime, was laying plans for a swift move up the Hudson. When the sloop *Vulture* from which André landed was forced by an American battery on Tellers Point to drop down the river, the decision was made for André to return to the British lines by land. He was carrying in his pocket a pass from Arnold and in his sock documents for Clinton written by Arnold. Captured on the way back by irregulars, André was turned over to American authorities when the documents were discovered. Luckily for himself, Arnold was apprised of the capture in time to dash to the *Vulture* in his barge. André subsequently went to his death as a convicted spy and Arnold passed out of American service.

The traitor received ample rewards from the British for his defection. He was given a commission as a British Provincial brigadier general, with solid footing as a cavalry colonel in the regular establishment, whose half-pay he drew after retirement for as long as he lived. Full pay as a colonel amounted to £450 a year, while as a Provincial brigadier he drew an additional £200. Though Arnold had failed to bring about the surrender of West Point and its garrison, Clinton granted him the full £6,000 that André had been commissioned to offer, plus £315 as expense money. The former Connecticut businessman at once invested £5,000 of the capital sum with the Court bankers for £7,000 in consolidated annuities at 4 per cent. The British likewise rewarded his family. In 1782, the King authorized an annual pension of £500 for Peggy. Each of Arnold's children by Peggy—and there were five who survived—received a pension of £100, while Arnold's three young sons by Margaret Mansfield were given commissions in the British army with half-pay as long as they should live. The Crown subsequently awarded the traitor and his family a total of 13,400 acres from among its lands in Canada reserved for American Tories.[31]

Generous as the British were to Arnold, they never completely trusted him as an officer in their service. Though he conducted a raid into Virginia and led the tragic expedition to New London, the British declined to give him an important command. After Cornwallis' surrender at Yorktown, Arnold took his family to London, where he encountered both respect and contempt but found no employment. Presently he moved to Canada—to St. John, New Brunswick—and entered the shipping business. The transplanted Tories in St. John hated him. On one occasion they blamed him for a fire that destroyed his warehouse, accusing him of wanting to collect the insurance, even though he was out of the country at the time.

Eventually Arnold moved his family back to London and tried to secure a command when the war with revolutionary France broke out. Denied a chance at another military career, he traded with the West Indies, where he was well thought of, and invested in privateering ventures which turned out badly. Rejected once again in his request for military service, he died in 1801, forlorn and almost forgotten in Britain.[32] His wife outlived him by only three years, but had the satisfaction of seeing her children started in respectable careers in which they were to attain a mild fame. Arnolds have performed well since then, and a number have risen to high rank in Britain's subsequent wars, including the Second World War. If none has achieved such military importance as their ancestor, the tireless and deadly "Dark Eagle" as the Indians called him, none has put self-interest or injured pride before honor.

FOOTNOTES

1. For Arnold's early life, see Willard M. Wallace, *Traitorous Hero: The Life and Fortunes of Benedict Arnold* (New York, 1954), pp. 5–37; James Thomas Flexner, *The Traitor and the Spy* (New York, 1953), pp. 3–19; Malcolm Decker, *Benedict Arnold, Son of the Havens* (New York, 1932), pp. 1–33; Isaac N. Arnold, *The Life of Benedict Arnold*, 3rd ed. (Chicago, 1897), pp. 15–36.
2. For Arnold's part in the seizure of Ticonderoga and his subsequent experiences in the Champlain area with Allen and others, see Wallace, *op. cit.*, pp. 37–54; Flexner, *op. cit.*, pp. 41–58; Justin H. Smith, *Our Struggle for the Fourteenth Colony*, 2 vols. (New York, 1907), I, 107–92; John Pell, *Ethan Allen* (London, 1929), pp. 74–108; *Collections of the Connecticut Historical Society* (Hartford, 1860), I, 165–88.
3. The best accounts are: Kenneth Roberts, *March to Quebec, Journals of the Members of Arnold's Expedition* (New York, 1947); Justin H. Smith, *Arnold's March from Cambridge to Quebec* (New

York, 1903); John Codman, *Arnold's Expedition to Quebec*, 2nd
ed. (New York, 1901).

4. Arnold's letters to Washington and Schuyler, both dated October
   13, 1775, may be found in Roberts, *op. cit.*, pp. 70–73.

5. *Ibid.*, pp. 301, 347–48, 552.

6. For Washington's letters to Arnold and Schuyler, both dated December 5, 1775, see John C. Fitzpatrick, ed., *The Writings of
   George Washington*, 39 vols. (Washington, D.C., 1931–44), IV,
   147, 148. Hereinafter cited as Washington, *Writings*.

7. Montgomery to Schuyler, December 5, 1775, in Peter Force, ed.,
   American Archives, 9 vols., 4th series (Washington, D.C., 1837–
   53), IV, 189. Hereinafter cited as *American Archives*.

8. Arnold to Hannah, January 6, 1776, in Roberts, *op. cit.*, p. 109.
   For the Quebec assault, see Arnold's letters of December 31, 1775,
   and January 2, 1776, in *ibid.*, pp. 102–06. See also, for letters of
   January 6 and 14, *American Archives*, 4th series, IV, 589, 674,
   and Carleton's report in *ibid.*, p. 656. For other accounts see Smith,
   op. cit., II, 113–47; Allen French, *The First Year of the American
   Revolution* (Boston, 1934), pp. 614–20; and North Callahan,
   Daniel Morgan, Ranger of the Revolution (New York, 1961), pp.
   100–08.

9. Arnold to Schuyler, April 20, 1776, in *American Archives*, 4th
   series, V, 1098–100.

10. *Ibid.*, 5th series, I, 1273.

11. Gates to John Hancock, September 2, 1776, in *ibid.*, 5th series, I,
    1268.

12. The Arnold–Gates correspondence may be found in *ibid.*, 5th series,
    II, 440, 481, 591, 1015.

13. For Admiral Mahan's opinions, see *The Major Operations of the
    Navies in the War of American Independence* (Boston, 1913), pp.
    13–26. For other accounts, see Christopher Ward, *The War of the
    Revolution*, John Richard Alden, ed., 2 vols. (New York, 1952),
    I, 393–97; Gardner W. Allen, *A Naval History of the American
    Revolution*, 2 vols. (Boston, 1913), I, 161–79; Wallace, *op. cit.*,
    pp. 110–20.

14. Gaillard Hunt, ed., *Journals of the Continental Congress*, 34 vols.
    (Washington, D.C., 1904–37), VIII, 132–33; hereinafter, *Journals
    of Cont. Cong.*

15. Washington to Arnold, March 3 and April 3, 1777, in Washing-
    ton, *Writings*, VII, 234, 352–53.

16. Washington to Richard Henry Lee, March 6, 1777, in *ibid.*, VII,
    251–52.

17. Arnold to Washington, March 14 and 26, 1777, in Jared Sparks, ed., *The Writings of George Washington,* 12 vols. (Boston, 1835), IV, 345–46.

18. Charles Francis Adams, ed., *Familiar Letters of John Adams and His Wife Abigail Adams during the Revolution* (New York, 1876), p. 276.

19. Carl Van Doren, *Secret History of the American Revolution* (New York, 1941), p. 159.

20. *Journals of Cont. Cong.,* VII, 372–73, VIII, 372–73, 382; Adams, *op. cit.,* p. 276.

21. Washington, *Writings,* VIII, 47–48.

22. The motion to restore Arnold's seniority was defeated sixteen to six, and Congressional comment was bitter, pro and con. Henry Laurens, of South Carolina, who thought "the reasoning upon this occasion was disgusting," said that Arnold was rejected "not because he was deficient in merit or that his demand was not well founded but because he asked for it and that granting at such an instance would be derogatory to the honour of Congress." See E. C. Burnett, ed., *Letters of Members of the Continental Congress,* 8 vols. (Washington, D.C., 1921–36), II, 585, 442, 445.

23. For the relief of Fort Schuyler, see Wallace, *op. cit.,* pp. 141–44; Flexner, *op. cit.,* pp. 163–67; Ward, *op. cit.,* II, 489–91.

24. Arnold's part in the action on September 19 is discussed in Hoffman Nickerson, *The Turning Point of the Revolution* (Boston, 1928), pp. 308–16, 473–77; Flexner, *op. cit.,* pp. 170–73; Ward, *op. cit.,* II, 504–12, 941–42; Wallace, *op. cit.,* pp. 146–48, 326–32.

25. Differing views of the Arnold–Gates quarrel may be found in Samuel W. Patterson, *Horatio Gates* (New York, 1941), pp. 159–63, and Wallace, *op. cit.,* pp. 149–53. For an especially sharp criticism of Arnold's role in the whole campaign ending at Saratoga, see Lynn Montross, *Rag, Tag and Bobtail: The Story of the Continental Army, 1775–1783* (New York, 1952), pp. 217–27.

26. Accounts of the action on October 7 may be found in Nickerson, *op. cit.,* pp. 356–68; Ward, *op. cit.,* II, 526–31; Flexner, *op. cit.,* pp. 180–84; Patterson, *op. cit.,* pp. 166–68; Wallace, *op. cit.,* pp. 1–2, 154–59.

27. For Arnold's courtship of and marriage to Margaret ("Peggy") Shippen, his commercial transactions, and his troubles with civilian authorities, see Wallace, *op. cit.,* pp. 162–92; Flexner, *op. cit.,* pp. 217–53; John C. Miller, *Triumph of Freedom, 1775–1783* (Boston, 1948), pp. 530–35; Van Doren, *op. cit.,* pp. 168–93; Arnold, *op. cit.,* pp. 222–64.

28. The most comprehensive study of treason during the Revolution is the excellent monograph by John Bakeless, *Turncoats, Traitors and Heroes* (Philadelphia, 1959).
29. Wallace, *op. cit.*, pp. 193–259.
30. See the accounts by Van Doren, *op. cit.*, pp. 193–371; Flexner, *op. cit.*, pp. 253–393; Wallace, *op. cit.*, pp. 193–259. See also Sir Henry Clinton, *The American Rebellion*, William B. Willcox, ed. (New Haven, 1954), pp. 214–18, 462–66.
31. Arnold's rewards are discussed in detail in Wallace, *op. cit.*, pp. 261–63, 365–66.
32. For Arnold's career after the treason conspiracy, see Willcox, *op. cit.*, 235–37, 243–44, 250–55, 276–78, 482–83, 505–06, 565–67; Arnold, *op. cit.*, pp. 329–98; Van Doren, *op. cit.*, pp. 371–88; Flexner, *op. cit.*, pp. 356–65; Wallace, *op. cit.*, pp. 260–309; J. G. Taylor, *Some New Light on the Later Life and Last Resting Place of Benedict Arnold and His Wife Margaret Shippen* (London, 1931).

BIBLIOGRAPHY

Callahan, North, *Daniel Morgan, Ranger of the Revolution*. New York, 1961. A biography of the officer closely associated with Arnold in the Quebec and Saratoga campaigns.

Clinton, Henry, *The American Rebellion*, William B. Willcox, ed. New Haven, 1954. A biased treatment, but of great value, by the British commander-in-chief, with discussions of Arnold's treason and his service in the British army following his defection.

Flexner, James T., *The Traitor and the Spy*. New York, 1953. A remarkably interesting, unique, tri-cornered study (despite the dual title) of Arnold, André, and Peggy Shippen, containing a good deal of original information.

Nickerson, Hoffman, *The Turning Point of the Revolution*. Boston, 1928. The most competent account of the Saratoga campaign, with a careful evaluation of Arnold's role.

Roberts, Kenneth, ed., *March to Quebec, Journals of the Members of Arnold's Expedition*. New York, 1947. A compilation of journals, some written on a daily basis under the most trying conditions, that makes fascinating reading.

Smith, Justin H., *Our Struggle for the Fourteenth Colony*, 2 vols. New York, 1907. A detailed and objective history of the attempt to acquire Canada, with attention to Arnold's early efforts on Lake Champlain, his march through Maine, and his subsequent experiences in Canada.

Van Doren, Carl, *Secret History of the American Revolution*. Garden City, 1941. Contains a superb close analysis of Arnold's treason, with the inclusion of the Arnold–André correspondence.

Wallace, Willard M., *Appeal to Arms: A Military History of the American Revolution*. New York, 1951. A useful one-volume history of the war.

————, *Traitorous Hero: The Life and Fortunes of Benedict Arnold*. New York, 1954. The most complete Arnold biography of recent years.

Benjamin Lincoln:

OLD RELIABLE

——•-•——

CLIFFORD K. SHIPTON

American Antiquarian Society

BENJAMIN LINCOLN as a soldier had all the traditional virtues of a New Englander—reliability, sobriety, and common sense. He took both victory and defeat in his limping stride, for he participated in the great victories at Saratoga and Yorktown, and, between them, had the dubious distinction of surrendering the Southern army at Charleston. After the Revolution he served with wisdom and success against Shays' rebels. Fat, lame, and undramatic, he has been neglected by historians who are naturally attracted by more dashing men.

He was born the son of Colonel Benjamin and Elizabeth Lincoln, of Hingham, Massachusetts, on January 24, 1733. The Colonel was a farmer and maltster by trade, but held an important political office on the colony's Council. After receiving "a good common education," young Benjamin took to farming for a living and prospered enough to marry Mary Cushing, of Pembroke, in 1756. The next year he was elected town clerk, an office his father and grandfather had held before him. He followed his father's footsteps in military as well as political circles. Appointed an adjutant in Colonel Lincoln's militia regiment, the Third Suffolk, he eventually worked his way up in the ranks to succeed his father as commander.[1]

With the advent of the Revolutionary War crisis, he took a

much stronger Whig position than most Hingham inhabitants, and this gave him much more influence than his native ability might have won for him. He served on the town's Committee of Safety and was sent as the Hingham representative to several provincial congresses. In October, 1774, he was elected commissary by the Massachusetts Provincial Congress.

In his new position, Lincoln pressed for the reorganization of the militia and helped to replace Tory officers with reliable Whigs appointed by the governor and Council. When fighting broke out, he mustered the Second Suffolk regiment on April 19 and marched to Cambridge. But on the news that the British regulars had retired into Boston, he left the regiment and rode up alone to take his place in the Provincial Congress.

At Watertown, Lincoln was promptly chosen muster master of the army of Massachusetts. By July he had been appointed president of the Provincial Congress, the chief executive post in the rebel government. When that Congress transformed itself into the General Court, Lincoln was elected to the Council. During the winter of 1775–76, he went home to make saltpeter and to strengthen popular sentiment. In May he headed a town committee which instructed the representatives to support independence if Congress declared it.

In 1776, Lincoln had his first taste of combat. The Council appointed him major general, and co-operating with Artemas Ward, who commanded the Continental forces in Massachusetts, he broke the blockade of the port of Boston, on June 13, 1776, by driving off H.M.S. *Renown*. After the Battle of Long Island, the General Court ordered him to take a draft of militia by way of Rhode Island to reinforce the army in New York. On Washington's orders he conferred with Governor Trumbull about attacking Long Island, but the situation of the commander-in-chief became critical before the assault could be mounted. Lincoln joined the Continental forces and commanded the right wing at the Battle of White Plains on October 28, 1776. Then, while the armies moved to winter quarters, he hastened back to Providence to get more militia.

In January 1777, Lincoln arrived at Peekskill and led the right wing in Heath's attempt to recapture Fort Independence. When this movement failed, he crossed the Hudson, and on February 11, led the first of his regiments into Washington's camp. General Charles Lee, who didn't like deacons in uniform, accused him of trying to prevent the sending of Massachusetts militia to join Washington,[2] but the commander-in-chief, although he didn't like other deacons, had no such doubts about this one. Writing to Congress about Lincoln, he said:

> I should not do him justice were I not to add that he is a Gentleman well worthy of Notice in the Military Line. He Commanded the Militia from Massachusetts last Summer . . . much to my satisfaction, having prov'd himself on all occasions an active, spirited, sensible Man. I do not know whether it is his wish to remain in the Military Line, or whether, if he should, any thing under the Rank he now holds in the State he comes from, would satisfy him; how far an appointment of this kind might offend the Continental Brigadiers I cannot undertake to say.[3]

Congress decided to ignore the feelings of the other generals, and on February 19, 1777, appointed Lincoln a major general in the Continental line.

The new general was stationed at Bound Brook, New Jersey, the post nearest the British army. At daybreak on April 13, 1777, a force under Cornwallis made a sudden attack. The American outposts ran without giving the alarm, and the British were within 200 yards of Lincoln's headquarters before he was warned. He mounted and galloped to rally his force; one of his aides who was a little slower in mounting was captured. Lincoln gathered his men, got them off before two converging columns of the enemy could close, and took up a position in a valley in which he could present a narrow front. Cornwallis ate his luncheon in the Bound Brook headquarters, and then retired to Brunswick taking Lincoln's baggage with him. The American general returned and ate his dinner as usual at headquarters.

Other generals experienced far worse defeats in the north,

where the evacuation of Ticonderoga so angered the New England leaders that they wrote to congressmen saying that the quota of militia called for by the Northern army could not be raised unless Lincoln was appointed to command it. Washington had already made up his mind to the same end, and had written Schuyler telling him he was sending Lincoln to command the militia:

> This Gentleman has always Supported the Character of a judicious, brave, active Officer, and as he is exceedingly popular and much respected in the State of Massachusetts . . . he will have a degree of influence over the Militia, which cannot fail being very advantageous. I have destined him more particularly to the command of them, and I promise myself it will have a powerful tendency to make them turn out with more cheerfulness, and to inspire them with perseverance to remain in the field.[4]

Washington might have added, as others did, that Lincoln had "gained the love and respect of all men" with whom he had served, and that his division was sorry to see him leave.[5] No one ever suggested that he was a brilliant soldier or a good judge of men; his popularity rested on his obvious integrity, and that was what the Northern army needed now that suspicions were being voiced that Schuyler was dealing with the enemy.

In July, 1777, Lincoln took up his station at Manchester, Vermont, rallied the fleeing inhabitants, served as contact between the army and the New England governments, and organized the militia as it came in. On the news of the Battle of Bennington he marched to join Stark, arrived after the fighting was over, and sent out three columns of militia which cut Burgoyne's lines of communication with Canada. He did this without informing his superior, Gates, lest news of the movement be intercepted.

In September, Lincoln joined Gates at Stillwater, where as second in command he led the right wing. During the Second Battle of Saratoga on October 7, he commanded the defensive works. That night he led out the force sent to relieve the troops who were holding the ground gained during the day. The next morning he led a reconnoiter which, considering the conflicting reports later circulated, had better be described in his own words:

> I entered an open cart path, which led through the wood, rode in it some distance, and did not discover any troops till I turned an angle in the road. Then a body of men opened to my view. At first, I could not distinguish them by their dress from our own troops, two of them having scarlet clothes, others being in blue, (the Hessian uniform), and some being clad like our militia. A few of our men, two or three in a company, had British uniforms taken in a prize; the other Continental troops were in blue, while our militia resembled in dress the people of the country who had joined the army. In this state of uncertainty I continued my route until I was within a few yards of them so near as perfectly to discover my error. As soon as the enemy perceived this, and that I was checking and turning my horse, I saw the two in British uniform present and fire.[6]

A ball shattered his right ankle. He exclaimed, "The rascals have struck me," [7] and rode back. The enemy could easily have captured him, but fearing that he was a decoy, did not follow.

Lincoln was carried to Albany, where part of the broken bone had to be cut out. Three months later he was taken home on a couch in a sleigh. For several years the wound kept breaking open and pieces of bone working out; when it healed the leg was two inches shorter than the other. Washington presented him and Arnold with "shoulder and sword knots" in recognition of their wounds and service. In September, 1778, Congress sent him to command in the Southern Department, where what was needed was not a brilliant soldier but a man who could gather and control the militia; any pitched battle was sure to be a disaster.

Lincoln arrived at Charleston on December 4, 1778, and set himself to the task of organizing an army. When he heard that the great British force which had sailed from New York had landed in Georgia, he started down to halt their northern advance, but the commanders in the upper country on whom he called for assistance could not help because their forces were being pinned down by loyalist companies. Still more frustrating, he reported to Washington, was the unco-operative spirit of the state government:

> I found . . . that the army, to use Major General Howe's own words, "has been in a state of abject dependence on the civil authority." Indeed the continental officer, commanding in this department, had not had it in his power, from the want of supplies which he could controul, to march the troops, without the consent of the President of South Carolina, however urgent the necessity. —I hope things will be better settled, and that I never shall be driven to the hard necessity of altercating with the civil power.[8]

Only three days later that hard necessity presented itself. He had requested President Lowndes to instruct the keeper of the state arsenal to issue arms and supplies to the North Carolina Continentals who had just arrived, and had been told:

> His Excellency cannot think of delivering these stores while this State is in so precarious a situation with respect to the enemy . . . it would be betraying a trust reposed in him to do it; —they were purchased for the defence of this State—it would never do to leave themselves defenceless— No: he would deliver them, should he receive an order of Congress for it.[9]

Besides this lack of co-operation, he complained, he was hindered by the vice and corruption which had sprung up during the war to such a degree that if the Americans were saved it would not be because of their merit.

Lincoln had hoped to invade East Florida, but the small forces he could raise could do no more than occupy upper Georgia. Even here he met with disaster, for at Brier Creek on March 3, 1779, the incompetence of General Ashe cost the Americans an estimated third of the Southern army. Instead of placing the blame on "that good man," where it really belonged, he sheltered Ashe from the wrath of his countrymen.[10] The Georgians, less charitable, hated him for a century.

Once more building up his army, Lincoln again moved into Georgia in April, 1779. General Prevost evaded him and made a feint toward Charleston which he turned into a serious invasion when he found a great part of the population neutral or friendly. Lincoln got there before him and formed a junction with the forces under Governor Rutledge and General Moultrie. Their combined force was greater than that of the British and loyalists, but the spirit was weak. A council, in which Governor Rutledge and a majority of the members of the upper house of the South Carolina legislature participated, authorized negotiations with Prevost on the basis of an agreement that the state stand neutral for the rest of the war. Before anything could be accomplished in this direction, Lincoln brought up his forces and compelled Prevost to retire to an island in the harbor, where he attacked him and could have captured his army had promised reinforcements come up.

Prevost escaped to Savannah, but Lincoln reported to Congress that his own troops were melting away and unless there were immediate reinforcements from the North there would soon be no army. Knowing that little would be done in this direction, he asked and received, in June, 1779, permission to retire and relinquish the command to Moultrie. However, that general and the Council of South Carolina unanimously asked him to remain; reluctantly he consented.

It is hard to see why General Lincoln was so popular in the South. He was not a romantic figure, for his weight was usually around 224 pounds, and it sagged. He was so methodical that he accomplished much with little inconvenience or hurry, and thus gave the impression of sloth. His manners were of a kind more common in New England than the South, for he was pious, and he always frowned on profanity and impropriety; he was temperate, frugal, and an early riser. He had no use for military affectations of honor, and refused to be provoked into duels. Once when a quarrelsome officer tried to goad him at headquarters table, he said coldly:

> I apprehend, Sir, you are disposed to take too much liberty. If you repeat any thing of this kind, I shall be obliged to tell this company facts, which I know respecting you, that will make their hair stand on end.[11]

This was enough to silence that officer. Of his military personality, there is much testimony like this:

> His composure and self-possession, his exemption from any apparent weakness or folly, uniform discretion and integrity made him revered, whilst the goodness of his disposition, and his frank and cordial manners, engaged affectionate regard. He knew how to exercise command without exciting aversion. Paying deference to the rights and feelings of others, whether present or absent, his own were not likely to suffer injury or insult. . . . By an expressive look, which was understood, by an anecdote, by pleasant irony, or more directly, he was sure to notice and to repress any symptoms of impertinence or rudeness which might show in his presence.[12]

Much of the civil war which the South was then suffering was waged, on both sides, more for plunder than for patriotism. But Lincoln did his best to suppress this "licenciousness" even at the risk of alienating the militia support which he so desperately needed. Denouncing both the cruelty and political stupidity of plundering, he insisted that individuals who collected Tory goods "forfeit them to the public." Equally troublesome at times was the social consciousness of the Southern officers. In the Northern army a militia captain might be a cobbler who would cheerfully repair the shoes of his men, but one of Lincoln's South Carolina captains was haled into a court of inquiry for "ungentlemanly Behaviour in associating with a private Soldier." [13] Because physical labor was the badge of the black man, the general found it very difficult to get his soldiers to work on the defenses which were everywhere necessary, and by way of setting an example, he would spend whole days with the work details, sometimes handling pick and shovel himself. Considering the climate and his weight, this was heroism. He could also be brutally hard when necessary; he ordered the instant hanging of a colonel apprehended in the act of riding out to the enemy with plans of the Charleston fortifications in his pocket.

When D'Estaing landed before Savannah in September, 1779, Lincoln marched at once to join in the siege. The count hoped to conquer Georgia for France, and in dealing with Prevost he

said, "I apprise your Excellency that I have not been able to re-
fuse the army of the United States uniting itself with that of the
King," and he demanded the surrender of Savannah "in the name
of the King of France." [14] Lincoln firmly protested this attitude
and insisted on being the spokesman for the allies. Prevost had
asked D'Estaing for permission to send the women and children
out of the city, but Lincoln tartly informed him that this was
only a transparent play for time, and that the blood of the civilians would be on the head of the British command. For this he
was denounced in the British press like "Beast Butler" of another
generation.

When it became apparent that Savannah could not be reduced
by siege, the allies planned an assault, which was promptly betrayed to the British. In the dark of the morning of October 9,
1779, Lincoln and D'Estaing led the main column, which in the
face of a withering fire fought its way through the abatis and
planted two standards on the parapet, but a second column led
by Count Dillon lost its way in the dark. After D'Estaing had
been twice wounded and Pulaski killed, the allies withdrew.
Because of the season the French fleet had to leave the coast, and
Lincoln sadly retired toward Charleston. A lesser man would
have blamed the count for the disaster, but Lincoln's report to
Congress was eminently fair:

> Our disappointment is great, and what adds much to our sense of
> it, is the loss of a number of brave officers and men. . . . Count
> D'Estaing has undoubtedly the interest of America much at heart,
> this he has evidenced by coming to our assistance, and his constant
> attention during the siege; his undertaking to reduce the enemy by
> assault, when he despaired of effecting it otherwise; and by bravely
> putting himself at the head of his troops, and leading them to the
> attack. In our service he has bled; I feel much for him, for while
> he is suffering the distress of painful wounds, he has to combat
> chagrin.[15]

Back in Charleston, Lincoln resumed the effort to get the state
to support the Continental effort. In vain he tried to get the

Assembly to permit the enlistment of Negroes, the draft of militia to fill the Continental battalions (general practice in the North), and the placing of the militia when in the field under the Continental articles of war. For fear of smallpox, masters refused to send their slaves to work on the fortifications, so the general himself spent every day from dawn to dark on the works. The Assembly made Governor Rutledge dictator and then dissolved, but Lincoln could get no more co-operation from the governor than from the legislature.

In February, 1780, Sir Henry Clinton had landed a great army and begun a slow advance toward Charleston. Lincoln had small hope of withstanding a siege, but he knew that if he withdrew the Continental forces to the up country, the state would make a separate peace. He had with him a large surplus of experienced Continental officers whom he might have sent away, but he still had some faint hope that the Carolinians would rally and send militia who might be placed under their command. He waited too long, and the officers were trapped with him when Clinton arrived before the town in April.

Lincoln rejected the first summons to surrender, but within two weeks failing food supplies compelled him to offer to evacuate the town if given a ten-day truce in which to withdraw his army; naturally the British rejected his proposal.[16] When word of this got out, a delegation of citizens appeared before the Council and informed the general that if he attempted to withdraw the troops and leave them to the British, they would cut up his boats and open the gates. After this there was nothing to do but make the best terms possible. On May 9, Clinton again demanded that the town surrender, but Lincoln replied that the proposed terms were inadmissible. The next day the civilians asked him to accept the British terms. The militia, meantime, seeing the flags passing back and forth, decided that it was all over, abandoned the defensive works, and straggled into town. Lincoln had himself been in the front lines night and day, and had not taken his uniform off for two weeks. When he dragged himself back into town he met the lieutenant governor and the

Council who joined in the demand that he surrender. Now he could only accept the inevitable. An amused British officer reported the events of the next day:

> The Lincolnade was acted on the 12th of May. General Leslie, with the Royal English Fusileers and Hessian Grenadiers, and some Artillery, took possession of the Town, and planted the British Colours by the Gate, on the Rampart, and Lincoln limp'd out at the Head of the most ragged Rabble I ever beheld. . . . They were indulged with beating a Drum, and to bring out their Colours cased. . . . The Militia, poor Creatures, could not be prevailed upon to come out. They began to creep out of their Holes the next Day.[17]

It was reported that the militia promptly took the oath of allegiance to the King and happily marched off with Cornwallis. When the news of the "Lincolnade" reached the back parts of South Carolina, one regiment of militia seized their officers, marched into Charleston, and surrendered them to the British.[18] Hundreds who had refused to serve under Lincoln flocked to enlist in the loyalist regiments, and some of the most trusted members of the Council who had worked with him now became willing collaborators with Sir Henry Clinton. The amused British reported that nothing could equal the hatred which the Carolinians now showed for the northern rebels, whom they blamed for misleading them.

It is an amazing fact that none of this hatred rubbed off on Lincoln as it did on Ashe. Francis Bowen, who was the last historian to read the voluminous Lincoln correspondence, declared that it did not show one word of reproach or complaint leveled against him by the Carolinians, indeed not even an insinuation that he had shown injustice, partiality, neglect, or incompetency.[19] Equally amazing is the fact that Lincoln never excused his defeat by pointing out the contrast between their lack of co-operation with him and their quick turn to loyalism. In later years when these Carolinians sent their sons to Harvard, it was Lincoln whom they asked to look after them.

Paroled and back in Philadelphia on June 23, 1780, Lincoln

asked for a court of inquiry to investigate his conduct at Charleston, but no one ever showed any interest in such a procedure. At the Harvard commencement a month later, when Benjamin Lincoln, Jr., took his M.A. in course, the general was voted an honorary degree. There were no qualifications to his welcome in Massachusetts; even so ardent a Whig as William Gordon urged that there was no better person than Lincoln to be the first governor under the new constitution.[20]

He had no political ambitions, however, and in September he was at Elizabethtown with the British Major General Phillips, negotiating a general exchange of prisoners which would release them both from their parole. When this was achieved, Washington wrote kindly to Lincoln:

> I am of the opinion, that your influence and exertions in procuring the State's quota of Troops for the War, providing funds for the subsistance of them, and Magazines, will be of infinitely more importance in your own State this winter, than it can be to become a mere spectator, or fellow-sufferer of hunger and cold . . . which I expect the small remains of our Army will have to encounter in a very short time, and more than probably to contend with during the winter. But at the same time I give this as an opinion; I leave you at full liberty to pursue the bent of your inclination and judgment.[21]

Lincoln spent the winter in Massachusetts, and in June, 1781, joined Washington's army on the North River. His first assignment was to cut off Delancey's loyalist regiments then at Morrisania, but they took alarm and escaped. In July, he tried in vain to draw the British out of their fortifications around New York. When in August word arrived of the opportunity to corner Cornwallis at Yorktown, Lincoln led the southward dash of the army. Six weeks later he opened the trenches before the town, and during the siege he commanded the allied right. On November 19, it was he who conducted the British garrison of Yorktown through the allied army drawn up in two lines to the field of surrender. The terms of capitulation were substantially those imposed upon him at Charleston the year before. Throughout the negotiations he was very careful not to "mortify" the conquered. Then he led the army back to the Hudson.

The system of committee management of the departments of the Federal Government had failed, and while Lincoln was busy at Yorktown he was appointed the first Secretary of War. The appointment was an excellent one, for more than anyone else he enjoyed the confidence of the army officers, who were bitter at what they considered to be the neglect of Congress. While most politicians were ardent supporters of the interests of their economic groups or geographical areas, Lincoln had more perspective. He felt keenly the situation of the poor debtors who had claims against the United States, but he also saw that their interests would not be served in the long run by policies which destroyed the public credit.[22] He spent two uncomfortable years in Philadelphia waiting for the peace which would permit him to resign. As he sat in his office, he pondered the preceding years and came to the conclusion that although the war had hurt his generation more than the British economic policy which had brought it on would have done, his children would reap the benefits. He did not share Washington's antipathy for the loyalists, but urged Massachusetts to encourage the return of all but the most recalcitrant. When he met returnees like Ward Chipman, he greeted them kindly and over a bottle of wine gave them the news of their Boston friends.[23] In October, 1783, Lincoln resigned from the War Office and returned to civilian life in Hingham.

With the outbreak of Shays' Rebellion in 1786, he was forced to don his uniform once more. Governor Bowdoin appointed him commander of the Massachusetts militia, one obvious reason being his popularity in the western part of the state as the result of his services in the Saratoga campaign. On January 20, 1787, he marched from Boston to relieve General Shepherd who was holding the arsenal at Springfield. As he rode through the snow with his plodding column, Lincoln watched curiously the expressions on the faces he passed, and at the first stopping place he reported back to Bowdoin:

There is now in this part of the Country a fine field for the sporting fancy of the Physiognomist, to range in: I never had any knowledge of the art, but since I left your Excellency, if I read truly, I have seen in many countenances the open smile of approbation and the most perfect good wishes that Heaven would prosper us, while in others a sullen anxiety marked every line of the faces, and they seemed to mutter a wish, that destruction might over take us. These however are few, and I think we shall in general receive the kindest welcome.[24]

And how did the people of that day see General Lincoln?

He was about five feet nine inches in stature, and of so uncommonly broad person, as to seem to be of less stature than he was. His gray hair was combed back from his forhead, unpowdered, and gathered in a long queue. His face was round and full, his eyes blue, and his complexion light. He was usually dressed in a blue coat, and light under clothes, and wore a cocked hat. . . . His speech was with apparent difficulty, as though he were too full. The expression of his countenance was exceedingly kind and amiable. His manner was very gracious. . . .[25]

The most significant quality of the Hingham Cincinnatus at this time was his entire lack of the usual military pomp, prolixity, and tediousness. When he spoke it was with brevity, and often with gentle wit. He liked people, particularly young people, and he concerned himself with their personal problems. He delighted in children, and they loved him in turn. Perhaps his most famous characteristic was his somnolency:

This was not occasioned by age, but was constitutional. In the midst of conversation, at table, and when driving himself in a chaise, he would fall into a sound sleep. While he commanded the troops against the Massachusetts insurgents, he dictated dispatches, and slept between the sentences. His sleep did not appear to disturb his perception of circumstances that were passing around him. He considered this an infirmity, and his friends never ventured to speak to him of it.[26]

As Lincoln plodded westward through the bitter January weather, he pondered the disadvantages under which he acted.

Chief of these was the fact that he moved under civil authority, so that when he came up with the insurgents he could, unless they fired upon him, do no more than read the Riot Act, upon which they could quietly disband to come together in some other place. He had a vision of marching around, Riot Act in hand, until his troops collapsed from exhaustion and the insurgents quietly took over the western counties. Fortunately Shays did not see this opportunity. On January 25, 1787, he sent Lincoln proposals that both armies should disband and all proceedings against the insurgents be suspended until the people could have a proper hearing before the General Court.[27] The general replied that he had no authority to compromise, and urged the rebels to submit. On January 27, he reached Springfield and without stopping to rest his exhausted troops, crossed the Connecticut and scattered the insurgents on the western side while another column of his army proceeded up the river on the ice.

Having thus cut the rebellion in two, Lincoln sat down at Hadley on January 30, 1787, and wrote to Shays:

> Whether you are convinced or not of your error, in flying to arms;
> I am fully persuaded that before this hour, you must have the full-
> est conviction upon your own minds, that you are not able to ex-
> ecute your original purposes. Your resources are few, your force is
> inconsiderable and hourly decreasing, from the disaffection of your
> men; you are in a post where you have neither cover nor supplies,
> and in a situation in which you can neither give aid to your friends,
> nor discomfort to the supporters of good order and government.
> Under these circumstances you cannot hesitate a moment to disband
> your deluded followers. If you should not, I must approach and
> apprehend the most influential characters among you. Should you
> attempt to fire upon the troops of government, the consequences
> must be fatal to many of your men the least guilty.[28]

When this message failed to produce a mass surrender, the general tried to divide the insurgents by offering to intercede with the government for any privates who might lay down their arms. To the representatives of the towns who came to him asking mercy for the insurgents, he replied that he felt keenly for the distress of those unhappy and misled men who were in arms against their country, and that in his effort to reclaim them without bloodshed he had hitherto restrained his troops from firing; the decision to shed blood would be made by Shays.[29]

This did not mean that Lincoln would not try to capture or scatter the insurgents without bloodshed, and on the night of February 3–4, 1787, he struck at their headquarters at Petersham. His own account is the best:

> At 8 o'clock, our troops were in motion; the first part of the night was light, and the weather clement, but between 2 and 3 o'clock in the morning, the wind shifting to the westward, it became cold and squally, with considerable snow: The wind arose very high, and with the light snow that fell the day before, and was falling, the paths were soon filled up, the men became fatigued, and they were in a part of the country, where they could not be covered in the distance of eight miles, and the cold was so increased that they could not halt in the road to refresh themselves. . . . We arrived here about nine o'clock, exceedingly fatigued by a march of 30 miles, part of it on a deep snow and in a most violent storm. When this abated the cold increased, and a great part of our men are frozen in some part or other. . . . We approached this town nearly in the centre where Shays had covered his men; and had we not been prevented by the steepness of the hill, and the depth of the snow, from throwing our men rapidly into it, we should have arrested very probably one half his force, for they were so nearly surprised as it was, that they had not time to call in their out parties, or even their guards.[30]

Having broken up the eastern army of insurgents, Lincoln moved quickly to the west. Setting up his headquarters in Pittsfield, he sent mobile parties in every direction, apprehending or disarming those who had "made an improper use of their arms." By February 20, he could report that the former rebels were hourly coming in to submit, and he pointed out to Bowdoin that a mild policy would check the flight of others from the state. The governor of Vermont agreed to disarm the refugees who might make trouble, and on Lincoln's request Governor George

Clinton led a body of New York militia nearly to the line in order to co-operate. There were still many armed insurgents hovering on the borders, many of them wishing to return and submit but still capable of throwing the whole region into civil war. Only Lincoln's "delicately Cautious" policy, as Bowdoin described it, prevented this and trouble with the other states. Writing of the impending trial of the captured insurgents before the Supreme Judicial Court, the general said:

> I hope they will [be merciful] and do it with a grace, and that she may evidence a disposition to forgive and to embrace Cordially those who are forgiven To regain the affections of the deluded and to bring them to order and to esteem government.[31]

In March, Lincoln was appointed by the General Court to head a commission that went through the insurgent regions, where it set at liberty most of the prisoners and collected the few ringleaders who were to be tried. There were still dangerous rebels in Vermont and New York, and Bowdoin asked Congress to commission Lincoln as an officer of the United States so that he might hunt them down, but fortunately this did not become necessary. On June 10, the general was allowed to resign his special commission, but he continued to serve as major general of the Suffolk militia.

In postwar politics, Lincoln's influence was not great because his attachment to Washington made the Hancock party suspicious of him. When the Constitution of the United States began to operate, the President appointed him the first collector of the Port of Boston. He also served the Washington administration as commissioner plenipotentiary to negotiate a peace with the Indians of the South, and, in 1793, to treat with the Western Indians at Sandusky. President Adams considered appointing him commander-in-chief, so naturally the Jeffersonians did not make use of his services. In 1809, he resigned the office of collector while under political fire, and on May 9, 1810, he died in the house in which he was born.

FOOTNOTES

1. Family manuscripts in the Massachusetts Historical Society contain some of Benjamin Lincoln's military commissions.
2. New York Historical Society, *Collections*, 1872, p. 273.
3. John C. Fitzpatrick, ed., *The Writings of George Washington*, VI, 408.
4. *Ibid.*, VIII, 459.
5. Timothy Pickering, October 22, 1777, in Pickering MSS, V, 59, Massachusetts Historical Society; hereinafter, Mass. Hist. Soc.
6. Francis Bowen, "Life of Benjamin Lincoln," in Jared Sparks, *The Library of American Biography*, 2nd series, XIII, 262.
7. Mass. Hist. Soc., *Collections*, 3rd series, VI, 284. Ebenezer Matoon's contradictory account apparently confuses the events of the seventh and the eighth.
8. Benjamin Lincoln, Letter Book, December 19, 1778, Mass. Hist. Soc.
9. *Ibid.*, December 22, 1778.
10. *Ibid.*, March 3, 1779.
11. Mass. Hist. Soc., *Collections*, 2nd series, III, 251.
12. *Ibid.*
13. *South Carolina Historical and Genealogical Magazine*, XVI, 179.
14. Bernhard A. Uhlendorf, *The Siege of Charleston* (Ann Arbor, 1938), p. 173.
15. Mass. Hist. Soc., *Collections*, 1st series, II, 180.
16. The documents exchanged during the siege are printed in *The Siege of Charleston* (Albany, 1867), p. 91 ff.
17. *Ibid.*, pp. 129–30.
18. *New York Royal Gazette*, June 8, 1780, 2/3; June 17, 2/4; July 1, 3/2.
19. Francis Bowen, *op. cit.*, pp. 352–53.
20. Mass. Hist. Soc., *Proceedings*, LXIII, 440.
21. A. J. Bowen, *Fifty-Five Letters of George Washington* (New York, 1907), p. 28.
22. Benjamin Lincoln to Artemas Ward, September 13, 1782, in Artemas Ward MSS, Mass. Hist. Soc.
23. Essex Institute, *Historical Collections*, LXXXVII, pp. 216–17.
24. Shays MSS, January 21, 1787, Mass. Hist. Soc.
25. William Sullivan, *The Public Men of the Revolution* (Philadelphia, 1847), p. 128.
26. *Ibid.*, p. 129.

27. The originals of this and a number of other key documents are in the Shays MSS, Mass. Hist. Soc.
28. Hartford *American Mercury*, February 5, 1787, 3/2–3.
29. Knox MSS, February 1, 1787, Mass. Hist. Soc.
30. Hartford *American Mercury*, February 12, 1787, 3/3–3.
31. Knox MSS, March 1, 1787, Mass. Hist. Soc.

BIBLIOGRAPHY

Adams, James T., *New England in the Republic 1776–1850*. Boston, 1926. Has a brief account of Lincoln's part in quelling Shays' Rebellion.

Alden, John R., *The South in the Revolution, 1763–1789*. Baton Rouge, 1957. Contains a short but accurate survey of Lincoln's southern campaigns.

Bowden, A. J., *Fifty-Five Letters of Washington to Benjamin Lincoln 1777–1779*. New York, 1907. A calendar of some interesting letters exchanged between the two generals.

Bowen, Francis, "Life of Benjamin Lincoln," in Jared Sparks, ed., *The Library of American Biography*. Boston, 1864, 2nd series, XIII, 205–434. Provides one of the longer and more complete accounts of Lincoln's life.

Lawrence, Alexander A., *Storm Over Savannah*. Athens, Georgia, 1951. Describes Lincoln's role in the Savannah campaign with Comte d'Estaing in 1779.

Nickerson, Hoffman, *Turning Point of the Revolution*. Boston, 1928. Highlights Lincoln's contribution to the victories in the Saratoga campaign.

Thacher, James, *Military Journal During the American Revolutionary War*. Boston, 1827, pp. 400–10. One of the earliest biographical sketches of Lincoln.

Uhlendorf, Bernhard A., ed., *Siege of Charleston*. Ann Arbor, 1938. Lincoln as seen through enemy eyes during the Charleston campaign.

Marquis de Lafayette:

EAGER WARRIOR

————•—•————

HOWARD H. PECKHAM

William Clements Library

OF THE twenty-nine major generals who served during the American Revolution, few were more devoted to the commander-in-chief than the Marquis de Lafayette. Certainly no one drew more expressions of affection from the forbidding dignity of George Washington than the ebullient young Frenchman. What began on Washington's part as the resigned acceptance of still another condescending French adventurer ripened into paternal attachment, nurtured by filial esteem and love. The relationship surprised Washington's compatriots and astonished Lafayette's friends. To be sure, Lafayette was the youngest of the generals, and Washington twenty-five years his senior. The difference in age no doubt helped to frame the father–son attitudes that developed, but it does not explain the warmth of regard on both sides. Nor is it enough to say that Washington represented the type of man Lafayette longed to be but never could because of his temperament—though it might be sufficient to say on the other side that the young marquis was the kind of son the Virginian would have loved to have had. It was the coincidence of Washington as a man and a symbol of an ideological struggle that made him the idol of this young aristocrat who was dissatisfied with himself.

Lafayette belonged to the rural aristocracy of his native land.

His father, the Marquis de Lafayette, was an army colonel and minor seignior with an estate at Chavaniac in Auvergne, in southern France. Gilbert de Motier was born in the family châteatu on September 6, 1757. His father was killed at the Battle of Minden two years later by a cannon ball allegedly from the British battery of Captain William Phillips, a name to remember. When Gilbert was eleven he was sent to Paris to be put in school. Two years later both his mother and his maternal grandfather died. Suddenly the young marquis came into great wealth which was ably managed and increased for him. Countryfied though he might be, he was richer by far than most of his noble acquaintances.

Early in 1772, when he was fourteen and a half, his greatgrandfather arranged for his marriage to Marie Adrienne de Noailles, aged twelve and a half. She was the daughter of the Duc d'Ayen, who was eager to tap the Lafayette fortune, and granddaughter of the noted Duc de Noailles. Adrienne was not told of the arrangement for more than a year. By that time she had become acquainted with Lafayette and was quite fond of him. The marriage ceremony, eagerly entered by both parties, took place on April 11, 1774, and the young couple set up residence in Paris.

Presumably Lafayette had reached his full growth by this time. He stood about five feet nine inches tall, was rather lanky and pale in coloring. His sandy hair verged on red, his eyes were hazel. More noticeable were a receding forehead and a pointed nose. No one called him handsome, yet he seemed to have an animated countenance and pleasant manner. Lafayette possessed few of the qualities required for the gay social life at Versailles: he was shy in company, awkward in sports and dancing, a poor drinker, and generally uncomfortable in the glittering royal court.

His youthful virtues are harder to fathom. Reserved though he appeared, he had a warm and affectionate nature capable of high enthusiasm and great devotion. He loved the military life. By it he hoped to achieve recognition and distinction, possibly to compensate for his feelings of inferiority at court. But after a long war with England, France was at peace. Lafayette had been made an officer in the Noailles regiment of dragoons and after his marriage was promoted to captain. Although he could look forward to gradual promotion, his career did not promise excitement.

There must have been more to the youth than this limited ambition. He probably did a great deal of reading on his own—especially in the military field. Otherwise, it is impossible to explain the ease with which he exercised a major general's command in the Continental army two years later. Similarly, there is no documentary evidence that Lafayette grew introspective about his wealth and position, or speculated on the rights of peasants and city populace, or was touched by the writings of such liberals as Rousseau or Voltaire. It is difficult, however, to believe that thoughts of social and political reform were utterly foreign to him. If so, then his enthusiasm for the American cause in 1777 was an incredibly sudden adoption of strange doctrine. Six or seven years later, Lafayette declared that he had always had republican leanings, but the statement has been suspect because it was written after the American Revolution ended victoriously. The truth is that what went on in Lafayette's mind—and it was an observant, active mind—between 1775 and 1777 is simply not known.

In the summer of 1775, he attended a dinner at which the revolt in America was discussed with admiration because of France's long enmity toward England. Lafayette thereafter seems to have followed Washington's campaigns. But at the end of the year a new minister of war determined to reform the French army, and one of his measures was to ease out those officers who had had no real military experience. Captain Lafayette found himself a reserve officer, with small prospect of promotion unless France went to war. Small wonder, then, that his interest in a distant war increased.

In July of 1776, Silas Deane arrived in Paris, the first representative of the American colonies sent abroad. On his own initiative, he began engaging European army officers to serve in America by promising them high rank and good pay in the Continental army. Deane was glad to sign up Colonel Johann Kalb, dubbed Baron de Kalb, who had served in the French army, and promised him a major generalship in America. By December 1, 1776, seventeen French officers were enlisted in addition to several who had crossed the Atlantic earlier. The example of these officers fired Lafayette's imagination. De Kalb took him to Deane. Rather surprisingly, the nineteen-year-old Lafayette asked for the rank of major general in America, largely to win his father-in-law's permission to go. He accompanied that request with another surprise: he would not take any pay, only expenses. The eager Deane agreed on December 7, 1776.

The party of French officers preparing to embark for America was stopped at Le Havre by the French government and returned to Paris. It was now hinted to Lafayette that if he would buy a ship for the voyage, the group could slip away secretly. The notion appealed to him; a merchant ship was found and the sale consummated early in March, 1777. Fifteen French officers and Edmund Brice, who was a friend of Deane's secretary, were to rendezvous at Bordeaux. After some delay the *Victoire* sailed on April 20 directly for Charleston, South Carolina. In Paris, Lafayette's defiant exploit made him a hero to all the liberals, just as he was considered an errant hothead in the salons of the conservatives.

In a letter to his young wife, Lafayette tried to excuse his leaving her so abruptly by declaring his devotion to liberty and calling America the hope of all humanity. If this was just an idea and not a philosophy, as his biographer Gottschalk insists, it is still difficult to believe that it was a rationalization that occurred to him on the high seas when he had time to think.[1] The coming change in his public character from what it appeared to his friends at home was even more startling.

Escaping all British cruisers, the *Victoire* anchored near midnight in Georgetown Bay on June 13, 1777. Lafayette, De Kalb, and Brice went ashore on North Island and found themselves on

the summer estate of Major Benjamin Huger of the South Carolina militia. That surprised southern gentleman readily played
host, and from this moment on Lafayette delighted in everything he saw in America.

What Lafayette and his companions did not know was that
the Continental Congress and General Washington were fed up
with French adventurers demanding high rank, some of them
bearing "contracts" from the enthusiastic Silas Deane. When
Lafayette and his friends reached Philadelphia, he was the only
one who impressed Congress. He was asked whether he would
accept a commission as major general dating from that day (so
he would not supersede any existing major generals), without
pay, and without claim to commanding a division. This was
hard bargaining, but Lafayette agreed.

Congress thereupon voted Lafayette the rank of major general
on July 31 and sent him a sash. That night he was invited to
dinner at the City Tavern to meet Washington, who had just
entered Philadelphia with some troops in search of the elusive
Howe. The commander-in-chief was prepared only to dislike
another Frenchman foisted on him, especially one so young and
inexperienced. But he was impressed by the earnest and respectful youth; by the modesty of his motives, his eagerness to learn,
his exquisite manners and his efforts to speak English. Lafayette
found his anticipation more than realized, for he believed he
could recognize true nobility in the face and demeanor of Washington. The Virginian made a point of speaking privately to
Lafayette, inviting the volunteer to mess at his headquarters and
to accompany him next day on an inspection of Philadelphia's
defenses. The young man was elated.

Lafayette's deference and charm soon made him the most popular man at headquarters. He risked this favorable impression,
however, by writing directly to Congress and hinting to Washington about getting a division to command. This was in complete disregard of the earlier stipulation to which he had agreed.
One of his motives for doing so was to make a place for some of
his French companions, who remained in Philadelphia begging

for commissions. His appeal was unexpectedly strengthened by
letters to Congress from Deane and Franklin saying that a warm
reception of Lafayette would help the American cause in France,
and a private letter to Washington from Franklin asking him
to take a personal interest in the youth so as to preserve him from
unnecessary risk. Along with these letters came Count Casimir
Pulaski, hero of the unsuccessful Polish war for independence,
who expressed a willingness to serve under Lafayette. In consequence of these endorsements, Washington explained to Lafayette that though Congress could not yet grant him a command, he himself would be glad to be regarded as the young
man's "father and friend." The marquis was more than satisfied
—he was deeply touched and honored. From this moment on he
had a living ideal before him, such as he had never known before.
The familiar relationship not only molded Lafayette's character
but even affected the self-possessed Washington by drawing a
rare ray of warm affection from him.

When the British transports headed up the Chesapeake, Washington moved his headquarters down to Wilmington on August
25. Lafayette took part in councils of war, marched and counter-
marched with various troop units. He observed his twentieth
birthday on September 6. Three days later a war council directed
the army to Chad's Ford on Brandywine Creek, 26 miles southwest of Philadelphia. Here was the spot where the British and
Hessian forces probably would try to cross. On the morning of
September 11, the enemy appeared marching in two columns.
The one commanded by Major General Wilhelm Knyphausen
stopped at Chad's Ford and made as if to cross. Cannon and
musket fire were exchanged.

Washington, with Lafayette at his side, grew more concerned
about the second column, under Lord Cornwallis, that marched
away from Chad's Ford. The commander-in-chief alerted Sullivan, who commanded his right wing, but Sullivan could not see
the column. Cornwallis continued far beyond Sullivan before
crossing the creek, then turned back, coming in sight of Sullivan's flank about four o'clock. Meanwhile, Lafayette, sensing

that Knyphausen did not intend to force a crossing, had obtained Washington's permission to move over to the right wing. He joined Stirling's division just before Cornwallis struck.

Although he had never been under fire before, Lafayette exhibited great bravery and command ability. Dismounting, he rallied the men in Conway's brigade to hold against the British. In the close fighting he was hit by a bullet that passed through his leg below the calf. Blood ran out of the top of his boot, and his aide Gimat insisted he remount and ride into the woods. Greene's brigade turned and came up just before Washington did. They held Cornwallis at bay until the American left wing could pull back. Knyphausen then crossed the ford, and the outgeneraled American forces fled toward Chester, 12 miles away. Dr. John Cochran, Washington's personal physician, slapped a hasty bandage on Lafayette's leg as they joined the retreat.

It was dusk when Lafayette reached the stone bridge across Chester Creek. He stopped and gathered up scattered fugitives, forming the men into lines and reassuring them. When Washington came up there was a semblance of order, and the flight was stopped. Lafayette was carried into a house and set on a table so that Dr. Cochran could finish attending to his wound. The marquis was voluble and in high spirits; he had demonstrated that he was no oranamental soldier. But Washington sent him to Philadelphia by boat.

While Lafayette was recuperating, Washington was pushed away from Philadelphia after warning Congress he could not protect the capital. Residents and delegates alike began to flee and Congress resolved to meet in York. A boat moved Lafayette up to Bristol on September 16. Congressman Henry Laurens did not leave Philadelphia until the nineteenth. He picked up Lafayette in his coach and deposited him two days later in Bethlehem, where the Moravian brethren were caring for American wounded.

Lafayette remained at Bethlehem about three weeks, captivating the Moravians by his admiration for their faith and institutions. On his return to headquarters about the middle of October, he still limped and could not wear a boot, but he was ready to take up military duties again. He was also something of a hero. De Kalb wrote home to the French War Department that "No one deserves more than he the esteem which he enjoys here. He is a prodigy for his age, full of courage, spirit, judgment, good manners, feelings of generosity and of zeal for the cause of liberty on this continent." [2] It was an accurate summary.

On November 20, General Nathanael Greene led a brigade into New Jersey to strengthen Fort Mercer against Cornwallis. Lafayette asked to join him. Four days later Lafayette took a detachment of 300, mostly militia, north of Gloucester to observe Cornwallis' camp. They ran into a Hessian outpost of 350 men with two cannon. Lafayette charged them and drove them back, then disengaged at dusk. The enemy lost 60 men in killed, wounded, and captured; Lafayette had one officer killed and five men wounded. He had conducted an independent command with skill and coolness, and his casual reference to the engagement in a letter to Henry Laurens, now president of Congress, earned him fresh regard: "I was there nothing almost but a witness, but I was a very pleased one in seeing the behaviour of our men." [3]

There was no holding the marquis from command of a division now. Washington did not want him to return to France in disgust and so with Congress' approval, Lafayette was given the Virginia brigades of Woodford, Muhlenberg, and Scott, formerly commanded by Major General Adam Stephen. The new command was announced on December 4.

Lafayette avoided the factions jealous of Washington because he recognized that Washington was the Revolution and that should he be reduced in power or replaced, the whole cause would collapse. Considering his age and experience, how Lafayette could handle himself so adroitly would be a mystery if he had not revealed his method in a letter to his father-in-law on December 16: "I read, I study, I examine, I listen, I think, and out of all that I try to form an idea into which I put as much common sense as I can. I shall not speak much for fear of saying foolish things; I will risk still less for fear of doing them, for I am not disposed to abuse the confidence which they have deigned to show me. Such is the conduct which until now I have followed and will follow." [4] To judge the young man by his enthusiasms or Gallic expression of his feelings is to miss the sober reflections of a maturing mind. Washington was a shrewd judge of character and never would have warmed to Lafayette if he had been only a superficial ingratiating romantic.

Lafayette scrupulously looked after his men, spending his own money when Congress failed to provide them necessities. Nor was he backward in suggesting to Washington certain changes and innovations from French military practice. The Board of War now proposed to Congress an expedition into Canada that won approval. Lafayette was given the command, to impress the French-Canadians.

Going to Albany to assume command, he consulted three fellow generals all of whom declared that the obstacles to success were insurmountable. The troops were less than half the number promised; no food, clothing, sleighs, or ammunition were ready, and soldiers in the Northern Department were long in arrears on their pay. Angry and deflated, Lafayette wrote to the Board of War for a new assignment. He happily rejoined Washington at Valley Forge on April 8, 1778, and saw what another adventurer, the pseudo-Baron von Steuben from Prussia, was doing toward training the troops.

Lafayette was soon overjoyed to learn that France had allied herself openly with the young republic. Announcement of the Franco-American treaty was made at Valley Forge on May 5. More than ever, the young marquis regarded himself as the spokesman for his country in America.

Lafayette next saw action during a probing march toward Philadelphia on May 18, when he went to discover what the enemy was doing. With a reconnaissance force of 2,200, Lafayette set out and, contrary to Washington's suggestion, established a camp on Barren Hill, halfway to the city. It was a good, defensible position, however, from which to reconnoiter. He posted some militia at Whitemarsh to protect two fords, but for reasons unknown they did not remain there. From a deserter Howe learned of this neglect and set out the next night to get behind Lafayette, using three columns of troops. Warned barely in time, Lafayette extricated himself from the trap, deceived one of Howe's columns, and forced the enemy to retire into Philadelphia chagrined. Moving in a circle, Lafayette returned to Barren Hill and then proceeded back to Valley Forge. If he erred in camping on the same spot two nights in a row and in trusting too much to militia, Washington was yet willing to say: "Upon the whole, the Marquis came handsomely off." [5]

It was now apparent to everyone that the British were going to evacuate Philadelphia. To the question of what the American army should do, the council of generals recommended following the enemy on its road of retreat without bringing on a set battle. Howe had resigned, and his second, Sir Henry Clinton, had become commander-in-chief. He "is a military pedant, somewhat blunderer, and nothing more," Lafayette characterized him, and it was not a bad estimate. [6]

By noon on June 18, Washington learned that the British had pulled out of Philadelphia, crossed the Delaware, and were marching northeast across New Jersey. Immediately he started six brigades in pursuit under Generals Lee and Wayne. At dawn the next day the main army marched out of Valley Forge led by Lafayette's division. When Lee came within striking distance of Clinton's column, he urged avoidance of a clash. Lafayette opposed him in council, and it was finally decided to send a small detachment to annoy the enemy's rear. The eager Frenchman begged to lead it. Washington agreed, asking only for Lee's consent. Lee readily granted it, since he did not want the blame that would come from failure of this effort. Washington then raised the "detachment" to 5,200 men and ordered Lafayette to pursue Clinton. When Lee learned of the increased size of the corps Lafayette was given, he was jealous and demanded that as second in command he should lead it. Washington hesitated, and Lee appealed to Lafayette to save his somewhat suspect "honor." The Frenchman was touched and said that if he did not meet the enemy within twenty-four hours he would turn over the corps to Lee.

Unfortunately for the American cause, Lafayette could not catch up to Clinton within the prescribed time limit. Despite intense heat he pushed his brigades to Hightstown and then onto the road to Monmouth Court House, getting ahead of his provisions. Washington ordered him to Englishtown and sent Lee to support him. The older man took command upon joining. So it was that on June 28, a cautious general was in charge when the American advance came up with the British near Monmouth. Lee developed no plan of action and had few orders to give. Getting into a favorable position to cut off Clinton's rearguard, he muffed the attack and ordered a partial withdrawal. His unit commanders were confused by his orders, and Lee permitted a general retreat, though he knew that Washington was coming up with the main army.

Washington appeared before noon and saw his advance force in retreat. Finding Lee, he rebuked him publicly, took personal command, and reversed the movement. He sent Lafayette back to the main army to form and command the second line of attack. At the front Washington pushed the advancing British back toward Monmouth. The dreadful heat took its grim toll, and the battle broke off with darkness. Clinton had no intention of renewing it, and at midnight he stole away, having suffered a great number of casualties.

Washington's horse had dropped dead from the heat, and when Lafayette came up to him, the two slept under a tree together. Lee was court-martialed and suspended from the army. The Continentals turned up to White Plains, New York, and encamped. Both sides were now back where they were in October, 1776. If only the incompetent Lee had been kept from command of the advance, there is little doubt that under Lafayette a vigorous thrust would have crippled Clinton and perhaps insured a decisive victory by Washington.

The French alliance soon produced its first joint military operation. Comte d'Estaing, who was both an admiral and a general, reached Maryland with sixteen ships and some French marines aboard. To everyone's disappointment, his largest warships were too big to enter New York harbor, and the French were directed to Rhode Island. Newport was garrisoned by 6,000 British, and Sullivan was encamped nearby with 3,000 Continentals and militia. Washington sent Lafayette and Greene with 2,000 reinforcements, and called for the New England states to supply more militia. D'Estaing indicated he would be happy to place his French marines under Lafayette's command.

The allied attack on Newport never materialized. D'Estaing was uneasy about being bottled up in Narragansett Bay by a British fleet. He had started to put some of his troops ashore, however, when Admiral Howe appeared on the horizon with thirty sail, on August 9, 1778, offering to do battle. D'Estaing immediately weighed anchor to meet the British, but a severe storm of gale force prevented a decisive sea fight. The storm scattered and damaged both fleets, and D'Estaing brought his crippled squadron back to Rhode Island only to inform Sullivan that he had to proceed to Boston for repairs.

Sullivan now had more troops than the British, and he tried to persuade D'Estaing to stay for a joint attack. But the admiral sailed away, much to Sullivan's disgust and Lafayette's embarrassment. Sullivan launched an unsuccessful attack on August 29. Lafayette was not present, having been dispatched on the twenty-seventh to Boston to learn what D'Estaing's intentions were. He felt himself very much in the middle, forced to defend D'Estaing and uphold the French alliance in the face of critical public outcry.

He remained on duty in Rhode Island until late September, when he asked for permission to go home for a visit. Washington readily assented, and Lafayette sailed from Boston on January 11, 1779, carrying messages from Congress to Franklin and from Ambassador Gérard to Foreign Minister Vergennes as well as testimonials of his own services to the American cause. The Atlantic was crossed in the short time of twenty-three days, the passengers surviving a brief mutiny.

Lafayette's reappearance in Paris was as dramatic as his exit from France. His cousin, the Prince de Poix, was giving a party on February 11, and suddenly about midnight Lafayette burst in, to be cheered and embraced by all the guests—an authentic hero and celebrity home from the wars. Officially he was still under the displeasure of the King for having run off without royal permission, but a week of house arrest placated His Majesty. Lafayette then was free to be lionized. Indeed, the King promoted him from a reserve captain to lieutenant commander of the King's Dragoons, which, in European fashion, cost him 80,000 livres for the commission.

Lafayette and Franklin met at last, and each was taken by the other. John Adams was now also in Paris. As requested by Congress, Lafayette spoke to them about the previously planned invasion of Canada with French help. Franklin approved, but Adams preferred that France help America with her navy. Premier Maurepas and Vergennes heard the persuasive youth, but were not moved. Lafayette himself soon became diverted by the prospect of a more exciting venture, and in a few months learned that the Continental Congress had changed its mind about Canada.

The new venture planned by the ministry involved Spain, which declared war on England in June, 1779. French troops had been quietly gathered in Normandy and Brittany for an invasion of England. Lafayette was named aide to the commander. This bold undertaking was to begin as soon as the combined French and Spanish fleets had cleared the English Channel. Lafayette worked feverishly at Le Havre gathering supplies for a force of 30,000.

Admiral d'Orvilliers finally sailed into the Channel in August with a combined fleet of 66 French and Spanish ships. He blockaded Plymouth for three days while the French army made ready to embark for Falmouth. Then a severe storm blew the navy out of the Channel, and a British squadron sailed in. D'Orvilliers returned for a decisive engagement, but the smaller British force skillfully avoided battle. The French admiral gave up the chase early in September. His fighting strength reduced by sickness and dangerously low on his supply of stores, D'Orvilliers disgustedly returned to France.

It was November before the invasion army was disbanded and Lafayette could leave Le Havre. He was now showing a genuine interest in human rights—Irish discontent and the condition of his own serfs—but his fondest dream was still to lead an expeditionary force to America. Premier Maurepas was reluctant to send off a French army, but Vergennes favored it because he believed that America was the best place to strike England. A letter received from Washington in January, 1780, said he would welcome such military aid. The ministry acceded to the new appeal, but hesitated over the commander. Their decision was to ask Lafayette to resume his rank in the American army and to name the Comte de Rochambeau to command the expeditionary force. Rochambeau was fifty-five years old, a veteran of the Seven Years' War, and had been a major general for nineteen years.

Jaunty as ever, Lafayette was not offended, as he recognized that his youth and lack of experience were against him. He was instrumental in having Rochambeau's instructions include the stipulation that the French army should act only under the orders of Washington so as to prevent its falling under the authority of Congress. Moreover, he won the promise of clothing and munitions for American troops. He was to set off at once to carry the good news to Washington.

Arriving in Boston at the end of April, 1780, Lafayette was welcomed by cannon, bells, bands, and officials. Although he drank up this tribute, he was not happy by what he saw and heard. The country was just emerging from a particularly harsh winter, taxes and prices were exorbitant, paper currency had depreciated greatly, the Congress was held in low regard, the army was hungry and small. Charleston, South Carolina, was under siege by the British.

The main army was at Morristown, New Jersey, and Lafayette set off on the long ride. Washington did not try to hide his delight that the marquis was coming back. No doubt he had missed his youthful confidence and high spirits, his warm and loyal devotion, and his faith in the common cause. Lafayette reached the Morristown camp on May 10, to be welcomed by all.

His message to Washington prompted the commander-in-chief to plan an attack on New York as soon as Rochambeau should arrive. In the meantime the Continental army would have to be enlarged, and Washington could think of no one better qualified than Lafayette to go to Philadelphia and gain authorization from Congress. Then came news that General Lincoln had surrendered Charleston on May 12, and that Clinton was returning to New York. Washington still persevered in his plan to attack New York, but Rochambeau's army of 5,000 men did not arrive at Newport, Rhode Island, until mid-July. The delay had enabled an English squadron to reach New York, and an attack on the city seemed out of the question.

Rochambeau requested a personal meeting, but as Washington was conferring with a visiting committee from Congress, he sent Lafayette instead. The marquis soon discovered there was a problem of divided command. The French admiral, Du Ternay, insisted on superiority at sea before he would blockade New York, and Rochambeau would not act without naval control in local waters. This meant asking Paris for more ships and troops. It was clear that nothing could be attempted that summer. Lafayette again was disappointed by his countrymen, because he believed New York could be taken by an attack on land by the combined armies. The stalemate continued.

Lafayette was given command of a new corps of 1,850 light infantry, a kind of elite mobile division. Divided into two brigades, it included a cavalry unit under Major "Light-Horse Harry" Lee. Lafayette worked to develop an *esprit de corps* and spent his own money on uniforms and equipment. The war news almost countered his efforts. In August, Gates was routed by Cornwallis in Camden, South Carolina, in a battle that cost the life of Lafayette's old friend, Baron de Kalb. Lafayette was sufficiently discouraged to wish that Washington would make

himself dictator for the sake of the public welfare. His democratic faith at this point was not unshakable.

In the middle of September he and several officers accompanied Washington to Hartford for a meeting with Rochambeau
and Du Ternay. On the way they learned that the English naval
force at New York had been reinforced. The commanders agreed
that unless the French could gain naval superiority around the
city, the allies should attempt an expedition somewhere in the
South.

On their way back to camp, Washington's party again stopped
off at West Point, where Arnold commanded, on the fateful
twenty-fifth of September. Arnold had held a treasonable meeting with Clinton's adjutant general, Major John André, and
arranged to surrender West Point and its garrison to the British
for handsome pay and honors. Word was now received by Arnold
that André had been captured within the American lines on the
Hudson, and that suspicious papers in his boot were being forwarded directly to Washington. Fleeing from his quarters just
before Washington rode up, Arnold took to a boat and was
rowed down the Hudson to a British ship. Washington was
shocked and numbed by Arnold's defection. Lafayette, along
with thirteen other officers, tried André and sentenced him to
hang as a spy.

After this excitement, matters reverted to normal idleness,
broken only by Admiral de Ternay's sudden death in December.
Lafayette was mortified by Rochambeau's cautiousness. He
feared for the alliance and the honor of France if some action was
not taken in 1781. Action was just as necessary for America;
Lafayette could see that his friends were plainly running out of
funds. He put these arguments together in an urgent code letter
to Vergennes, another to the Prince de Poix, and another to
Franklin. He asked for men, ships, and cash. His pleas were
echoed by Washington and Rochambeau.

In the interim of waiting, Lafayette's constitutional impatience
and his eagerness to provoke battle asserted themselves in proposals for several small attacks. Washington, always more real-

istic, admired Lafayette's boldness but cautioned him that "we must consult our means rather than our wishes; and not endeavour to better our affairs by attempting things, which for want of success may make them worse." [7] This attitude was foreign to the youth, but instructive.

Lafayette also sharpened his comprehension of political liberty by talking with the Duc de Chastellux and writing to a new friend, Dr. James McHenry. Though still a defender of French institutions, he was learning from his American experience to question and to doubt.

In February, 1781, Washington decided to help Virginia, which had been invaded by a British force under the turncoat Arnold. Lafayette marched south at the head of 1,200 Continentals to reinforce Steuben and try to bottle up the British inside Portsmouth so that a French fleet on its way could close the door of an escape by sea. He proved to be a master at wheedling supplies where none seemed to exist. In mid-March, the incoming French fleet was attacked by a British squadron and forced to turn north. Arnold was able to receive reinforcements and supplies, and the contemplated allied clamp was broken. The marquis' hopes of gaining glory by bagging Arnold were dashed.

Lafayette went back to Annapolis, where his men were waiting. General Nathanael Greene in the meantime was in North Carolina pleading for reinforcements, and Washington ordered Lafayette to go to his assistance. At first Lafayette was loath to stay in the South, fearing he would be too far away when French reinforcements arrived and the long delayed attack on New York took place. Then he learned that the commander of the reinforcements brought to Arnold was Major General William Phillips—the man whose battery had killed his father in 1759. Lafayette took after him in a hurry. To reach Richmond with greater speed, he impressed wagons and had half of his men ride and half walk, with the two changing positions at regular intervals. He arrived at Richmond in the last days of April, barely before the British. Steuben, whose militia had dwindled to a thousand men, kept falling back slowly up the James River until he joined Lafayette. The British came within sight of the city, burned some hogsheads of tobacco, swore at Lafayette, then turned back down the river.

The military maneuvering continued, though most of it was inconclusive. As tensions tightened on him, Lafayette was not without humorous self-knowledge. "I have so many Arrangements to make, so many difficulties to Combat, so many enemies to deal with," he wrote to Alexander Hamilton, "that I am just that much of a general as will make me an Historian of misfortunes, and nail my name upon the Ruins of what good folks are pleased to Call the Army of Virginia . . . To speak truth I was afraid of myself as much as of the Enemy. Independence has rendered me the more cautious, as I know my warmth." [8]

By mid-May, the situation in Virginia had altered considerably. Lord Cornwallis, moving up from North Carolina, took over command of those British forces that had lost their leader when General Phillips died of fever. Convinced that British control in the deep South could not be restored while Virginia remained a major supply and training base, Cornwallis was determined to make the state a major theater of operations. There was a rapid British buildup of forces, and Cornwallis soon had 7,200 men to mop up Virginia. Lafayette, who by this time held practically an independent command in the state, could muster no more than 2,500—half of whom were militia. Yet the young man whom Cornwallis sneeringly dubbed "the boy" proceeded to teach the veteran lord something of a lesson in the war of maneuver. "I am therefore determined to scarmish, but not to engage too far," he wrote to Washington, adding with a wink, "I am not strong enough even to get beaten." [9]

Lafayette had to abandon Richmond as Cornwallis approached, moving northward in a line parallel to the British but holding himself between them and certain American supply depots. He was maneuvering also in the direction of his coming reinforcements. Near Fredericksburg, Wayne joined him with 900 veterans in early June. Then Colonel Campbell, who had fought at King's Mountain, arrived with 600 mounted riflemen. Lafayette called also for General Daniel Morgan, who was home on sick leave.

After failing to catch the Frenchman, Cornwallis raided deep into Virginia. He sent Tarleton riding off to Charlottesville in a wild attempt to capture Governor Thomas Jefferson. The results were almost successful, but Tarleton bagged only a few lowly legislators rather than a governor. A force of British rangers under Major John Simcoe set off in pursuit of Steuben, but the Prussian eluded the stab and marched his 450 men toward Lafayette. As the young marquis was reinforced and more militia began turning out to halt the British invasion, Cornwallis decided to move back toward Williamsburg where he expected to find new orders. Lafayette, his force now swelled above 5,000, discarded the role of rabbit and turned upon the hounds.

When Cornwallis first veered toward a supply depot at Albemarle Old Court House, Lafayette by forced marches beat him to it. Cornwallis pulled away toward Richmond, and then to avoid battle, began marching eastward toward Williamsburg. Lafayette followed on his heels. Five miles from the old colonial capital, there was a small clash on June 26, but it was the British who broke it off. As Professor Gottschalk has pointed out, most Americans believe that Cornwallis ran because Lafayette chased him, whereas in reality Lafayette chased him because he ran.[10] The marquis gave out the former impression to raise the morale of Virginia. Throughout this phase of the campaign he had handled himself admirably, and no one could have done better. Washington was not flattering when he wrote to a friend: "He possesses uncommon Military talents, is of a quick and sound judgment, persevering, and enterprizing without rashness, and besides these, he is of a very conciliating temper and perfectly sober, which are qualities that rarely coincide in the same person." [11]

At Williamsburg, Cornwallis found frantic letters from Sir Henry Clinton. The British commander-in-chief had never given His Lordship permission to leave the Carolinas, and as he was planning to strike at Philadelphia again, he did not want to get committed in Virginia. Therefore he ordered Cornwallis to take up a defensive post on the coast and send part of his army up to New York for the Philadelphia project.

Clinton had no sooner posted these orders than he found his plans overturned. News came from France to Rochambeau that a large French fleet would reach America in July or August. Washington met with the French general at Wethersfield, Connecticut, and they perfected plans to attack New York City. Washington wrote this news to Lafayette, and Clinton read the intercepted letter. Panicked, Clinton wrote again to Cornwallis that he needed all the men from Virginia who could be spared. The irritated Cornwallis decided to move to Portsmouth and headed for the James River.

Lafayette was right after him. At the crossing on July 6, Wayne rushed up on what he thought was the rearguard, but the main body of British lay hidden just beyond them. When they burst out on Wayne's 900 men, he realized that to call retreat would bring on a rout. So he bluffed the enemy and ordered an attack! Lafayette came up and helped the men when they recoiled from overpowering numbers. The Pennsylvanians pulled back half a mile in good order, and Cornwallis resumed his crossing of the river. Lafayette had two horses shot out from under him and suffered casualties of 139 killed, wounded, and captured. The British losses were less.

As the Virginia militia began to go home, Lafayette established a camp at Malvern Hill, halfway between Williamsburg and Richmond, and kept Wayne reconnoitering on the south side of the James. Having calmed down, Clinton changed his mind and told Cornwallis to keep his troops and occupy a port that would provide a good naval station for warships, preferably on the Chesapeake. Not knowing of these fresh orders, Lafayette was puzzled when on the last day of July, Cornwallis shifted his men by water to Yorktown and the hamlet of Gloucester, across the York River.

Lafayette moved his troops eastward to the head of the York River and set about badgering and imploring General Nelson, who had succeeded Jefferson as governor, for men and supplies. He could not understand why Cornwallis was fortifying himself, but soon after the middle of August he received exciting news from Washington. The French fleet under Admiral de Grasse was coming up from the West Indies to the Chesapeake; Lafayette must not let Cornwallis escape and might expect aid from the North. Lafayette acknowledged "the most beautifull prospect that I may ever behold." [12]

To prevent Cornwallis' escape southward, he shifted men south and east around to Portsmouth and alerted the North Carolina militia. His intelligence service now included one of Cornwallis' servants. Arrival of General du Portail, Washington's best engineer, about August 26, gave Lafayette the latest news. Not only was De Grasse coming, but so was the Rhode Island squadron, and so were the combined armies of Rochambeau and Washington! Lafayette drew his noose tighter. On August 30, De Grasse hove in sight—34 ships, 3,100 marines, and crews of several thousand. Cornwallis' hope of rescue by sea was gone.

A tardy British fleet appeared on the horizon on September 6, and De Grasse sailed out of the lower bay to meet it. An all-day battle damaged the English seriously and they broke off, though they hovered around several days before turning back to New York. De Grasse returned to the bay. Lafayette fell sick with the fever, but he got up on September 14, to rush out and embrace Washington and Rochambeau, who had arrived ahead of their troops. Late that night after a joyful reunion supper, De Grasse sent word that the Rhode Island squadron had joined him with siege guns.

With American and French forces pouring in, the siege of Yorktown began. The presence of Major General Lincoln, who outranked Lafayette, placed the marquis under him in command of two brigades, including his old light infantry. It fell to Lafayette's division to storm one of the British redoubts outside the Yorktown wall. The assault was capably handled by Lieutenant Colonel Alexander Hamilton in a matter of minutes on the night of October 14. The French seized the other redoubt, and both

were incorporated into the tightening ring Washington drew
around the beleaguered post. The next night Cornwallis tried a
sortie that failed. On the seventeenth he opened negotiations to
surrender, and on the nineteenth he signed the capitulation. Lafayette insisted that the British be allowed no honors because
they had denied Lincoln the same privilege at Charleston the
year before. No one viewed the surrender ceremonies with more
pleasure and satisfaction than the marquis. It was the glorious
culmination of a long wait.

After the fall of Yorktown, Lafayette applied for a furlough
for France. He was to seek reinforcements for Rochambeau and
another fleet. Stopping at Philadelphia, he was thanked by
Congress for his services and asked to consult with Benjamin
Franklin in Paris about getting a loan from France. Lafayette proceeded to Boston, where he boarded the *Alliance* commanded by
Captain John Barry. They sailed on December 23, and Lafayette
was back in Paris on January 20, 1782. The King promptly promoted him to *maréchal de camp* (major general) in the French
army. He was honored and congratulated by everyone, and
crowds gathered wherever he made an appearance.

Franklin, now troubled by the gout, made good use of the
young man in obtaining a loan. The ministry agreed also to reinforce Rochambeau. Then England's war ministry fell, and the
British began to show signs of desiring peace. During the negotiations, Lafayette did yeoman service as liaison between the
French foreign minister and the American peace commission
composed of Franklin, John Adams, and John Jay. By stalling,
the American commissioners forced England to recognize American sovereignty before negotiating a treaty.

France and Spain in the meantime had decided to send
D'Estaing to the West Indies and offered Lafayette command of
the troops aboard the French fleet. He set off for Cadiz in November. Late in December, word reached the fleet that a preliminary treaty of peace had been signed between England and
the United States. France signed a separate treaty on January
20, 1783, and the expedition to Cadiz was called off. Lafayette,

who had consciously tried to model his deportment as a diplomat after Washington, sent his congratulations to his idol. "I cannot but envy the happiness of my grand children when they will be about celebrating and worshipping your name. To have one of their ancestors among your soldiers, to know he had the good fortune to be the friend of your heart, will be the eternal honour in which they shall glory. . . ." [13]

Both Lafayette's energy and his humanitarianism asserted themselves in a peacetime proposal he made to Washington: he and the Virginian should purchase together a small plantation and experiment in employing freed Negroes as tenants. It would be a demonstration of how slavery might be abolished. Matured by his experience and observations in America, Lafayette was on his way to becoming a true and thoroughgoing liberal. America, indeed, shone as the example to French radicals of what might be done by a transfer of political power from the King and nobles to the people. There was a great difference, however, in the two peoples, and Lafayette's political efforts in France were destined for disaster.

The young marquis returned to America in August, 1784. Beginning with an ovation in New York, he was wildly received by everyone. Washington entertained him at Mt. Vernon, fulfilling a wartime promise. Three states made him and all his male heirs citizens. When he returned to Paris, he threw himself into various reform movements and ably assisted Jefferson in promoting increased trade with the United States.

With the outbreak of the French Revolution, Lafayette was recognized in the initial stages as a national leader. In 1790, he was probably the most popular person in France. But he was a moderate, and as the revolution fell into excess he was denounced by the terrorists and imprisoned from 1792 to 1797. Although President Washington sought his release, it was Napoleon who finally had him freed. Settling down in La Grange, forty miles from Paris, he retired from public life for a short time. The years had taken his fortune, but the United States Congress now voted him almost $25,000 for his unpaid services and later gave him 11,500 acres of land in Louisiana. His wife died in 1807. After Napoleon's defeat at Waterloo, Lafayette sat in the Chamber of Deputies from 1818 to 1824, always voting on the liberal side.

In 1824, President Monroe invited the aging warrior to visit America as the nation's guest. His triumphal tour has never been matched. Most of his distinguished colleagues were dead and some were forgotten, but Lafayette's name was still a household byword. He moved through the southern states to the Mississippi, then up that river and the Ohio, across New York and into New England. The great circle tour lasted a year. He was greeted everywhere with banquets, balls, parades, fireworks, special music, speeches, and testimonials of respect and affection. Congress restored his fortune by voting him the sum of $200,000. Fifty-five towns and counties were named in his honor. He was touched, inspired, proud, and grateful. His charm enchanted everyone.

Lafayette had less success with his republican ideas in France than abroad. In the 1830 revolution he was offered the presidency of the French Republic but decided his country was not yet ready for that form of government. Instead he accepted Louis Philippe as "King of the French" hoping for a monarchy with republican institutions. His idea was doomed to fail. He died on May 20, 1834, still dreaming of a pure republic for France. He was buried in Paris, his grave covered with soil from Bunker Hill, a gesture by which the United States laid claim to him.

What remains to be said of this exuberant Frenchman who was an American major general? Perhaps he was bumptious in regarding himself as the spokesman and representative of France in America, but his presumption was so infused with good will that few could take offense. He did, in fact, succeed in promoting better relations between the two countries. Throughout the war he showed a remarkable facility for being amiable to all factions in Congress and in the Versailles court. For his diplomatic services alone, Lafayette is deserving of high praise.

He was equally untiring in concocting schemes for military

offensives. Personally brave to the point of recklessness, he gave watchful care to his men and actually held them in high regard, contrary to most foreign officers. In battle he displayed good judgment, matching his field generalship with a talent for wheedling supplies from barren cupboards. Like Washington, he respected the democratic process while pushing against its slowness. Devoted to the American cause, he not only risked his life but opened his ample purse. His motive was partly glory for the sake of reputation, yet it was not all self-promotion. There was also idealism and commitment to principles. Although he learned the weaknesses of republics and the pitfalls of liberty, his faith in self-government remained. He outlasted and outshone the self-righteous Jacobins of his own country.

In speaking of himself he was modest, even deprecating, but it was more humorous than truthful. When he asked for something for himself, he revealed immense self-assurance. It is difficult in assessing one so young to say whether his American experience changed his character or hastened its liberal growth. If at the beginning of 1777 he was only a wealthy aristocrat, shy and without social conscience, as innocent of political philosophy as he was of military operations, by the end of the year he was revealed as aggressive in manners, courageous in perils and proposals, enthusiastic about the libertarian ends of the Revolution, and devoted to Washington as a person and as a symbol. The contrast appears too great for a harvest from barren ground. Clearly he developed rapidly under Washington's tutelage and returned to France a ready leader of men and ideas in the movement to liberalize the French monarchy.

FOOTNOTES

1. Louis R. Gottschalk, *Lafayette Comes to America*, pp. 137, 141.
2. Gottschalk's translation in *Lafayette Joins the American Army*, p. 53, of a letter from De Kalb to St. Paul, November 17, 1777, in *American Historical Review*, XV (1910), 563.
3. *South Carolina Historical Magazine*, VII (1906), 55.

4. Quoted in *Lafayette Joins the American Army*, p. 92, from Lafayette's *Mémoires*, I, 133–34.
5. Washington to G. Morris, May 29, 1778, in John C. Fitzpatrick, ed., *The Writings of George Washington*, XI, 485; hereinafter cited as Washington, *Writings*.
6. Lafayette to Laurens, June 12, 1778, *South Carolina Historical Magazine*, IX (1908), 4.
7. Washington to Lafayette, October 30, 1780, in Washington, *Writings*, XX, 267.
8. Lafayette to Hamilton, May 23, 1781, in Harold C. Syrett and Jacob E. Cooke, eds., *The Papers of Alexander Hamilton*, II, 643–44.
9. May 24, 1781, in Gottschalk, ed., *The Letters of Lafayette to Washington*, p. 198.
10. Gottschalk, *Lafayette and the Close of the American Revolution*, pp. 270–71.
11. Washington to Joseph Jones, July 10, 1781, in Washington, *Writings*, XXII, 353.
12. August 21, 1781, in *The Letters of Lafayette to Washington*, p. 220.
13. February 15, 1783, in *ibid.*, p. 259.

BIBLIOGRAPHY

Chinard, Gilbert, *The Letters of Lafayette and Jefferson*. Baltimore, 1929. These letters reveal much about Lafayette's services to the United States after his return to France.
Gottschalk, Louis R., *Lafayette Comes to America*. Chicago, 1935. Gottschalk's four volume work is by far the best source for Lafayette's activities in the American Revolution and this essay has drawn heavily on it.
———, *Lafayette Joins the American Army*. Chicago, 1937.
———, *Lafayette and the Close of the American Revolution*. Chicago, 1942.
———, *Letters of Lafayette to Washington*. New York, 1944. The preface to this volume carries an incisive essay on the relations between the two men.
———, *Lafayette Between the American and French Revolution, 1783–1789*. Chicago, 1950.
Loth, David, *The People's General*. New York, 1951. Emphasizes the personal aspects of Lafayette's life.

238 GEORGE WASHINGTON'S GENERALS

Nolan, J. Bennett, *Lafayette in America Day by Day*. Baltimore, 1934.
A compilation of Lafayette's movements in America.

Sedgwick, Henry D., *Lafayette*. Indianapolis, 1928. More of a character study.

Tower, Charlemagne, *The Marquis de La Fayette in the American Revolution*. Philadelphia, 1895. An older work that is still interesting and reliable.

Henry Knox:

AMERICAN ARTILLERIST

———•———

NORTH CALLAHAN

New York University

ONE of the most impressive developments in the Continental army was the creation of the artillery arm. Not even in existence at the beginning of the war, this branch of the service grew to a point where big guns became the decisive factor in the Yorktown campaign. A portly but energetic young officer named Henry Knox was the person primarily responsible for this amazing expansion. Inside of six years, Knox rose from a civilian bookseller in Boston to become the youngest American major general in the army.

"Henry Knox," Washington Irving once observed, "was one of those providential characters which spring up in emergencies as if formed by and for the occasion." He was born on July 25, 1750, in Boston, a collateral descendant of the famous Scottish reformer, John Knox. Before reaching his teens, he was forced to drop out of school to support his mother, who had been deserted by her husband. Knox started working in a local bookstore—an occupation he found interesting because it gave him time to read and to satisfy his inquiring mind. He was present at the Boston Massacre and tried, without success, to restrain the British from firing into the mob. As a result of this episode among others, he became committed to the patriot cause.

Love knows no loyalties, however, and Knox soon was at-

239

tracted to Lucy Flucker, the plump daughter of a prominent Tory. Thomas Flucker, the royal secretary to the Massachusetts colony, cared neither for the politics nor social station of his daughter's suitor. It was Lucy who finally resolved the matter. She embraced the patriot cause, married Knox in 1774, and fled from Boston the following year, never to see her parents again.

Knox cut a fine figure as a man and no doubt it was his military bearing that first caught Lucy's eye. He was already inclined to that stoutness for which he was well-known in later life. But his six-foot-plus frame with its broad shoulders always seemed to carry its great weight with such verve that one almost forgot he was fat. His merry, handsome face set off by sharp though genial gray eyes, gave him an air of sociability that delighted all he met. In fact, before the war his English-educated patrons made a habit of meeting their friends in Knox's bookstore because of the fine companionship and stimulating conversation the proprietor provided.

When Knox offered his services to Washington in the summer of 1775, the newly appointed commander-in-chief received him with greater cordiality than he had accorded to most New Englanders entering the army. Washington was impressed because he learned the young bookseller had read widely about British theories on the use of artillery. Knox already had put some of his ideas to the test with the Boston militia. Consequently, Washington was favorably disposed when John Adams suggested that Knox be given the rank of colonel and made chief of the Continental army artillery. There was only one slight problem—the army had little or no artillery to command.

Knox then proposed a plan that was to earn him his first fame —a trek to Ticonderoga to bring back some captured artillery with which to blast the British out of Boston. Washington quickly agreed and directed Knox to go after the guns. Before leaving Cambridge, Knox expressed his contempt for the British artillerymen who had fired over one hundred rounds at the Americans at close range. "And did what?" Knox asked sarcastically. "Why scraped a man's face with the splinters of a rail fence . . . nor am I afraid they will hit me, unless directed by the hand of Providence." [1]

Upon reaching Ticonderoga in December, 1775, Knox quickly surveyed the captured artillery and found that many of the guns were too worn for more use. He sorted out some three score usable pieces, ranging from 4-pound to 24-pound guns, as well as a number of howitzers and mortars. Altogether the guns weighed more than 120,000 pounds and they had to be hauled almost 300 miles through the snow and ice.

Rounding up a small task force of soldiers, hired civilians, horses and oxen, Knox started back to Massachusetts with a long caravan of 42 sledges, bearing 59 fieldpieces. Hauling the heavy cannon was hard, back-breaking work, but with shouting drivers cracking whips the column slowly inched its way across the frozen countryside. The work was not only difficult but dangerous. To prevent runaway sledges from crashing downhill upon the men in front, drag chains and poles were thrust under the runners, and check ropes were fastened around the trees along the way to hold back the heavy cargo. As an early January thaw set in, some of the big guns broke through the ice on the rivers and lakes. But the "drowned cannon" were laboriously recovered in almost every case. Making its way along the Hudson and then turning eastward through the Berkshires, the column finally emerged from the mountains entering upon an old Indian trail running across Massachusetts. Upon reaching Springfield, however, the snow was almost gone and Knox could proceed no farther. Fortunately the weather turned cold again and as the ground froze the column lurched on toward Cambridge.

By early February, Knox completed his journey and delivered to Washington a "noble train of artillery." It is a feat at which soldiers and engineers still marvel. Washington promptly placed the cannon atop Dorchester Heights where they could fire down upon the British troops, forcing General Howe to evacuate Boston. There was rejoicing in the streets as the American army triumphantly trooped in. As befitted the important part he played in driving the British out of Boston, Knox rode beside Washington at the head of the army. The occasion was not without its humor. As the procession passed by the celebrated, punning Tory clergyman Mather Byles, he was heard to exclaim loudly on seeing the portly artilleryman: "I never saw a (Kn)ox fatter in my life!"

From the outset of the war, Knox was forced to struggle along with a collection of ill-assorted cannon of various caliber. Besides captured British cannon, he had French fieldpieces and some guns cast in crude American foundries. At no time during the war was Knox able to achieve uniformity in the Continental army's artillery. The cannon also used different types of ammunition; some fired solid cast-iron shot, others grapeshot, still others canister. Guns varied so in size that ammunition usually was not interchangeable. Despite these difficulties, Knox put together a formidable force and rightfully deserves his reputation as "father of the American Army Artillery."

When the scene of fighting shifted to New York in the spring of 1776, Knox participated in the preparations to fortify Manhattan Island. Following a careful reconnaissance, he reported to Washington that there were 120 light and heavy cannon mounted and ready for action in and around New York City. About 1,200 artillerymen would be needed to man these guns, but Knox's own regiment numbered only 520. He recommended, therefore, that additional men be drafted from other units to make up the difference. Under the supervision of the commander-in-chief, Knox also helped to fortify Fort Washington, which lay on the east bank of the Hudson a short distance above the city.

Although there were rumors for some time that General Howe had left Halifax and was sailing toward New York, Lucy Knox was determined to be with her husband. She travelled down from Connecticut and joined him in New York City. One bright morning in early July as they were seated at breakfast, the young couple looked up to see a huge British fleet sailing toward them down the Narrows between Staten Island and Long Island,

on a fair wind and rapid tide. As Knox wrote to his brother
William:

> . . . one could scarcely conceive the distress and anxiety Lucy then
> had. The city in an uproar, the alarm guns firing, the troops repair-
> ing to their posts, and everything in the height of bustle, I not at
> liberty to attend her, as my country calls loudest. My God, may I
> never experience the like feelings again! They were too much; but
> I found a way to disguise them, for I scolded like a fury at her for
> not having gone before.[2]

After scolding Lucy, he sent her packing back to New England.

Knox, along with other American officers, was stunned at the
size of the British armada sent to seize New York. Besides a powerful British fleet, there were more than 150 transports and
10,000 men. After landing on Staten Island, Howe began a rapid
military buildup, massing more than 32,000 men before he was
through. New York harbor swarmed with masts as men-of-war
and transports kept shuttling in troops. It was the largest expeditionary force ever seen in American waters. To oppose this
invasion, the Americans had about 20,000 troops, many of whom
were untrained and poorly armed.

The first indication of impending disaster came when British
ships sailed boldly up the Hudson and East rivers in defiance of
the patriot batteries. Knox reported that his cannon opened fire
on two or three vessels moving up the Hudson, but they kept so
close to the Jersey shore as to be out of reach of his short-range
guns. In fact, Knox lost six men as the result of the bombardment. His crude cannon were apt to burst upon firing, maiming
or killing the gun crews. In this instance, defective Continental
cannon caused more casualties than did the fire from British
ships.

General Howe began his campaign for capturing New York
City by landing a large force on the western tip of Long Island.
After defeating the patriots in the Battle of Long Island in late
August, the British began preparing for an amphibious attack on
the lower end of Manhattan Island in mid-September. Washing-
ton, rather than risk being trapped in the city, started his troops

moving toward the hilly terrain on upper Manhattan. But before the retreat was completed, the British struck. Landing one-third of the way up the island, Howe threatened to cut off a large section of the American army still straggling out of the city. Knox was among those in the winding, sweating column as it made its way up the island. All day the column was in danger of being caught, but as night fell the weary soldiers finally slogged safely into the American camp on Harlem Heights. Almost the last man to arrive was Knox, who was welcomed joyously by all, for he had been previously reported as captured.[3] "My constant fatigue and application to the business of my extensive department has been such," he wrote his brother, "[that] I have not had my clothes off anights for more than 40 days."[4]

After some sharp skirmishes on Harlem Heights in mid-September, the British and American armies settled down to a stalemate because each felt the position of the other was impregnable. During this lull in the fighting, Knox was busy on other matters. Having seen how totally unprepared the patriots were to wage war, he had been thinking for some time about the founding of a military academy to teach the theories of warfare. When a Congressional committee set out to explore the idea of an academy, John Adams, who knew of Knox's interest, asked him to submit a plan for such an institution. Taking advantage of this opportunity to call attention to the needs of his own corps, Knox modestly titled the plan "Hints for the Improvement of the Artillery of the United States," and included therein his specific suggestions for a military academy.[5]

Knox's plan first recommended the establishment of a number of laboratories for making artillery materiel. To be certain that these manufacturing centers would be beyond the reach of the enemy, they were to be located in parts of the country far removed from the fighting. The laboratories were to be furnished with raw materials for making cannon carriages, ammunition, and wagons and to contain foundries for casting cannon, mortars, and howitzers.

Besides producing equipment, Knox urged that artillery officers be trained at an academy where the "whole theory and practice of fortifications and gunnery should be taught." He recommended that such an academy be modeled along the same lines as the military school at Woolwich, England. Unless immediate steps were taken to make the military service sufficiently attractive, the armed forces would suffer from lack of leaders. Not only academies but every form of encouragement should be offered to attract qualified men. "As the army now stands," he stated, "it is only a receptacle for ragamuffins." Despite the costs involved, Congress should set up academies or else the war would be lost, Knox concluded. Thus he helped to give birth to the idea of the United States Military Academy at West Point. Although the Academy did not come into being until 1802, its pedigree in part can be traced back to Knox's proposal.

Knox was busily engaged also in changing the army's concepts on the use of artillery. He attacked the old idea of employing only heavy artillery and of placing emphasis on cannon primarily for siege operations. His trek from Ticonderoga had convinced him that artillery could be made to keep pace with marching regiments. He placed great stress on building and improving gun carriages to provide greater mobility for the cannon with Washington's army. In the next two major battles in which Knox was involved—the Battles of Trenton and Princeton—his idea paid off handsomely.

On a stormy Christmas night in 1776, Washington decided to cross the Delaware River to deliver a surprise attack upon the isolated Hessian garrison at Trenton. From the very start of the campaign, it was assumed that cannon were to play an important role in the assault. The most critical part of the entire operation came when Knox began to ferry his heavy fieldpieces across the ice-choked river with the help of Colonel John Glover's regiment of rugged Marblehead fishermen.

Knox seemed to be everywhere. Pacing nervously along the river's edge, he supervised the entire ferrying operation. His ringing bass voice was put to use as a kind of modern walkie-talkie as he shouted instructions to Glover's boat crews in their trips to and fro. For a time it appeared that the floating masses of ice might obstruct their passage, but as Knox observed later, ". . . perseverance accomplished what at first seemed impossible."

About 2,400 men were ferried across the river along with Knox's 18 pieces of field artillery. Such a heavy proportion of guns to men was almost unheard of in eighteenth-century warfare. Usually two or three cannon were employed per 1,000 foot soldiers. Washington's task force had three times the normal number. There were two sound reasons for this preponderance of fieldpieces. First, artillery was considered the army's wet-weather weapon because muskets in that day could be fired only when completely dry. Realizing December weather might bring storms that would render his men's muskets unusable, Washington was relying heavily on his artillery. Secondly, bringing along an abnormally large number of guns was as much a psychological as a military move. Knox's gunners were known to have high morale and could be depended upon to stand and fight. They would make their presence known with their booming cannon and thereby help to stiffen the resolve of the infantry.[6]

Once across the Delaware, the troops marched throughout the night in good order toward the small village of Trenton. As wet snow started to fall, Knox's guns took on an increased importance. A violent sleet storm developed and began blowing upon the backs of the trudging Continentals. But snow flew into the faces of the Hessian sentries and they failed to see the American soldiers emerging out of the early morning air until it was too late. During the fighting that followed, the shoulder weapons of both sides were largely useless because of wet firing pans. It was the artillery that bore the brunt of the battle.

Knox was able to move some of his batteries into position at the head of the two main streets—King and Queen streets— which almost ran together at the head of the village. By controlling this crucial location, his gunners were able to dominate the fighting. As enemy soldiers came stumbling sleepily out of their houses into the street, Knox's cannon cut them down. The Hes-

sian cannon were only able to fire a few rounds before they were
knocked out of action.

At the other end of the village, the story was much the same.
The only escape route out of the village lay over the Assunpink
Bridge and American artillery soon commanded the strategic
spot. One artillery sergeant drew a graphic picture of what happened:

> We had our cannon placed before a bridge. . . . The enemy came on
> in solid columns . . . then by given signal, we all fired together. . . .
> The enemy retreated. . . . Our whole artillery was again discharged
> at them—they retreated again and formed. . . . We loaded with
> canister shot, and let them come nearer. We fired altogether again
> and such destruction it made, you cannot conceive—the bridge
> looked red as blood, with their killed and wounded and their red
> coats. The enemy beat a retreat. . . .[7]

Within an hour the battle was over and a brilliant victory
won. Knox bragged of his exploits to Lucy, but his pride was justified. His cannon had played a crucial role in the American
success. He was unaware at the time he had been promoted to
brigadier general of the artillery on December 27, 1776. The
Continental Congress had rewarded him even before they
learned of the remarkable contributions he and his gunners had
made at Trenton.

After both armies had maneuvered for about a week, the British general, Cornwallis, advanced upon Trenton where Washington had drawn up his army. Knox's gunners saved the army from
what might have been a disastrous defeat in this so-called "Second Battle of Trenton" on January 2, 1777. It took the entire
force of Continental artillery to throw back the British attack
across the Assunpink Creek after the enemy had taken most of
Trenton. Knox's massed artillery fire probably was the heaviest
ever delivered on any American battlefield up to that time.[8]

Knox's artillerymen barely had time to catch their breath before they plunged into the Battle of Princeton. On January 3,
the night after the second Trenton battle, Washington slipped

quietly around Cornwallis' army and engaged some British reinforcements on their way to Cornwallis. For a fleeting moment,
the fate of American independence hung in the balance as the
patriot vanguard was routed and the Continental army was on
the verge of defeat. Then Knox's gunners came to the rescue by
holding back the British attack, thereby giving Washington's
forces a chance to rally. The tide of battle turned and the Americans went on to win overwhelmingly.

Washington withdrew his tired troops from the field and soon
took up quarters at Morristown, New Jersey, for the remainder
of the winter. The cessation of hostilities during the winter
months gave the American commander a chance to bolster his
military strength, and he sent Knox back to Massachusetts to
oversee the casting of cannon and production of gunpowder.
Knox was overjoyed at the assignment because it gave him an
opportunity to see his beloved Lucy. The sturdy horse he rode
to Boston was not spared. Once back in his home state, Knox
scurried about trying to round up supplies. He wrote Washington that in his judgment Springfield, Massachusetts, was the
best place in all the four New England states for a cannon fac-
tory. Washington thereupon issued the necessary orders and the
Springfield arsenal of the United States Army remains there to
this day.

Upon his return to the army at Morristown, Knox was involved in an event that rocked the army's high command. One
of the problems Washington had to face was that of finding
places in the Continental army for foreign officers who secured
military commissions from American diplomats stationed in Europe. Silas Deane, who was representing this country in France,
for example, sent over one Philippe du Coudray who held a rank
somewhat higher than that of an American brigadier general.
Du Coudray, an arrogant troublemaker, was soon styling himself
as the new "commander-in-chief of the Continental Artillery"
and hinted he had a contract with Deane making him chief of
the artillery arm. Washington was alarmed and quickly wrote
to Congress in Knox's defense. He praised Knox as a valuable

officer with sound judgment, clear conception, and one who was widely read in military matters. If he were superseded, said Washington, the artillery would be "convulsed and unhinged," for it was Knox who had placed this part of the army on firm footing. The letter was one of the most glowing Washington ever wrote on behalf of one of his generals.

But such high praise was not enough. Du Coudray showed his commission from Deane which revealed that he was to become general of the artillery and ordnance with the rank of major general, and Congress took the matter under advisement. Knox promptly wrote to Congress asking that he be retired if Du Coudray were placed in command. Because Du Coudray's commission would affect their seniority, Generals Greene and Sullivan wrote similar letters to Congress. Members of Congress resented these blunt letters which disregarded the normal channels of communication, but after some delay they agreed to let Knox remain on as head of the artillery. Du Coudray was given another command and shortly thereafter lost his life in an accident.

Knox's next major campaign against the British took place in the fall of 1777, when General Howe sought to take the American capital, Philadelphia. By September 11, the two armies which had been marching toward one another made contact and the Battle of Brandywine was on. While Lord Cornwallis led a wide flanking movement to strike the main blow on the American right, the Germans under General von Knyphausen attacked the center at Chad's Ford. Although the patriots suffered a defeat, Knox's artillerymen gave an unusually good account of themselves. Washington reported to Congress that his artillery delivered its fire with better aim than did the British batteries. He had personally gone among Knox's guns while the battle was in progress and was pleased with what he observed. At times during the fighting the British overran American artillery positions, but most of the gunners stayed by their cannon until shot down or forcibly removed from their stations. When the British reported they had captured "five French brass guns, three Hessian and three American pieces," it gave some indication of the motley collection of cannon Knox had to depend upon during the early years of the war.

"My dear girl will be happy to hear of her Harry's safety," wrote Knox to his wife, "for, my Lucy, Heaven who is our guide has protected him in the day of battle." He described the battle as "the most severe action that has been fought this war," and boasted, "My corps did me great honor." Nor was Knox alone in his pride. One newspaper noted that "The regiment of artillery, with their general, behaved with their usual coolness and intrepidity. Some of them could scarce be prevailed on to quit their guns, even when surrounded by the enemy and forsaken by our infantry." [9]

For a young man only twenty-seven years of age, Knox had demonstrated remarkable powers of military organization and administration. By choosing his officers carefully, he had built up an efficient arm that was second to none in Washington's army. His gunners possessed an *esprit de corps* that was truly unusual. Few American generals had been able to accomplish so much with so little in such a brief space of time. [10]

After Howe captured Philadelphia, Washington brought on another engagement by attacking the British main camp at Germantown on October 4. During this battle there occurred an episode that was to be one of the low points in Knox's army career. In the initial stages of the fighting, the Americans had the British on the run and victory seemed within their grasp. But Colonel Thomas Musgrave with some British infantry barricaded themselves inside a large stone structure known as the Chew House which lay directly in the path of the advancing Americans and resisted all attempts to root them out. From the second story of the house, Musgrave's men poured a hail of fire upon the vanguard of patriot troops and finally forced them to take cover. The American attack rolled to a halt and Washington considered the situation so serious that he held a staff conference on the battlefield. Some generals were all for leaving a regiment behind to immobilize the garrison inside the house and for pushing on. Knox thought differently. In his study of mili-

tary classics in his Boston bookstore he had read that while penetrating an enemy's country, you must never leave an occupied
castle to your rear. Washington, always respectful of Knox's
military knowledge, agreed with him. An officer carrying a
white flag was sent out to demand surrender, but Musgrave's men
fired and killed him.

Knox then threw his artillery in a circle around the building.
His cannon pounded away, blowing in the front door, smashing
windows, and piercing the roof. But the house was built with
thick stone walls which resisted the battering by cannon balls.
Here was a situation which military books failed to cover. Knox's
guns opened up again, but they failed once more. After repeated
barrages, the Chew House stood rugged and unyielding. This
delay, among other factors, turned victory into defeat. In his
report to Congress, however, Washington blamed the early
morning fog that confused his troops for the defeat more than
the Chew House incident.[11]

With the coming of cold weather, campaigning ceased and
Washington's army headed for its winter quarters at Valley
Forge. As soon as he had established the artillery park in camp,
Knox set out for Boston once again to round up supplies and
men. But he found prices in and around his native city so high
that he hesitated to place orders for supplies. Moreover, many
civilians were reluctant to work for the government. Knox informed Washington that wages were so high in New England
that the artificers at the Springfield arsenal whose contracts were
expiring spurned the thirty dollars a month plus clothing and
rations he offered them. "As the necessity is so great," he wrote,
"I shall be obliged to offer them, besides the above pay and clothing, one-half ration and a jill or half pint of rum per day." [12]
Knox found that recruiting also was difficult despite the bounties
being offered.

Upon his return to Valley Forge, Knox decided that Lucy
should come to stay with him at camp. Martha Washington, Mrs.
Greene, and Lady Stirling were already there and with Lucy's
arrival the drab routine of army life would be brightened a bit.

Lucy quickly became a social leader and her lively if sometimes meddlesome disposition and boundless energy almost matched that of her husband. Both were jovial people and Nathanael Greene commented that the Knoxes were "a perfect married couple."

But there was always business amidst the social pleasures. Washington was soon asking his generals whether the patriots should attack the British in Philadelphia. Knox was ready with his answer. Once again he turned to military books for his solution to the problem. Quoting from *Mes Rêveries,* written by Maurice Saxe, marshal of France in the early eighteenth century, Knox advised against an attack. The English historian, George Trevelyan, commenting on the soundness of Knox's views a century later wrote: "Henry Knox, the best artilleryman and almost best tactician in the Confederacy, pronounced such an attack on Philadelphia impossible." [13]

When the British gave signs that they were evacuating Philadelphia in mid-June, Washington again called a council of war to decide what to do. Some generals favored bringing on an engagement. Knox believed "it would be the most criminal madness to hazard a general action at this time." Why fight for the city, Knox asked, when it soon would be abandoned and turned over to the Americans anyway? How apt this question was may be judged by the fact that on the very day Knox asked it—June 18, 1778—the British left Philadelphia. Once the British army was on the move toward New York, Washington started after them in eager pursuit. Upon overtaking the enemy near Monmouth Court House early on June 28, Washington attacked. The training Knox had given his artillerymen during the long months at Valley Forge began paying dividends. His gunners were so mobile with their cannon that they were able to shift their artillery support to different units as needed in quick order. On the battlefield Knox's cannon were directly under the command of his brigade adjutant, Chevalier de Plessis.

Knox himself dashed about the battlefield, reconnoitering the enemy here and directing the movement of guns there. The artillery was on both flanks of the main action and performed magnificently. Henry Dearborn wrote later that "the briskest cannonade occured on both sides . . . the finest music I ever heard." Knox's leadership was so conspicuous that he was singled out for special mention. "In the hard-fought contest of Monmouth," wrote one army surgeon, "no officer was more distinguished than General Knox. In the front of the battle, he was seen animating the soldiers and directing the thunder of their cannon. His skill and bravery were so conspicuous that he received the particular approbation of the commander-in-chief in the general orders issued on the day succeeding the battle."

Monmouth was to be the last major battle of the war in the North. During the months that followed, Knox spent most of his time training his troops. In the winter of 1779, while at Pluckemin, New Jersey, he established what might be termed a forerunner of the United States Military Academy. Knox, in fact, called it "the academy" and used the camp to instruct military personnel. The physical arrangement was appropriate, the big guns being arranged in a neat row, huts for the personnel in an opposite line, while in the center was located a large building, wider and taller than the others. From an elevated platform in the main room in this building, Knox gave military lessons on gunnery, tactics, and related subjects. His corps was in better shape than ever before; but how much better it had become could be judged by the decisive role his artillery played at the Yorktown campaign in the fall of 1781.

Yorktown turned out to be the American artillery's sternest test because the campaign developed into a full-scale siege operation. Lord Cornwallis was bottled up on the Yorktown peninsula between the Franco–American forces on land and De Grasse's fleet on the water. Siege guns were placed into position to fire into the British camp and Knox issued precise orders on the procedures to be followed. One field officer was to be appointed each day to command in the trenches for each 24-hour period. He was to see that the guns were well-directed and to report the number of shots fired and the apparent effect on the enemy's works. Ricochet firing of shot and ball was to be employed. By this method, cannon balls bounced along the ground taking off the arms and legs of enemy soldiers. Only battalion officers were to level pieces. Strict silence was to be maintained at all times and sentries in sandbag observation posts were to shout a warning of any artillery fire from the British lines.

With his preparations completed by the afternoon of October 9, Knox opened up on Cornwallis' position. The first shots were said to have crashed into the house where British staff officers were gathered for mess, killing Commissary General Perkins and wounding three of his companions. The combined artillery fire from French and American cannon was devastating. Houses came tumbling down, cluttering the streets of Yorktown with debris. The ricochet firing that Knox had ordered sent cannon balls bounding along the ground filling the British camp with mangled soldiers. As one enemy soldier reported:

> One could not avoid the horribly many cannon balls either inside or outside the city. . . . Many men were badly injured and mortally wounded by the fragments of bombs which exploded partly in the air and partly on the ground, their arms and legs severed or themselves struck dead. . . . One saw men lying nearly everywhere who were mortally wounded.[14]

With his artillery so destructive at distances of 800 to 1,200 yards, Washington hastened to open a second siege line in order to achieve even better results at closer range. Work on the new line began on the night of October 11, and continued for three days as Knox hauled his guns forward. The second siege line was completed and despite a British night attack to spike some of the guns, the cannon were soon delivering a withering fire. One American officer observed:

> It is astonishing with what accuracy an experienced gunner will make his calculations, that a shell fall within a few feet of a given point, and burst at the precise time, though at a great distance . . . The whole peninsula trembles under the incessant thunder of our infernal machines.[15]

The American fire throughout the campaign was, indeed, very accurate. Lord Cornwallis himself was almost hit by a cannon ball and at one point had to seek refuge under a cliff. British ships in the harbor were pinpointed, struck, and started burning. The emotional and expressive Lafayette was watching the fire of the American guns one day and turned to Major Samuel Shaw, aide to Knox, to say, "You fire better than the French." Shaw secretly agreed but diplomatically made a polite remonstrance to the Frenchman. "Upon my honor, I speak the truth!" cried Lafayette. "And the progress of your artillery is regarded by everyone as one of the wonders of the Revolution." [16]

The enemy's works were tumbling into ruins. Not a gun could be fired in reply, for the British artillerymen could not approach their cannon because of the murderous fire from the second siege line. At ten o'clock on the morning of October 17, the fighting came to an end. Cornwallis decided to surrender. Knox wrote exultantly to Lucy two days later:

A glorious moment for America! This day Lord Cornwallis and his army march out and pile their arms in the face of our victorious army. They will have the same honors as the garrison at Charleston, that is, they will not be allowed to unfurl their colors *or play Yankee Doodle.*[17]

Both friend and foe alike praised Knox's artillery at Yorktown. As one observer noted, "The English marveled no less at the extraordinary progress of the American artillery and at the capacity and instructions of the officers." [18] The crowning tribute to Knox was Washington's comment in his report to Congress that "His genius supplied the deficit of means." [19] The commander-in-chief recommended Knox for a promotion to major general in November and he shortly became the youngest American general to hold that rank in the Continental army. One of Washington's last official acts in the army was to designate Knox to succeed him as commander.

When it came time for Washington to take leave of his officers, he met with them at the picturesque Fraunces Tavern near the Battery on the southern tip of Manhattan Island. The usually composed and reserved commander-in-chief entered the room with deep emotion showing in his face. "I cannot come to each of you," he said brokenly. "But I shall feel obliged if each of you shall come and take me by the hand."

Henry Knox being nearest to him was the first to come forward, and fittingly so. He was the one senior officer who in eight years of faithful service had never given Washington a moment's worry and had remained completely devoted. When the tender-hearted Knox, his own eyes brimming with tears, took Washington's hand, the commander-in-chief was so overcome he threw his arms around him and wept.

Knox went on to serve as Secretary of War under the Confederation government. In this capacity he set forth a memorable plan for a national militia which set a precedent for our peacetime military training for over a century and a half. Some of his ideas are still expressed in our National Selective Service manuals to this day. Immediately after the war, Knox also helped to form the fraternal organization of Continental army officers called the Society of the Cincinnati. Named after the famous farmer-general Cincinnatus, who left his plow in Roman times to lead his countrymen to military victory, the Society soon became a controversial one in American affairs. Although ostensibly formed to perpetuate wartime friendships, the organization briefly played a political role that many considered dangerously antidemocratic.

Knox, a strong Federalist, personally took part in many of the major political events of the postwar period. As Secretary of War, he was instrumental in helping to suppress Shays' Rebellion in Massachusetts in 1786-87. Disappointed in the weaknesses of the Confederation government, Knox submitted a "rude sketch" for a stronger central government to Washington even before the latter attended the Constitutional Convention in Philadelphia in 1787. While the convention was in session, Knox's friend, Rufus King, kept him posted on the proceedings. Once the Federal Constitution was written, Knox became one of its staunchest supporters and helped to get the document ratified in Massachusetts.

When Washington was elected President he named Knox Secretary of War, and the two men collaborated as well on governmental affairs as they had on military matters. Knox proved quite competent at his post. He negotiated a series of treaties with southern Indian tribes, urged the establishment of a strong navy, and sought to build a chain of coastal fortifications for the country's defense. After six years in the cabinet, he retired to private life in 1794.

His remaining years were spent near Thomaston, Maine, where he settled on a huge estate inherited by his wife. Here he lived in an imposing mansion called "Montpelier," living in baronial splendor, and carrying on business affairs in land speculation, ship-building, lumbering, and brick-making. From time to time he sat on the Massachusetts General Court and served on several important state commissions. When war with France threatened in 1798, he was appointed a major general by President John Adams. He then had a falling out with General Washington, who had been called out of retirement, over the question of rank. Fortunately, the two old friends patched up their differences before Washington died in 1799. Knox himself died unexpectedly seven years later at the age of fifty-six as the result of swallowing a chicken bone.

Of all Washington's generals, Knox was, without doubt, the most faithful. Only a youth in his mid-twenties when he first reported for military duty, Knox quickly became one of Washington's most loyal friends and trusted advisers. He was probably closer personally to Washington as commander-in-chief and President than any other man. One of the qualities that appealed most strongly to Washington was Knox's great optimism. Like the commander-in-chief, his courage never flagged even during the darkest days of the Revolution. By his able administration of the artillery he created a formidable branch of service in the Continental army and contributed greatly to the winning of America's independence.

FOOTNOTES

1. North Callahan, *Henry Knox: General Washington's General* (New York, 1958), p. 37.
2. Knox to William Knox, July 11, 1776, Knox Papers, Massachusetts Historical Society; hereinafter, Mass. Hist. Soc.
3. Extract of anonymous "Letter from Harlem," September 16, 1776, *American Archives*, Peter Force, ed., 4th series, II, 352.
4. Callahan, *op. cit.*, p. 70.
5. Knox to William Knox, September 23, 1776, Knox Papers, Mass. Hist. Soc.
6. Jac Weller, "Guns of Destiny: Field Artillery in the Trenton–Princeton Campaign 25 December 1776 to 3 January 1777," *Military Affairs*, XX (Spring, 1956), 7–8.
7. Callahan, *op. cit.*, p. 88.
8. Weller, *op. cit.*, p. 2.
9. *Independent Chronicle*, October 2, 1777.
10. Weller, *op. cit.*, p. 12.
11. Callahan, *op. cit.*, p. 122.
12. *Ibid.*, p. 137.
13. George O. Trevelyan, *American Revolution* (London, 1909–14), IV, 305.
14. Callahan, *op. cit.*, p. 185.
15. *Ibid.*, p. 187.
16. Shaw to Knox, April 15, 1792, Knox Papers, Mass. Hist. Soc.
17. Callahan, *op. cit.*, p. 189.
18. Marquis de Chastellux, *Travels in North America in the Years 1780, 1781 and 1782* (London, 1787), I, 150.
19. Washington to President of Congress, October 31, 1781, in John C. Fitzpatrick, ed., *The Writings of George Washington* (Washington, D.C., 1931–44), XXIII, 308.

BIBLIOGRAPHY

Allis, Frederick S., Jr., ed., *William Bingham's Maine Lands 1790–1820. Publications of the Colonial Society of Massachusetts, Collections,* XXXVI–XXXVII. Boston, 1954. Of special interest for Knox's speculations in Maine lands.

Becker, John, *The Sexagenary*. Albany, 1833. Contains considerable information regarding Knox's trek from Ticonderoga.

Billias, George A., *General John Glover and His Marblehead Mariners.*

New York, 1960. Shows the importance of Knox's role at the Battle
of Trenton.

Brooks, Noah, *Henry Knox: A Soldier of the Revolution*. New York,
1900. An older work on Knox's life, but still valuable for some of
the letters quoted therein.

Callahan, North, *Henry Knox: General Washington's General*. New
York, 1958. The most recent biography of Knox's career.

Drake, Francis S., *Life and Correspondence of Henry Knox*. Boston,
1873. Valuable for the Knox letters it contains.

Ford, Worthington C., "Henry Knox—Bookseller." *Massachusetts Historical Society Proceedings*, VI (Boston, 1927–28), 227–303. An
interesting account of Knox's prewar occupation.

Starrett, Lewis F., *General Henry Knox; His Family, His Manor, His
Manor House, and His Guests*. Rockland, Maine, 1902.

Weller, Jac, "Guns of Destiny: Field Artillery in the Trenton–Princeton Campaign 25 December 1776 to 3 January 1777." *Military Affairs*, XX (Spring, 1956), 1–15 Contains a brief but accurate
survey of the field artillery used by both armies in this and other campaigns.

Whitcomb, Joseph W., *Memoir of General Henry Knox of Thomaston,
Maine*. Bangor, 1890. Contains the eulogy delivered at Knox's funeral
and a copy of his will.

Anthony Wayne:

MILITARY ROMANTICIST

————◆————

HUGH F. RANKIN

Tulane University

ANTHONY WAYNE was an anachronism in the eighteenth century. A knight errant riding forth to do great and noble deeds, he was five hundred years too late to don shining armor. His reckless courage, dash, and daring in the Revolutionary War were reminiscent of a romanticism found back in the days of chivalry.

In the sturdy stone house built by his grandfather at Waynesborough, Pennsylvania, Anthony was born January 1, 1745, the son of the brusque Isaac and the gentle Elizabeth Iddings Wayne. Sent to his uncle Gilbert Wayne's school, young Anthony's interest lagged except when the reading concerned military matters. The fancies of his nephew led the harassed uncle to complain to Anthony's father:

> What he may be best qualified for I know not. He may perhaps make a soldier. He has already distracted the brains of two-thirds of the boys under my charge by rehearsals of battles, sieges, etc. During noon, in place of the usual games of amusement, he has the boys employed in throwing up redoubts, skirmishing, etc.[1]

Eventually Isaac sent his volatile son off to the Academy at Philadelphia, where the youth became something of a dandy and a frequenter of taverns. Still, Anthony absorbed enough knowledge of mathematics to establish himself as a moderately successful surveyor at East Town in Chester County, Pennsylvania. In the spring of 1765, when he was twenty, he began courting a slim blonde girl of sixteen, Mary "Polly" Penrose, whose parents were disturbed by the uneasy reputation of her suitor. Anthony and Mary were persuaded to postpone marriage until his future was more certain.

It was during this same year that Wayne was employed by a Philadelphia syndicate (which included Benjamin Franklin) to survey the 200,000 acres they hoped to acquire in Nova Scotia. Working swiftly through the autumn, the lovesick youth returned to Pennsylvania in late December to press his suit with Mary. A promising future softened family resistance, and on March 25, 1766, Anthony carried her off as his bride to Waynesborough.

Later that spring he went back to Nova Scotia, but rising tensions between the mother country and her colonies caused the syndicate to lose interest in land speculation. Anthony returned to Waynesborough; he cultivated his farm and built a thriving tannery upon it. As he prospered, his family grew larger. In 1768, there was a daughter, Margaretta, and four years later, a son, Isaac.

By 1774, Anthony had fallen heir to his father's fortune. He was now quite successful—enough so that he had already taken on the swagger which he affected the rest of his life. Although only of medium height, he appeared taller because of his commanding presence. His handsome features were so clear-cut they seemed almost chiseled from stone and his dark hair, aquiline nose, and penetrating brown eyes added to his good looks. His personality bordered on the quixotic, for he was vain, impulsive, and given to the use of hyperbole. But he had great qualities of leadership and was most popular in the community where he lived.

With his educational background, natural talents, and attractive personal characteristics, Wayne soon emerged as a leader of the patriot cause. He was elected chairman of the Chester County Committee of Safety in 1774 and headed the local committee chosen to carry out the provisions of the boycott on British goods proposed by the First Continental Congress. In January, 1775, he represented his community in Pennsylvania's Provincial Congress, arguing the virtues of greater efforts for home manufactures. Yet he never allowed politics to overshadow his periodic exercises with the militia.

Although the ranks of the local regiments filled very quickly after the outbreak of war, Wayne was not commissioned colonel of the Fourth Battalion of the Pennsylvania line until January 3, 1776. When his command was ordered to join Washington around New York, he complained that at least one-half were armed with little more than "damned tomahawks." His Pennsylvanians had encamped on Long Island only a short time before orders came to relieve the sagging Canadian expedition. The American efforts to take Quebec had suffered a severe setback in December, 1775. Brigadier General Richard Montgomery had fallen victim to British bullets and Benedict Arnold had retreated to Montreal with the small force that had managed to escape capture.

Under Washington's mandate that the Quebec "misfortune must be repaired," [2] the first objective became the reportedly lightly-held post of Trois Rivières, halfway down the St. Lawrence between Montreal and Quebec. Wayne was ordered to serve under General William Maxwell along with Arthur St. Clair and William Irvine. Disembarking from their bateaux some three miles above the town at three in the morning of June 8, 1776, the Americans were discovered and fired upon by enemy vessels in the river. Led astray by their guide, the troops were soon lost and floundering belly-deep in the midst of "the most Horrid swamp that ever man set foot in."

It was nearly eight in the morning when Wayne and his 200 men broke into the clearing before the town, only to discover that redcoated regulars were driving down upon them. Wayne's muddy troops sent the enemy reeling back with a well-directed volley. British light artillery was brought up and this, added to the fire from boats on the river, swept the field clean of invaders.

A second British force was set ashore upstream to cut off the retreating Americans. The swamp offered the only route of escape. Other fugitives staggered in, their faces puffed from the "stings of Musketoes of a monstrous size and inumerable numbers." Rallying as many of his disorganized soldiers as possible, Wayne, limping from a "Slight touch in my Right leg," led them at last to safety across the New York border. There was more than a trace of egotism in Wayne's letter to Franklin, "I believe it will be Universally allowed that Col. [William] Allen & myself have saved the Army in Canada."

Even in the retreat down Lake Champlain, the dandy in Wayne showed itself when he ordered that a barber be appointed for every company and prescribed punishments for those soldiers who appeared shaggy or dirty. As he explained to General Washington:

> I have an insuperable bias in favour of an elegant uniform and a soldierly appearance, so much so that I would rather risk my life and reputation at the head of the same men in an attack, clothed and appointed as I could wish, merely with bayonets and a single charge of ammunition, than to take them as they appear in common with sixty rounds of cartridges. It may be a false idea, but I cannot help cherishing it.

Wayne was made commandant at Ticonderoga, the key fortress on the lakes in northern New York, in the fall of 1776 and readied his troops for what he grandly called "Death or Glory." But he had earlier lamented to his Polly that "Fortune has heretofore been a fickle Goddess to us—and like some other females changed for the first new face she saw." Sectionalism was rampant in the ranks. The Pennsylvanians had little use for the "damn'd Yankees," as they termed the New Englanders, and there was one mild riot involving some gunfire when the "leveling principle" of the northern troops became too much for the more class-conscious Pennsylvanians.

The discipline and uniformity so ardently desired by their colonel seemed remote for the Pennsylvanians. One teamster noted: "The vices of insubordination, gambling & rioting marked their battalion, and we ourselves had great trouble with them." Conditions inside Ticonderoga were such that it was hard to boost morale. Wayne dubbed the fortress a "Golgotha" and felt that if God had any hand in its being, "it was surely done in the dark; it is one confused jumble of stones, without order, beauty or profit." During the winter, the men within its walls shivered with cold. There was little food, and clothing fell into rags. The British were expected to come pouring down the lake with warmer weather. Discontent became vocal and Wayne's men began calling him a "tyrant." One company of infantrymen maintained their enlistments had expired and were driven back as the angry colonel thrust a pistol into the chest of the sergeant leading the malcontents; when there were increasing whispers of mutiny, the ringleader was publicly slapped across the cheek and sent to Albany for court-martial.[3]

On February 21, 1777, Wayne was promoted to brigadier general, and two months later received instructions to rejoin Washington's army at Morristown. But sad news from home took some of the edge off the joy of impending combat. His farm was being badly managed in Wayne's absence; no provisions had been made to educate his children while he was away; and politics in Pennsylvania were in a "sickly state." War, however, had become too fascinating a game to abandon, and his domestic concerns were drowned in a torrent of flowery words as he assured his harried Polly that he was indispensable to the army and elaborated upon the "pristine Lustre" of the "Blessings of Liberty."

When General Howe, in June, 1777, began the evacuation of British posts in New Jersey, Nathanael Greene's division was ordered to harass them on their march. After numerous delays and frustrations, only the troops led by Wayne and Daniel Morgan managed to reach the area, on June 22, in time to be of any service. They advanced on the British redoubts on the left bank of the Raritan and, in general, according to Washington, "behaved in a manner that does them great honor."[4] Writing to a

friend, Wayne proudly exulted: "This Howe who was to March
through America at the head of 5000 men had his coat much
Dirtied, his Horses taken off, and himself badly Bruis'd for having the presumption at the head of 700 British Troops to face
500 Penns'as." Wayne was inclined to make too much of his
small success. When Polly wrote pleading letters asking that he
come home to handle pressing problems, he justified his reluctance to request leave with the assertion that he was doing the
work of three general officers and was "peremptorily forbid by
His Excellency to leave the Army." He had, indeed, entered upon
a new phase of his career, for he began serving as a division commander with Washington's main army.

When finally it became evident that Howe's objective was
Philadelphia, Washington decided to make his stand on the east
bank of the Brandywine. Wayne, enthusiastically citing Caesar
and Marshal Saxe, proposed that he lead a surprise attack against
the marching enemy and perhaps throw them into "Confusion,
Disorder or Retreat." The commander-in-chief, however, was
in no mood to gratify Wayne's whims and stationed the spirited
Pennsylvanian at Chad's Ford—the logical spot where the stream
might be crossed. For an officer of limited combat experience
Wayne did well, throwing a series of light, jabbing probes
against Knyphausen's Hessians to keep them off balance. His
defense of the ford was later termed "most conspicuous" by
Henry Lee. Only after a sizable segment of the army had been
outflanked by Cornwallis and a general retreat had been ordered,
did Wayne and Maxwell fall away from their positions under
the full fury of enemy artillery and musketry.[5] It is not unreasonable to suppose that Wayne's tenacious resistance at Chad's
Ford may have helped to save Washington's army from envelopment.

Wayne's new-found fame was followed by one of the more
shameful episodes in his career. As Washington withdrew from
the Brandywine, Wayne's detachment of 1,500 men and four
fieldpieces was sent to the neighborhood of Warren's Tavern near
Paoli, close to Wayne's own home and only three miles from the

left flank of the enemy. There, in the skirt of a thick wood, they lay awaiting a British move. When and if Howe marched, the Americans might fall upon his rearguard and baggage train. Wayne's position was not a well-kept secret, but he could see little reason for alarm and reported that the "enemy are very quiet, washing and cooking." In fact, he considered them ripe for a "fatal blow" and dispatches to Washington urged, "for God's sake push on as fast as possible." [6]

The British struck even as Wayne dreamed of victory. Major General Charles Grey, leading a detachment whose arms had their charges drawn or flints removed, slipped silently through the night of September 20–21, 1777. Some time after nine o'clock, a Mr. Jones, "an Old Gent'n" of the neighborhood, came into the American encampment with the information that the British had planned a surprise assault. Additional videttes and pickets were thrown out, but when nothing happened Wayne ordered Major Francis Nicholas "with some degree of anger to go to bed—for having made a mistake."

At about eleven o'clock that night, the British burst upon the camp from out of the shadows and caught the Pennsylvanians as they were crawling out of their blankets groggy with sleep. Wayne declared later that he had stationed his troops in some semblance of order, but neither the British narratives nor American casualties bear out this assertion. Major John André implied that the surprise was complete, while a fellow officer referred to the so-called "Paoli Massacre" as "a dreadful scene of havoc," marked by "shrieks, groans, shouting, imprecations, deprecations, the clashing of swords and bayonets." Not a shot was fired by the disciplined British regulars and they depended exclusively upon their bayonets. The American artillery was brought off with some difficulty, but eight supply wagons were lost to the enemy. Estimates of casualties were indefinite, ranging all the way from Howe's 370 to Elias Boudinot's 25 or 30. Historians have generally agreed that Wayne's losses were about 150, while those of the British seem to have been no more than 10. [7]

Thus did Anthony Wayne suffer a deflation of ego, personally more damaging than his military defeat. Although he was exonerated by a court of inquiry, the persistent accusations of Colonel Richard Humpton of the Eleventh Pennsylvania "that he had timely notice of the enemy's intention to attack" and had done nothing, led Wayne to demand a court-martial. He was acquitted "with the highest honor." [8] Physically worn out by this ordeal, Wayne began to entertain serious doubts as to whether he should continue in service. Yet wounded vanity demanded that he vindicate himself. As the two armies maneuvered, Wayne bombarded Washington with proposals that he be allowed to lead a flank attack upon the enemy.

He was soon to have his revenge. At the Battle of Germantown, on October 4, 1777, Wayne went charging into the British lines like a whirlwind. In the early morning hours, British officers were startled from their sleep by ringing cries of "Have at the bloodhounds, revenge Wayne's affair!" [9] Revenge must have been sweet. Wayne's men killed some British soldiers even after they had thrown down their arms and offered to surrender, but the Pennsylvanian only noted piously: "Our people Remembering the Action of the Night of the 20th of Sep'r . . . pushed on with their Bayonets—and took Ample Vengeance for that Nights Work. Our Officers Exerted themselves to save many of the poor wretches who were Crying for Mercy—but to little purpose; the Rage and fury of the Soldiers were not to be Restrained for some time—at least not until great numbers of the Enemy fell by our Bayonets."

From the patriot point of view, the Battle of Germantown was one long string of mistakes. Some of the blame must fall upon Washington, whose orders were so confusing that even the guides lost their way. The battle plan, classic in conception, was based on four pincer columns which, marching through the night, were to converge upon the British lines from different directions. At sunrise Wayne's troops, in Sullivan's division, drove the British before them with bayonets, but many units soon became separated in the dense morning fog. Wayne, hearing artillery and musketry to his rear, thought Sullivan was in trouble and turned back. A dim and distant line of men was faintly out-lined through the mist. Both sides fired. Both were Americans, although Wayne later claimed that the other group was dressed in red coats. The battle which had begun with such great promise quickly came to a disastrous end. Nathanael Greene furnished cover for the subsequent retreat, which was described as be-yond all "powers of description: sadness and consternation ex-pressed in every countenance."

The troops wandering through the fog and fired on by Wayne's men had been under the command of Adam Stephen. Stephen, who was to be accused of drinking heavily that day, argued that Wayne's troops had brought on the exchange of shots when they fired on a British group who were coming forward to surrender. Stephen, however, was later found guilty of "Unoffercerlike con-duct" and "drunkenness" and dismissed from the service.[10] Had Wayne been able to pursue his initial assault without interrup-tion, he might well have pierced the British center and won the battle out of hand.

The fog, insisted Wayne, had been responsible for the defeat that had flirted with victory—a victory which he declared "in all Human probability would have put an end to the American War." He scarcely mentioned Washington's willingness to listen to those officers who protested leaving "a castle in our rear" when a detachment of the enemy sought refuge within the sturdy stone walls of the Chew House. Nor would he admit that even after two years of war there was still such a woeful lack of ex-perience that officers found it necessary to quote from military textbooks when making tactical decisions.

One of the American positions that had withstood the enemy assault near Philadelphia was Fort Mifflin—a bastion located on Mud Island below the city, which denied the British passage far-ther up the river. Wayne, continually searching for military im-mortality, pleaded that he be allowed to lead a relief expedition to the fort. Instead, Washington called a council of war, a prac-tice Wayne felt "was the surest way to do nothing." When Fort

Mifflin fell in mid-November, Wayne still urged the commander-in-chief to take the field: "You will not be in a Worse Situation, nor your Arms in less Credit if you should meet with a Misfortune than if you were to Remain Inactive." If nothing else, he argued, constant action should be maintained against the enemy's outposts. In the end no action was taken, and it was said that Wayne was the one who suggested Valley Forge as winter quarters because of its proximity to the enemy.

Perhaps it was the pain of being ignored or the growing tradition of defeat surrounding Washington that finally led Wayne to nurture doubts as to the ability of the commander-in-chief. After Gates's victory at Saratoga, Wayne wrote that "whether I shall remain longer in the service than this Campaign depends on Circumstances—there are certain Generals—as *Lee—Gates—Mifflin* &c^a. who will point out by their Conduct the line which I shall follow. . . ." Washington, on the other hand, had bungled his opportunities at the Battles of Brandywine and Germantown, and Wayne complained "if our Worthy General will but follow his own good Judgment without listning too some Council. . . ." [11] Being headstrong and bold himself, Wayne wanted Washington to assert more vigorous leadership.

Wayne was disenchanted too with the vaunted riflemen by whose efforts so many had expected to win the war. He expounded to a friend on a theme that had been preying on his mind for over a year:

> I don't like rifles—I would almost as soon face an Enemy with a good Musket and Bayonet without ammunition—as with ammunition without a Bayonet for altho' there are not many Instances of bloody bayonets yet I am confident that one bayonet keeps off an Other—and for the Want of which the Chief of the Defeats we have met with ought in a great measure to be Attributed—the Enemy knowing the Defenseless State of our Riflemen rush on— they fly mix with or pass thro' the other Troops and Communicate fear that is ever incident to a retiring Corps—this Would not be the Case if the Riflemen had bayonets—but it would be still better if good muskets and bayonets were put into the hands of good

Marksmen and Rifles entirely laid aside—for my own part I never Wish to see one—at least Without a Bayonet.

With the days growing warmer, Wayne was sent into New Jersey to round up some cattle for feeding the army. It was a task he considered beneath his dignity as a soldier. But the scattered contacts and skirmishes he had with the enemy fired his ambition to a point where he again began bombarding Washington with suggestions for striking at the British.

By June, 1778, it became known that Sir Henry Clinton had replaced General William Howe as commander-in-chief of the British army, and the bustle in Philadelphia suggested an evacuation of the city. When Clinton's army and extensive baggage train stretched itself into a slow crawl across New Jersey, Washington promptly called a council of war—a council characterized by such caution on the part of his generals that Alexander Hamilton sarcastically noted it "would have done honor to the most honorable body of midwives, and to them only." [12] Wayne along with General John Cadwalader urged an immediate attack on the premise that it would be impossible to overcome the enemy once they reached New York. Even if Clinton did gain the advantage, they argued, he would be unable to pursue the American army because of his baggage train. An attack by Washington, however, would make it appear that the enemy was fleeing before him. [13] Charles Lee wavered as to whether he would accept the command of the vanguard in an attack upon the baggage train, an attack he was convinced would be futile, but he finally assumed command of the advance corps in what came to be called the Battle of Monmouth.

Even as they marched, Alexander Hamilton reported back that "General Wayne's detachment is almost starving and seems both unwilling and unable to march farther till they are supplied." [14] Yet Wayne bullied his troops forward and after contact was made, Washington, despite the reluctance of his council, decided to attack in force. On the morning of June 28, 1778, Lee appeared to be maneuvering his troops aimlessly in the

vicinity of the Monmouth Court House with "no plan of attack."
Wayne's troops bore the brunt of the fierce fighting that followed
until, in the confusion and amidst a flurry of contradictory orders, Lee ordered a retreat.

Washington appeared on the scene and after some hot words
with Lee took command of the situation. The commander-in-
chief rallied the retiring troops and instantly ordered a new line
formed on Wayne's men, who had taken up a position in an
orchard at the edge of a road between two hills. Three times the
British came rushing along the low ground hoping to drive
through Wayne. Each time they were driven back with heavy
casualties as Wayne held his fire until the last minute. When
the British formed for a fourth assault with a body of troops so
large as to outflank both ends of his position, Wayne withdrew
in good order inside the main lines of the American army. Wayne
was satisfied; he had met and bested the flower of the British
army. "Among them are Numbers of the Richest blood of England," he wrote. "Tell the Phil'a ladies," he added sarcastically,
"that the heavenly, sweet, pretty red Coats—the accomplished
Gent'm of the Guards and Grenadiers have humbled themselves
on the plains of Monmouth." At Monmouth, Wayne had found
at last the glory that had eluded him so long.

Charles Lee, smarting under a reprimand from Washington,
began a vicious tirade against the commander-in-chief. Because
of his disrespect toward Washington and formal charges of misconduct on the battlefield by Wayne and General Charles Scott,
Lee was court-martialed. Wayne and Scott became important
witnesses for the prosecution.

Lee, fighting for his military reputation, railed against false
intelligence and, in part, blamed his difficulties on "the temerity,
folly and contempt of orders of General Wain. . . ." Wayne, on
the other hand, testified that Lee was dilatory in both decisions
and actions upon the battlefield. In the opinion of some historians, politics was the prime factor in Lee's conviction; his
biographer concluded that "the court-martial sacrificed Lee be-

cause of partisan passions in the army and a belief that the public welfare should override all other considerations." [15]

Lee was his own greatest enemy; he wrote and talked too much. His tart remarks brought a challenge from Von Steuben and a duel with John Laurens, aide-de-camp to Washington. While Lee was recovering from the slight wound received in the Laurens duel, Wayne, in early January, 1779, demanded satisfaction for Lee's strictures upon his conduct at Monmouth and the "ungenerous tho' free Manner in which you Affect to treat my Opinion & military Character. . . ." [16] When Lee explained that he was only defending his own reputation and that no personal affront or animosity was intended, Wayne was satisfied and dropped the idea of a duel.

Wayne had likewise suffered a blow to his pride—a blow that may have made him sensitive enough to challenge Lee. The gradual decline in numbers had made it necessary to reorganize the Pennsylvania line. Some of his enemies gained the upper hand in his state and Wayne, a brigadier general, was replaced by Major General Arthur St. Clair. His bitterness was compounded by humiliation, being "superseded at this late hour by a man in whose conduct and candor I have no confidence hurts me not a little." Wayne's sense of personal injury became so great that he "therefore determined to return to domestic life, & leave the blustering field of Mars to the possession of Gentlemen of more worth."

He was not to sulk for long. When an elite corps of Continental light infantry was formed, made up of veterans who were picked from the regular regiments on the basis of youth, agility, and daring, Wayne intrigued for the command. Of special interest to him was the fact that these select troops were to be rigorously drilled in the use of the bayonet. Wayne wanted the command so badly, he threatened to resign unless awarded the post. Daniel Morgan was another contender for the command. The very day that Wayne's appointment was announced in June, 1779, Morgan submitted his resignation and went home, "deeply affected with this Injury done my reputation." [17]

Wayne's popularity among the Pennsylvania troops became

evident when large numbers expressed a desire to follow him into the light infantry. One and a half battalions of Pennsylvania troops were included in the 2,000 soldiers who were planned for this new command, "preferable to any in the army." It was with these elite troops that Wayne was to tread the paths to glory.

Wayne was eager to commit the new corps to combat as soon as possible. "I believe that sanguine God is rather thirsty for human gore," he wrote grandly. Stony Point, the British strongpoint below West Point on the Hudson was selected as his objective. Serving as the southern gate to the Hudson Highlands, this position was of great strategic and economic significance. To Wayne it was much more. Stony Point was to furnish him with final retribution for Paoli. He had learned much from that night of misery and was determined to repay the enemy in kind by relying upon the bayonet as his weapon of victory in storming the garrison. For two days prior to the assault, it is said, American patrols killed every dog along the route of approach, and all communications with Wayne's men were halted to preserve secrecy. After dark on the night of July 15, 1779, the march began. One account stated that a soldier who refused to believe that a post could be taken with empty weapons stepped from the ranks to load his piece and was immediately run through by his captain.[18]

A man of Anthony Wayne's temperament would have considered himself negligent of the demands of posterity had he not composed words for the ages. To his friend Sharp Delany he wrote as one who felt death's chill breath, expressing the fear that his wife would die of grief, and requesting that Delany educate his children. After berating "the parsimony and neglect of Congress," he added the flourish, "I am called to Sup, but where to breakfast, either within the enemy's lines in triumph or in the other World!"

Approaching silently in two columns, with a third unit under Henry Lee demonstrating in front of the post, Wayne's men began their assault about a half-hour past midnight. A bullet crease along his skull allowed Wayne to indulge his flair for the dramatic. Crying out that the wound was fatal, Wayne asked that he be carried inside the fortress walls to die. His soldiers gave a shout, charged up the slope of Stony Point bearing their commander on their shoulders, and swept over the crest of the ramparts.

In less than a half-hour, the entire fort had been overrun. It was a feat that Nathanael Greene said would "for ever immortalize Gen. Wayne, as it would do honor to the first general in Europe." The light infantry, despite the large number of Pennsylvanians within the ranks, displayed a quality of mercy that led one British naval officer to comment: ". . . they showed at this moment a generosity and clemency which during the course of the rebellion had no parallel." As one American officer explained, ". . . the usage of arms justifying, and the *lex talionis* demanding, a carnage, yet that humanity, that amiable weakness, which has ever distinguished Americans, prevailed." [19] Over 500 prisoners, 15 cannon, and a quantity of valuable military stores had been taken.

Although Stony Point was abandoned after the victory, the legend of Anthony Wayne is based on this triumph. His first dispatch to Washington, though brief, boasted, "This fort & Garrison with Coln. Johnson are our's. Our Officers & Men behaved like men who are determined to be free." The conquest, said Washington, "will have a good effect upon the minds of the people, give our troops greater confidence in themselves and depress the spirits of the enemy proportionately." [20] Even British accounts conceded that "considered in all its parts and difficulties, it would have done honor to the most veteran soldiers." And, unbeknownst to Washington, the time the British consumed in reoccupying and rebuilding Stony Point, forced Clinton to abandon plans for a new offensive. [21]

In the opinion of certain of his officers, the glory of the day had not been properly shared by Wayne. Replying to Lieutenant Colonel Isaac Sherman's "You have not arrived beyond the regions of censure," Wayne penned an angry "I put up with no

man's Insults." But the grousing soon disappeared, possibly because of the breakup of the light infantry.

Success has a way of healing old wounds, and Stony Point was
instrumental in mending the breach between Wayne and Charles
Lee. Insisting that he had "no intent in paying court to any individual," Lee lauded the conqueror of Stony Point as "a brave
officer, and an honest man," and referred to his recent success as
"not only the most brilliant, in my opinion, through the whole
course of this war, on either side, but that it is the most brilliant
I am acquainted with in history. . . ." The vaulting ambition of
Anthony Wayne would not allow him to overlook such "en-
comiums." His reply was a bouquet of similar strain, most appre-
ciative of Lee's sentiments "because they come from a Gentleman
of the first experience—whose military abilities stand high in this
age of the World." [22]

Although the light infantry had proved its worth, Washington
decided to break up the corps after Congress had detached one
of the most serviceable regiments for other duty. In December,
1779, with his former officers expressing "that confidence essentially necessary to ensure success in military operations," Wayne
retired to Waynesborough. There he battled boredom until May
18, 1780, when he received Washington's "I shall be happy to
see you in camp again, and hope you will, without hesitation,
resume your command in the Penn'a line."

Once back in the army, Wayne was put to work harassing
some of the outlying British posts along the lower Hudson and
in New Jersey. One objective Washington ordered him to attack
was the enemy position at Bull's Ferry at Bergen, four miles north
of Hoboken. This strong blockhouse, "Garrisoned by the Refugees & a wretched banditti of Robbers horse thieves &c" not only
sheltered woodcutters for the British army and protected the
cattle in the area, but served as a repository for the booty taken
by local Tory raiders. Wayne, leading the First and Second
Pennsylvania Regiments, attacked the blockhouse during the
night of July 21, 1780. For an hour, light artillery pounded the
log walls without effect. Then, with the enemy rushing forward

reinforcements, there was a charge through the abatis to the stockade wall. This rash act which Wayne attributed to the "enthusiastic bravery of all ranks of officers and men," resulted in 65 casualties.[23] The attack ended in a stalemate and all Wayne succeeded in doing was to burn a few boats and drive off some cattle before he withdrew.

The failure to repeat the conquest of Stony Point stimulated a bit of notoriety that Wayne did not relish. Major John André, Clinton's adjutant general who fancied himself a poet, composed a frothy rhyme called "The Cow Chace." The poem, ridiculing Wayne, ended with these oft-quoted lines:

> And now I've closed my epic strain,
> I tremble as I show it,
> Lest this same warrier-drover Wayne
> Should ever catch the poet.

The last canto, ironically, was published the same day that André was captured at Tarrytown and held as a spy for assisting Benedict Arnold. Although some biographers claimed that Wayne did not gain the prefix "Mad" until after the war or certainly no earlier than the summer of 1781, it appears that the nickname was already associated with him. One line in "The Cow Chace" referred to "mad Anthony's fierce eye."

There was considerable unrest and discontent in Wayne's command during the summer of 1780. A dispute arose over the command of a new corps of light infantry that was to be created from the ranks of the Pennsylvania line. Faced with a rash of resignations, Wayne resorted to his entire repertoire of rhetorical grandiloquence by appealing to the friendship, honor, and patriotism of his officers. His address ended on this stirring note: "For God's sake, be yourselves—and as a band of Brothers—rise superior to every Injury—whether real or imaginary—at least for this Campaign which probably will produce a Conviction to the World—that America owes her freedom to the temporary sacrifice you now make." Fortunately the plan to organize the new corps was abandoned and the problem resolved itself.

When Benedict Arnold attempted to deliver West Point to the enemy in September, 1780, Wayne's quick move to that post prevented a British occupation. Leaving his tents standing at Tappan on the Hudson at two in the morning, he raced his Pennsylvanians northward to Haverstraw—a distance of sixteen miles—in less than four hours. Washington thought the feat "fabulous" and received Wayne "like a God," exclaiming "All is safe, and I again am happy." Once West Point was secure, Wayne bitterly denounced the traitor Arnold, claiming "that honor & true Virtue were Strangers to his Soul . . . he never possessed either fortitude or personal bravery—he was naturally a Coward, and never went in the way of Danger but when Stimulated by Liquor even to Intoxication. . . ."

But Wayne was soon to discover that Benedict Arnold was not alone in his dissatisfaction with conditions in the Continental army. In December, 1780, there was a great deal of grumbling in the Pennsylvania line. Wayne's soldiers were unhappy for a variety of reasons—their clothing consisted of tattered rags, the food was poor, there was no rum, and no one had seen "a paper dollar in the way of pay for near *twelve months*." By mid-December, Wayne was warning Joseph Reed, president of the Pennsylvana Executive Council, that the British were aware of this restlessness and were circulating tracts among the troops urging them to desert. He was beginning, Wayne said, to fear the "Ides of Jan[uar]y." [24] There were complaints also that those who enlisted "for three years or during the war" were being held in service longer than three years—the term that the troops interpreted as the limit of their obligations. Tempers were brought to a boil when it was discovered that new recruits were being offered an enlistment bonus of twenty-five dollars, "hard money," while veteran troops remained unpaid.

New Year's Day, 1781, dawned bright and clear, but the fine day proved a false omen for the events that followed. With his troops encamped at Mount Kemble near Morristown, Wayne had established his headquarters east of the bivouac in the house of the staunch loyalist Peter Kemble. There he spent the day with

his field officers discussing the new "arrangement of the Line."
As a New Year's treat each soldier had been issued a half-pint of
spirits and those who had money purchased more at local taverns.
Officers in the camp found their pleasure in "an elegant regimental dinner and entertainment." About eight in the evening,
a few huzzas rose from the Eleventh Regiment area. Within an
hour all was quiet again and the outburst attributed to an over-
indulgence in strong drink. Around ten o'clock a general huz-
zaing began to roll from one side of the camp to the other.
Lieutenant Enos Reeves dashed onto the parade "and found
numbers in small groups whispering and busily running up and
down the line." A musket fired, and a skyrocket split the night.
It was mutiny!

Wayne galloped in with several officers. Colonel Richard Butler joined him in a futile haranguing of the troops. Three of the
more energetic officers already had been wounded, one fatally.
The mutineers insisted they had been wronged in their pay and
other matters and demanded a hearing with their state officials.
Wayne argued that he would endeavor to remedy their griev-
ances. The reply was that their dispute was not with him and
could be settled only by the Congress. When Wayne persisted in
standing in their path, a volley whistled over his head. In a melo-
dramatic gesture, Wayne threw open his tunic and shouted: "If
you mean to kill me, shoot me at once—here's my breast." The
mutineers replied that they had no intention to harm any officer,
"two or three individuals excepted."

Part of the Fourth Regiment was paraded and ordered to
charge the malcontents. They refused. Around two in the morning, formed in platoons and with drums throbbing and fifes
squealing, the Pennsylvania line marched out of camp. Wayne
made his stand at the Chatham–Princeton crossroads, some say
with pistols drawn, determined to dissuade them should they turn
left in a mass desertion to the British. They answered him with
assurances that their march was to the Congress at Philadelphia,
and should the enemy sally forth to seek advantage from their
defection they would turn back to fight. "If that is your senti-

ments," said Wayne, "I'll not leave you, and if you won't allow
me to march in your front, I'll follow in your rear." It was later
reported that he not only offered them advice, but also forwarded
provisions in order to prevent any depredations upon private
property.[25]

True to their word, the mutineers not only made no attempt
to reach the enemy but turned over two British emissaries to be
hanged as spies. Their appeals were forwarded to Congress as
they halted at Princeton for an answer. Lafayette and Arthur St.
Clair rode out to negotiate, but they were requested to leave.
The insurgents declared that they would deal only with Wayne,
Walter Stewart, and Richard Butler, or the Congress.

In Philadelphia there was a near-panic. Some even suggested
that the Congress flee the city. Joseph Reed went with a committee from Congress to start negotiations. The committee remained at Princeton while Reed, Wayne, Stewart, and Butler
opened discussions with the sergeants at Trenton. A settlement
was finally reached calling for payment of all arrears in pay plus
depreciation, and the issuance of all articles of clothing to which
the soldiers were entitled. Any soldier who had enlisted on an
option of three years' service or the war's duration could be discharged at the end of three years. In the absence of documentary
proof, a man's oath was to be considered sufficient.[26]

By January 29, 1781, nearly 1,250 men had been discharged
from the Pennsylvania line—a large number swearing falsely
they had been in the service for three years. On February 20,
1781, the Congress resolved that all Continental troops from
Pennsylvania to Georgia were to be included in the Southern
army. Without consulting Washington, Congress ordered the
Pennsylvania line to the South as soon as it could be rebuilt.
Wayne was confident he could raise his command to its old
strength, but Washington commented, "I fancy he rather over-
rates the matter."

In the days that followed, matters went from bad to worse.
Perhaps the mutiny had rubbed tempers that were already raw,
for not only did Alexander Hamilton resign in a huff from

Washington's staff, but there are indications that Wayne had a tiff with the general and was nursing a bruised ego. Nevertheless he spent much of his time lobbying with the Pennsylvania Executive Council and the Continental Congress. However, he soon reported sadly, "They all present me that Gorgon Head, an empty treasury." [27] The Council did pardon some convicts on condition that they enlist in the line, and some of those soldiers recently discharged re-enlisted to receive the bonus.

When Wayne arrived at York, Pennsylvania, on May 19, he found what he termed a "little well appointed army." Inclement weather caused a three-day delay in his plans to march for Lafayette's army in Virginia. Then it happened once again—mutiny!

This time the discontent seems to have arisen from wages paid in the "Ideal money" of Pennsylvania, worth about one-seventh as much as specie. It was not a full-scale revolt, and varying reports confuse the events. Six soldiers were charged with such crimes "as exciting mutiny as far as in his power," for "mutinous expressions such as asserting that if any officer dared touch him he would shoot him," while one soldier, who later claimed he was drunk at the time, shouted in the hearing of the officer of the day, "God damn the officers, the buggers." Of the six mutineers, Wayne pardoned two, while the remaining four were executed by firing squad in "a most painful scene." And, according to one account, "The Line marched the next day southward, mute as fish." [28]

By June 10, 1781, Wayne's Pennsylvanians, almost 800 strong, were with Lafayette in Virginia. One observer described their elegant appearance to his wife in these words:

> They were a splendid and formidable corps. If the laurels which they win bear any proportion to the plumes they are adorned with, the heroes of antiquity will soon sink into oblivion. Were I a native of Laputa, with the assistance of a quadrant I might possibly calculate the altitude of that which nods over the brow of their General. Their military pride promises much, for the first step to make a good soldier is to entertain a consciousness of personal superiority;

and this consciousness is said to prevail in the breasts of these men, even to the meanest private in the ranks.[29]

Despite the Pennsylvanians and their magnificent plumes, Lafayette's army was too weak to do little more than dance away before Lord Cornwallis. On June 26, there was a skirmish at Spencer's Ordinary, but it ended only in a tangle of crackling musketry and plunging horses.

Finally at Green Spring, near Jamestown, on Friday, July 6, 1781, Anthony Wayne "pick'd a Quarrel [with] the British. . . ." Ostensibly, Cornwallis had ferried most of his troops across the James River; actually only the baggage and a mounted detachment were on the far side. Wayne assumed he was attacking the rearguard when he sent forward several hundred riflemen to harass the British while the Pennsylvanians advanced across a morass. Resistance by Banastre Tarleton's legion screened the major force of the enemy from view. When Lafayette threw in the Pennsylvanians still held in reserve, Cornwallis sallied forth with his entire army. What had been a supposed rearguard action turned into a full-scale battle.

Wayne, fearing to give the order to retreat lest it become a rout, impulsively ordered a bayonet charge. A heavy discharge of musketry and grapeshot brought it to an abrupt halt 200 yards from the enemy. Cornwallis could not but take this bold advance as a presage of a much more formidable attack. He hesitated and took up a defensive position waiting for the main blow to fall. For the next quarter-hour, as darkness began falling, the fighting grew fierce. Two British regiments, the Seventy-sixth and Eightieth, reported they gave the Pennsylvanians "a trimming" and claimed that they would have captured the whole corps had there been a little more daylight. Eventually Lafayette rode forward and ordered a retreat. Newspapers boasted of "Wayne, with a handful of Pennsylvanians, frightening the whole of Cornwallis' army of 'undaunted Britons.' " Others were less laudatory. Dr. Robert Wharry was even bitter: "I make no doubt, but you have heard of the Brush we had with the whole British Army; I was brought to bed with a Disappointment, another blockhouse affair—Madness—Mad A———y, by G—— I never knew such a piece of work heard of—about eight hundred troups opposed to five or six thousand Veterans upon their own ground." Ebenezer Wild commented, "General Wayne, being anxious to perform wonders! attacked the whole British Army with about 1000 men." French military censure was milder with General Rochambeau referring to Wayne as a *"brave homme, mais très ardent."* Even Wayne's friends voiced some apprehension as Nathanael Greene wrote of Lafayette's "military ardor, which no doubt is heated by the fire of the Modern hero, who by the by is an excellent officer. . . ." [30]

As Cornwallis maneuvered through the Virginia tidewater before fortifying the little village of Yorktown, Wayne's troops relaxed. Some even began to pay court to the Virginia belles. Wayne narrowly missed death when a befuddled sentry fired into the darkness wounding him in the thigh. The injury healed enough for Wayne to realize his "hope to participate in the glory attending the capture of Lord Cornwallis and his marauding army."

The Yorktown siege was dull in comparison with the actions that had gone before. Brigaded with Virginia troops in Steuben's division, Wayne found few opportunities to distinguish himself. When two redoubts were overrun in the most spectacular action of the siege, the Pennsylvanians remained in reserve. But in the colorful Steuben, Wayne found a kindred soul. After the completion of the second siege parallel, Wayne and Steuben were in the trenches together when a British cannon ball fell near by. The baron fell flat as Wayne tripped and sprawled across him. "I always knew you were a brave man," said the amused German, "but I did not know that you were so perfect in every point of duty: you cover your general's retreat in the best possible manner." [31]

Wayne believed, and undoubtedly hoped, that Cornwallis would not surrender nearly 6,000 troops without a "severe sortie." He was still awaiting such action when a chamade was beat on October 17, calling for a parley. The only compensation was that Wayne's troops were in the trenches when terms were requested. After the capitulation, Cornwallis was besieged with so many invitations that he was forced to decline Wayne's request to come to dinner.

On November 1, 1781, the Pennsylvania line, with St. Clair as major general and Wayne as brigadier, marched to South Carolina to reinforce Greene's Southern army. Henry Lee recorded his impressions of this "Irish" unit which could well be interpreted as a reflection of Wayne's personality:

> Bold and daring they were impatient and refractory; and would always prefer an appeal to the bayonet, to a toilsome march. Restless under the want of food and whiskey; adverse to absence from their baggage; and attached to the pleasure of the table; Wayne and his brigade were more encumbered with wagons than any equal portion of the army. The general and his soldiers were singularly fitted for close and stubborn action, hand to hand, in the centre of the army. . . ." [32]

After a leisurely march, the Pennsylvanians joined Greene on January 4, 1782. Within a short time Wayne was detached with 170 inexperienced men—and as many militia as could be persuaded to take the field—into Georgia. Taking post at Ebenezer, twenty-five miles above Savannah, he was soon sending dispatches to Greene, begging for some of his Pennsylvanians "who have fought and bled with me during my campaigns."

On February 19, he decoyed a large party of Indians into a trap, capturing the provisions they were taking to the enemy in Savannah. He sent the Indians back to their tribes, telling them that Savannah would soon fall to the Americans and that they had best remain neutral for the duration of the war. On May 21, the Savannah garrison under Colonel Thomas Brown made a sortie. Acting on the maxim that "the success of a night attack depends more on the prowess of the men than their numbers," Wayne marched four miles in the darkness across a narrow causeway through a swamp. A sudden charge, and Brown's force of cavalry, infantry, and Indians were sent fleeing into the night.

Three nights later some of the more defiant of the Creek Indians, led by the intrepid Guristersijo, turned the tables by surprising Wayne's camp. After the first recoil, Wayne rallied his troops and a sudden charge not only threw the savages into the swamp, but left Guristersijo among the slain. At daylight the British sallied out in support, but were driven back by a vigorous counterattack. "Our trophies," bragged Wayne, "are an elegant standard, 107 horses with a number of packs, arms &c. and more horses are hourly secured and brought in."

When the British evacuated Savannah on July 11, 1782, Greene wrote, "Georgia is ours, and Wayne has acquitted himself with great honor." [33] There was even a note of pride in Wayne's complaint:

> The duty done by us in Georgia was more difficult than that imposed upon the children of Israel. They had only to make bricks without straw, but we have had provisions, forage, and almost every other apparatus of war to procure without money; boats, bridges, &c. to build without materials except those taken from the stumps, and what was most difficult of all, to make Whigs out of Tories.

In August, 1782, after his return to South Carolina, Wayne fell victim to the same fever that was ravaging the rest of the Pennsylvania line. He doctored himself in the usual manner with "Frequent emetics & constant application of the Peruvian bark." While recovering, he managed to negotiate a treaty with the Creeks and Cherokees that helped to bring greater peace in Georgia.

On December 14, 1782, when Charleston was evacuated, Greene granted Wayne the privilege of leading the American troops into the city. The subsequent period of marking time until the formal peace was anticlimatic—winning independence was more exciting than the realization. In response to rumors that he was contemplating a future life on the plantation given him by the grateful citizens of Georgia, his fellow Pennsylvanian, Benjamin Rush, urged him to "Come and let the name of Wayne descend to posterity in your native State."

Wayne did return to Pennsylvania, having been promoted, by brevet, to major general. Still in poor health, he was elected, in 1783, to the Council of Censors, a watchdog organization whose duties were to determine if the provisions of the Pennsylvania Constitution of 1776 were being carried out. In 1784 and 1785, he was elected to the Assembly from Chester County, and vainly attempted to mollify retaliatory actions taken against the loyalists of the state.

By 1786, his financial problems had become critical. He sojourned south in an effort to make his Georgia plantation pay. Down the river was the plantation of Nathanael Greene, and when his general died in June, 1786, Wayne was at his bedside, distressed "because I have seen a great and good man die." [34]

Debt became an intolerable burden and Wayne took it as a personal insult when his creditors attempted to collect their money. Back in Philadelphia he became a member of the Pennsylvania Convention that ratified the Federal Constitution, but he returned to Georgia in 1788 in an attempt to bring some order out of the chaotic conditions on his plantation. He was bored, and proved to be an indifferent planter: "God, how tired I am of being buried in a damned rice swamp. I want a more active scene!" Overwhelmed with self-pity, he quoted the following lines from "The Old Soldier" to his wife:

> Ungrateful country! when the danger's o'er,
> Your bravest sons cold charity implore.
> Ah! heave for me a sympathetic sigh
> And wipe the falling tear from sorrow's eye.

The plantation was sold to satisfy his creditors, but his popularity was such that he became president of the Georgia Society of the Cincinnati. After a spirited campaign, he was elected a member of the House of Representatives from Georgia in 1791. He served only from March 4, 1791, to March 21, however, as his defeated opponent protested so loudly and presented such damaging evidence of fraud that the election was voided.

After Generals Josiah Harmar and Arthur St. Clair suffered

defeats by the Indians in the Northwest Territory, President Washington weighed the merits of his old officers as possible successors to the western command. Seemingly against his better judgment, Washington appointed Wayne to the post. Confirmation was not easily obtained, for too many in the Senate remembered that he was a business failure and a repudiated congressman. But Washington prevailed. Created a major general, "Mad Anthony" built an army around the riflemen of the frontier. Although this was a different type of warfare, Wayne still stressed the musket and the bayonet as the "most formidable weapons." Despite factions created among the officer corps by his subordinate, Brigadier General James Wilkinson, Wayne still managed to win a brilliant victory against the Indians in the Battle of Fallen Timbers in the summer of 1794. His triumph was gained through a volley and a charge with the bayonet. A year later, he was able to dictate the terms of the Treaty of Greenville that opened up the Northwest for settlement to a land-hungry people.

Because his victory brought an end to Indian resistance and gave additional stability to the government, Wayne easily overcame the charges of James Wilkinson, who spoke of him as "a liar, a drunkard, a Fool, the associate of the lowest order of Society, and the companion of their vices . . . my rancorous enemy, a Coward, a Hypocrite, and the contempt of every man of sense and virtue." Wayne's popularity was so great that he was able to dismiss such carping as "the idle Phantom of a disturbed imagination." [35] Indeed, in view of Wilkinson's subsequent duplicity in selling out to the Spanish for gold, his description of Wayne might easily have been applied to himself.

Upon Wayne's return to Philadelphia, he received the one thing he had sought and fought for all his life—adulation as a military hero. John Adams was to report one gathering: "General Wayne was there in glory. The man's feelings must be worth a guinea a minute." There was even talk that Wayne would become Secretary of War, although there were those who feared "we should be reduced to a State of insolvency" should he be appointed.[36]

But Wayne was worn out at fifty-one. When Jay's Treaty called for the evacuation of British posts in the Northwest, he hurried westward again. Upon his taking possession of Detroit, Congressman William Vans Murray mused, "Wayne! ah could we both have but seen W's Entre into Detroit! when he pranced over the Barbacon." Wayne soon busied himself with the inspection of posts. All the while he suspected his old enemy Wilkinson of intrigue with the Spanish, but never was able to furnish proof. It was to be 150 years before documents in the archives of Madrid would establish Wilkinson's treacherous intrigues with the Spanish governor of Louisiana. At Presque Isle, Wayne's health broke under what was termed "a severe fit of gout." [37] On the evening of December 15, 1796, Anthony Wayne suffered the indignity of dying in bed.

"Mad Anthony" seems particularly appropriate for the man. Proud, quick-tempered, impetuous, and even arrogant, he was consumed by a hero complex. His flaming and often uncontrolled temper revealed openly his passionate likes and dislikes. His entire life was a parade, with even a strut in his correspondence. Yet he was a useful man to have around during a rebellion, for his patriotism made him an inspiring leader on the battlefield. Homer surely had such a man in mind when he wrote, "Men grow tired of sleep, love, singing and dancing sooner than of war."

His comrade-in-arms came closest to describing Wayne's true character. Henry Lee, whose own temperament was not unlike Wayne's, said, "General Wayne had a constitutional attachment to the sword, and this cast of character had acquired strength from indulgence, as well as the native temper of the troops he commanded." [38] And George Washington, when searching his memories for a general in the Northwest, was more perceptive than is sometimes realized. Wayne, he noted, was "More active & enterprising than Judicious & cautious. No economist it is feared: —open to flattery—vain—easily imposed upon and liable to be drawn into scrapes. Too indulgent . . . to his Officers and men— Whether sober—or a little addicted to the bottle, I know not." Yet, Washington concluded, ". . . under a full view of *all* circumstances, he appeared most eligible. . . . G.W. [General Wayne] has many good points as an officer, and it is to be hoped that time, reflection, good advice, and above all a due sense of the importance of the trust which is committed to him, will correct his foibles, or cast a shade over them." [39] At places like Monmouth Court House, Stony Point, and Fallen Timbers, Anthony Wayne had more than met the "trust" committed to him, leaving behind a record of service that is hard to equal in America's military history.

FOOTNOTES

1. Charles J. Stillé, *Major-General Anthony Wayne and the Pennsylvania Line in the Continental Army* (Philadelphia, 1893), p. 6. All quotations in this essay are from Stillé's *Wayne* unless otherwise noted.

2. John C. Fitzpatrick, ed., *The Writings of George Washington, from the Original Manuscript Sources, 1745–1799*, 39 vols. (Washington, 1931–44), V, 78–79. Hereinafter cited as Washington, *Writings*.

3. Peter Force, ed., *American Archives*, 5th series, 3 vols. (Washington, 1848–53), I, 130; C. H. Jones, *History of the Campaign for the Conquest of Canada* (Philadelphia, 1882), pp. 122–23; "Memoirs of Brigadier-General John Lacey, of Pennsylvania," *Pennsylvania Magazine of History and Biography*, XXV, No. 4 (1901), 513.

4. Washington, *Writings*, VIII, 282, 292.

5. Henry Lee, *Memoirs of the War in the Southern Department of the United States*, Robert E. Lee, ed. (New York, 1870), p. 89. Hereinafter cited as Lee, *Memoirs*; James McMichael, "Diary of James McMichael of the Pennsylvania Line, 1776–1778," *Pennsylvania Magazine of History and Biography*, XVI (1892), 150.

6. William B. Reed, *Life and Correspondence of Joseph Reed*, 2 vols. (Philadelphia, 1847), I, 312–13. Hereinafter cited as Reed, *Reed*.

7. John André, *Major André's Journal*, Henry Cabot Lodge, ed., 2 vols. (Boston, 1903), I, 94; J. Smith Futhey, *Paoli Massacre* (West Chester, Pa., 1877), pp. 47–48; Benson J. Lossing, *Pictorial Field Book of the Revolution*, 2 vols. (New York, 1852), II, 370.

8. Washington, *Writings*, IX, 352, 361, 421, 422, 491.

9. "Extract from the Diary of General Hunter, originally printed in the *Historical Record of the 52d Regiment*," *Historical Magazine*, IV (1860), 346–47.

10. Washington, *Writings*, IX, 436.
11. Wayne quoted in Broadus Mitchell, *Alexander Hamilton: Youth to Maturity* (New York, 1957), p. 135.
12. *Lee Papers, New York Historical Society Collections*, 4 vols. (1871–74), II, 468.
13. John Richard Alden, *General Charles Lee: Traitor or Patriot* (Baton Rouge, 1951), p. 205.
14. *Lee Papers*, II, 420.
15. Alden, *op. cit.*, p. 242.
16. *Lee Papers*, III, 291.
17. Don Higginbotham, *Daniel Morgan: Revolutionary Rifleman* (Chapel Hill, 1961), pp. 95–97
18. William Abbatt, ed., *Memoirs of Major-General William Heath, By Himself* (New York, 1901), p. 193.
19. Josiah Quincy, ed., *The Journals of Major Samuel Shaw, the First American Consul at Canton* (Boston, 1847), p. 63.
20. Washington, *Writings*, XV, 451.
21. *Annual Register for 1779* (London, 1779), p. 193; Douglas S. Freeman, *George Washington: A Biography*, 7 vols. (New York, 1948–57), V, 140.
22. *Lee Papers*, III, 357, 375–76.
23. Jared Sparks, ed., *Correspondence of the American Revolution*, 4 vols. (Boston, 1853), III, 39–40.
24. Reed, *Reed*, II, 315–17.
25. "Extracts from the Letter-Books of Lieutenant Enos Reeves, of the Pennsylvania Line," *Pennsylvania Magazine of History and Biography*, XXI, No. 1 (1897), 72–74; *Journals of Major Samuel Shaw*, pp. 85–86.
26. Edmund C. Burnett, ed., *Letters of the Members of the Continental Congress*, 8 vols. (Washington, 1921–36), V, 514–41.
27. Washington, *Writings*, XXI, 145–46, 173; Wayne quoted in Carl Van Doren, *Mutiny in January* (New York, 1943), p. 233.
28. Van Doren, *op. cit.*, pp. 233–36, 251.
29. St. George Tucker to his wife, June 24, 1781, *Magazine of American History*, VII (September, 1881), 204.
30. Cornwallis to Leslie, July 8, 1781, Cornwallis Papers (Public Record Office, London, 30/11/85); "Letters to Dr. Robert Beatty," *Pennsylvania Magazine of History and Biography*, LIV, No. 2 (1930), 160; Ebenezer Wild, "Journal of Ebenezer Wild," *Massachusetts Historical Society Proceedings*, 2nd series, VI (Boston, 1891), 144; Frank Moore, *Diary of the Revolution*, 2 vols. (New York, 1860), II, 450; Comte de Rochambeau, *Mémoires Militaires, Historiques et Politiques*, 2 vols. (Paris, 1831), I, 284; Greene

quoted in Bernard C. Steiner, *The Life and Correspondence of James McHenry* (Cleveland, 1907), p. 38. Hereinafter cited as Steiner, *McHenry.*

31. Friedrich Kapp, *The Life of Frederick William Von Steuben, Major General in the Revolutionary Army* (New York, 1859), p. 457.
32. Lee, *Memoirs*, p. 420.
33. Greene quoted in Reed, *Reed*, II, 471.
34. George Washington Greene, *The Life of Nathanael Greene, Major-General in the Army of the Revolution*, 3 vols. (New York, 1871), III, 534.
35. Anthony Wayne quoted in James Ripley Jacobs, *The Beginnings of the U. S. Army, 1783–1812* (Princeton, 1947), p. 190.
36. John Adams to his wife, February 12, 1796, *Pennsylvania Magazine of History and Biography*, XXI, No. 1 (1897), 33; Steiner, *McHenry*, p. 165.
37. James Craig to James McHenry, December 9, 1796, *Pennsylvania Magazine of History and Biography*, XV, No. 2 (1891), 247–48.
38. Lee, *Memoirs*, p. 420.
39. "Washington's Opinion of General Officers," *Magazine of American History*, III (1879), 82–83.

BIBLIOGRAPHY

Boyd, Thomas, *Mad Anthony Wayne*. New York, 1929. This biography though colorfully written contains the flavor of fiction.

Moore, H. N., *Life and Services of General Anthony Wayne*. Philadelphia, 1845. One of the earliest attempts at a Wayne biography and now largely superseded.

Pratt, Fletcher, *Eleven Generals*. New York, 1949. Contains a most interesting chapter on Wayne.

Preston, John H., *A Gentleman Rebel: The Exploits of Anthony Wayne*. New York, 1930. Written in flamboyant phraseology and probably contains fabrications of colorful events.

Spears, John R., *Anthony Wayne*. New York, 1903. A short standard account of Wayne's life.

Stillé, Charles J., *Major-General Anthony Wayne and the Pennsylvania Line in the Continental Army*. Philadelphia, 1893. The best over-all study of the man. Despite his tone of rampant patriotism, Stillé made careful transcriptions of Wayne's letters, and his book contains much that is useful for any student of the Revolutionary War.

Wildes, Harry E., *Anthony Wayne: Troubleshooter of the Revolution*. New York, 1941. Wildes added little that was not known about Wayne other than a suggestion of a love affair with Mary Vining.

Daniel Morgan:

GUERRILLA FIGHTER

———•••———

DON HIGGINBOTHAM

Louisiana State University

NEARLY a century and a half ago Karl von Clausewitz, the Prussian military theorist, wrote that when war is mainly carried on by an armed citizenry rather than by professionals, "warfare introduces a means of defense peculiar to itself." Whenever men with little or no formal training in combat play a key role in dislodging an invader, they usually resort to tactics that reflect their immediate, local experience. The Revolutionary War in many ways was that kind of struggle. True, American military efforts sometimes followed the Old World pattern in the coastal areas: certain generals such as Lee and Gates had been trained in the British army, and native American commanders like Knox and Greene had read professional military treatises published in Europe. But by their frequent use of thin skirmish lines, highly mobile forces, night marches, winter campaigns, and hit-and-run tactics, the Americans revealed New World fighting methods alien to the conventional eighteenth-century practice.

Today, actions of this nature are called guerrilla or partisan warfare. The guerrilla—in the American Revolution, or in the mountains of Yugoslavia in World War II, or in the jungles of Southeast Asia in the 1960's—has attempted to confuse, harass, and destroy by methods his opponent does not understand. In the war for independence, such activity was most prevalent in the backwoods, and the American general who achieved the greatest success as a guerrilla fighter was a Virginia frontiersman named Daniel Morgan.[1]

Much of Morgan's early life is shrouded in mystery. His parents, farming people, were apparently Welsh immigrants living in New Jersey at the time of Morgan's birth, about 1735. At seventeen, after a quarrel with his father, Daniel fled to the frontier—a common practice among the restless, high-spirited youths of that day. By the spring of 1753, he was in Winchester, Virginia, a remote western settlement and the seat of Frederick County.

His awkward speech, coarse manners, and homespun clothing were not handicaps to the newcomer, who was to make his home in Frederick County. The English, Scotch-Irish, and German inhabitants of the county and surrounding area known as the Valley of Virginia were simple people. Life was hard with its exacting demands for survival—cutting timber, rooting stumps, planting crops, and erecting houses. Such a life sharpened the self-reliance of the settler and put a premium on initiative. Here law and order meant little when it prevented rough frontiersmen from getting the necessities of life, be they land, liquor, or women. If one can believe the tales of pious Moravian missionaries, scarcely a hardier breed of men existed than those on the fringes of western Virginia. Compounding the frontier disorder was the threat of Indian assaults as Valley men encroached on the redman's hunting lands in the Ohio country.

For Morgan, the alarms and excursions of war began in 1755. By that time, the French had started moving forces south from Canada to make good their King's claim to the Ohio Valley. Morgan, a teamster, secured employment from Major General Edward Braddock, sent from England to repulse the French tide. At Fort Cumberland, Maryland, Morgan and his fellow Virginia wagoners exasperated imperious British officers by their drinking, brawling, and lusty flirtations with Indian women. Once, when a redcoat reprimanded Morgan, the fiery young teamster knocked the man down—an offense which brought a drum-head court-martial sentence of several hundred lashes.

If, as Morgan claimed, he retained consciousness throughout the ordeal, it was a tribute to his superb physique. Standing six feet tall, with broad shoulders and massive arms, he was certainly capable of enduring great pain. Even so, he bore the scars from that beating the rest of his life, and with them he carried a firm conviction that the lash was a brutal, inhumane form of punishment. It was a kind of discipline he subsequently refused to use as an officer in the American army.[2]

Morgan learned still another lesson from the campaign when Braddock suffered his catastrophic defeat near the Monongahela River in southeastern Pennsylvania. Braddock's vain attempt to maintain line fire and regular formations against his French and Indian assailants, fighting from behind trees, bushes, and rocks, proved that European military methods were often futile in a wilderness setting. Later in the French and Indian War, Morgan served with the Virginia rangers. Once he was shot through the mouth and narrowly escaped death when he eluded capture by the Indians.

The years following "the French War" were carefree and roistering ones for Daniel Morgan. He was constantly in trouble with the law either for brawling in taverns or for not paying his liquor bills and card debts. But by 1763, when Morgan formed a common-law union with sixteen-year-old Abigail Curry, his conduct underwent a marked change. He settled down, purchased a farm, acquired some slaves, and began enjoying a more prosperous and peaceful existence. His changed way of life soon gained him the respect of the more important members of his rural community. The justices of the peace appointed him to several minor administrative posts, and in 1771 he was made captain in the militia.

Captain Morgan saw strenuous duty in 1774 when the white man's intrusions into the Ohio Valley set off another Indian conflict known as Lord Dunmore's War. He was a member of a special expedition under Major Angus McDonald which marched into the Ohio homeland of the Shawnee Indians, destroying crops and burning villages. Afterward Morgan participated in a similar mission that razed the lands of the Mingo, allies of the Shawnee. This campaign was among the last in Virginia's victorious war against the redman.

By the eve of the Revolution, the forty-year-old Morgan had been tested and tempered as a frontier fighter. The Indians, all unwittingly, had schooled him and countless others in the ways of wilderness warfare.[3] He had become proficient with the scalping knife and tomahawk, in addition to the so-called Kentucky rifle, a long, slender weapon designed by German gunsmiths. In the field he wore Indian leggings and moccasins and a hunting shirt, dyed the brownish color of a dry leaf. When the war clouds, hanging over the colonies since Parliament's passage of the "Intolerable Acts," finally burst at Lexington and Concord, Morgan found new opportunities to practice his military skills.

In June, 1775, the Second Continental Congress resolved that ten companies of light infantry be raised, including two from Virginia. The legislators were not thinking of the traditional European light infantry of the eighteenth century. They desired, said Richard Henry Lee, men who were known for their "amazing hardihood" gained through "living so long in the woods." Such veteran Indian fighters and hunters could travel far without provisions. They could perform remarkable feats with the rifle, allegedly hitting targets 200 yards away, whereas musketmen were ineffective at only half that distance. As snipers and woods-fighters, they could assault enemy supply trains, disrupt communications, and harass enemy armies as they marched into the interior.

Morgan, with his physical stamina, his experience in Indian warfare, and his knowledge of the rifle, was as well prepared to lead frontier light infantry as any colonial American. He was selected to head one of the Virginia companies authorized by Congress, and the rest of his Revolutionary War assignments, save one, involved light infantry. After recruiting ninety-six men, Morgan raced to Washington's camp outside Boston in amazing time, covering the 600 miles from Frederick County, Virginia, to Cambridge in three weeks.[4] Morgan may well have been acquainted with Washington before their meeting at Cambridge, for both Virginians had served with Braddock. In any event, the commander-in-chief took a genuine interest in the riflemen, for they were the first troops to come from his own colony. Washington, moreover, had spent much time in Frederick County and had once represented the region in the Virginia Assembly.

When the commander-in-chief organized an army under Colonel Benedict Arnold to invade Canada by way of Maine, three rifle companies, including Morgan's, were selected as part of the expedition. From the beginning, Arnold considered Morgan a valuable officer and appointed him to command all the riflemen. After plunging into the tangled Maine forests, Morgan led the forward units, while Arnold directed the bulk of the force composed of New England farmers and fishermen. As Arnold conceded later, no one did more to get the little army to the shores of the St. Lawrence—after traversing exhausting portages, rampaging streams, and deep swamps—than Daniel Morgan.

Stripped to the waist, attired in leggings and breech clout, Morgan toiled with his men as they cleared a rough trail for the troops behind them. Youthful Joseph Henry, a Pennsylvania rifleman, marveled at Morgan's strength and stamina. Henry's lone criticism was that the husky rifle captain demanded the same endurance from his men. On reaching the formidable Height of Land, which drops away toward the Canadian plain, Morgan insisted that his Virginians carry their heavy boats, for they would be needed on the north-flowing Chaudière and the St. Lawrence. The four-and-a-half-mile snow-covered trail crossed ravines and underbrush. Henry declared that Morgan's men had the flesh "worn from their shoulders, even to the bone." Yet Henry admitted that only by such exertions did Arnold's gallant little army finally emerge on the Plains of Abraham before Quebec in November, 1775, a distance of over 350 miles from the Maine coast. Henry, without disparaging Arnold's magnificent leadership, wrote that the individual, unforeseen, day-to-day problems were "left to the energy of Morgan's mind, and he conquered." [5]

Early in December, Arnold was joined by Brigadier General Richard Montgomery commanding a second army that had invaded Canada. Montgomery's troops had proceeded northward from Ticonderoga, taking British forts on the Sorel River and capturing Montreal, before descending the St. Lawrence to unite with Arnold. In planning the Quebec attack, Morgan, though only a captain, continued to play a more significant part than his rank would normally allow because he alone among Arnold's officers had seen important military service.

Since Governor Guy Carleton's combined force of British regulars and Canadian militia inside the walls of Quebec was double the 975 men of Montgomery and Arnold, the Americans needed both luck and the element of surprise to succeed. Their plan, to go into effect on the first stormy night, called for Arnold and Montgomery to attack from opposite directions. Both columns moving simultaneously were to strike against the Lower Town, a narrow strip along the river that was not as well protected as the rest of the city.

As snow whirled down in blinding intensity on the night of December 30, Arnold's men began their advance, with their commander and Morgan in the lead. One moment they were picking their way around the ice cakes thrown up by the river, the next they were scrambling out of the snowdrifts as they stumbled into the Lower Town. Sighting a barrier at the far end of the dark street, Arnold called for a frontal assault, since his only cannon had been abandoned in the deep snow. But a whirring musket ball tore into his leg, and he fell heavily to the ground. At this point, Arnold persuaded Morgan to take over. Arnold, the short, stocky apothecary from Connecticut, and Morgan, the tall ex-teamster from Virginia, came from different worlds, and on the wilderness trek and the Plains of Abraham they had had their differences. Yet as soldiers they had genuine respect for each other; both were brave, oblivious to personal danger, and, most important, both were leaders capable of arousing intense loyalty in their men.

Now all was up to Captain Morgan. Yelling for the rest to follow, he dashed toward the barrier. His performance in the moments that followed was one of the great personal deeds of the war. Setting a ladder against the barrier, Morgan scampered to the top. First a musket ball ripped through his hat, then a second creased his cheek. Falling backward into the snow, he lay there an instant, then he rose and bounded up and over the wall. Luckily he fell beneath a cannon which offered momentary protection from the thrusts of enemy bayonets. Riflemen, pouring over the wall, quickly overcame the opposition and saved him from harm.

Morgan had entered the Sault au Matelot, a narrow street where Arnold's division was to await Montgomery's force before the two would drive into the Upper Town. Finding no resistance, Morgan was convinced that the enemy was surprised and disorganized and that he should push on without waiting for Montgomery. But he soon discovered that Arnold's officers who outranked him disagreed. Although Morgan had assumed a colonel's command, he was still only a captain.

Even while the Americans stood quarreling in the streets, their attack was doomed to failure. Montgomery, after cutting a swath through two undefended palisades, had been shot down. His timorous subordinate, Lieutenant Colonel Donald Campbell, had beaten a hasty retreat. With Montgomery's troops out of the picture, Carleton dispatched units to the previously undefended barrier at the Upper Town end of the Sault au Matelot, while at the same time he sent a Captain Laws out the Palace Gate with instructions to hit Arnold's command from the rear.

Spotting the British activity at the second barrier, Arnold's field officers finally agreed to support Morgan and asked him to serve as their leader. Morgan, accompanied by Lieutenants Heth, Humphreys, and Steele, planted ladders and went up the wall; but they did not go over. A synchronized volley hurled them back. From upper-story windows on the British side of the barrier, musket flashes lit up the cold, gray dawn. Morgan, his stentorian voice sounding above the wind and musketry, rallied the Americans for repeated tries at the barrier—two, three, four, and more—all without success. He seemed to be everywhere, dashing here and there, now carrying a wounded comrade to shelter, now calling for still another assault at the wall. Morgan, declared one of his riflemen, was "brave to temerity," a sentiment echoed by another who wrote in his journal that "Betwixt every peal the awful voice of Morgan is heard, whose gigantic stature and terrible appearance carries dismay among the foe wherever he comes." [6]

As the British brought up an artillery piece, Morgan pulled his men back down the street toward the first barrier, hoping desperately that Montgomery would appear. At that point Laws's flanking unit from the Palace Gate swung into the street. The Americans were hemmed in front and rear—"caught as it were in a trap," wrote Carleton. Morgan begged to lead an attempt to fight their way out, an appeal Arnold's subordinates refused to heed. The Americans threw down their arms. Shouting, raging, tears streaming down his leathery cheeks, Morgan braced his back against a building and pulled out his sword. Which of the redcoat scum would try and take his sword, he yelled. When they threatened to shoot him, he told them to go ahead. At last, sighting a priest in the milling throng, he handed the astonished cleric his sword; at least no British "scoundrel" would take "it out of my hands." [7]

Morgan's anguish must have deepened when he later learned he had been accurate about the confusion among the British during the initial stages of the battle. A British officer, Major Henry Caldwell, declared that had Arnold's column pushed on, as Morgan had urged, the city might possibly have fallen. As it was, approximately 100 Americans were killed and wounded and 400 captured, compared to Carleton's loss of only 20.

Morgan and his fellow prisoners passed long months of confinement, until August, 1776, when Carleton released the Americans on condition they would not fight again until formally exchanged for Britons in Washington's hands. Though the labors of Montgomery, Arnold, and Morgan had failed to wrest Canada from the Crown, Morgan's role in the ill-fated Quebec venture brought him well-deserved recognition. Once he reached the American lines, he was promoted to colonel and slated for an important command.

In June, 1777, Washington gave Morgan a special corps of light infantry composed of 500 picked Continentals—men from the western counties of Maryland, Pennsylvania, and Virginia. Officially known as the rangers, more commonly called Morgan's riflemen, this unit compiled a spectacular record, scarcely excelled by any regiment in the Continental army. Outfitted with hunting shirts and rifles, these men included such celebrated backwoods fighters as Timothy Murphy, who during the Revolutionary War reputedly killed forty redmen and scalped twenty. The commander-in-chief considered Morgan's force a psychological as well as military weapon; they could serve to unnerve British soldiers who fancied all New World inhabitants as barbarians. In his first assignment, Morgan dressed his men in Indian garb and war paint before skirmishing with General Howe's forward units near New Brunswick, New Jersey. Let them shout and whoop, Washington added slyly; ". . . it would have very good consequences." [8]

Valuable as the riflemen were to Washington in the summer of 1777, as he and Howe engaged in a game of cat-and-mouse in the Jerseys, Washington agreed to a Congressional request that Morgan's unit be sent to upper New York. Morgan was to assist the American Northern army, then feebly contesting the southward drive from Canada of General John Burgoyne's Anglo–German army, supported by Tories and Indians. Just as Burgoyne's Indians had intimidated the New Yorkers with their scalping knives and hatchets, so Washington felt the same methods, if employed by Morgan's men, would demoralize the British and their allies. Horatio Gates, recently appointed commander of the Northern army, even hoped an American hatchet might find its way into Burgoyne's skull.

"Gentleman Johnny," the gay, wine-loving, playwright-soldier, kept his scalp but lost his military reputation. Later he frankly admitted Morgan's part in his undoing. Burgoyne, advancing through the red and gold of the autumn wilderness, had already overextended his supply lines from Canada. A force of British and Indians under Colonel St. Leger that was to drive from Oswego eastward along the Mohawk Valley to meet Burgoyne and Clinton at Albany, had been defeated near Oriskany. And one of his flanking parties already had been repulsed by a body of patriot irregulars at Bennington. But his situation deteriorated even further because of harassment from Morgan's forest-wise riflemen. They so terrorized his redskin scouts that not one could be brought within the sound of a rifle shot—a fact which seems to explain why the British moved to within three miles of Gates's encampment at Bemis Heights on September 18, 1777, without having any specific idea of the American general's whereabouts.

Even so, Burgoyne groped forward for an attack on the morrow. Gates, entrenched on Bemis Heights, held his main force inside his fortifications, but he wisely sent Morgan's riflemen into the woods in front of his lines to retard the enemy's progress. As a tactician, Morgan was best at woods-fighting. Here, as was customary with Morgan, he grouped his men in thin skirmish lines, which could be shifted about in the rough terrain more easily than the bulky British linear formations. He instructed his sharpshooters to concentrate their aim at enemy officers. Later Morgan received criticism for encouraging this practice, for a kind of gentlemen's agreement existed in European wars to spare opposing leaders. But as an Indian fighter, Morgan had concluded there was nothing chivalrous about war: it was ugly business, with one's chances of victory enhanced by crippling an opponent in any way possible, not by observing time-honored rules and customs.

Having deployed his riflemen, Morgan took a position slightly to the rear of his main skirmish line: there, in his favorite battle station, he could obtain reports easily and keep contact with the greater part of his men. But when his advance parties collided with Burgoyne's pickets, the Americans in front broke ranks as the enemy pickets fell back. Morgan then blew his familiar "turkey-call," a shrill gobble, and his men gathered around him. By this time, Burgoyne was aware of Morgan's presence in the woods. In a clearing 350 yards long, known as Freeman's Farm, Burgoyne had drawn up his center column which was widely separated from the supporting columns to his left and right. Morgan, while arranging his men in the foliage just beyond the clearing, was joined by Continental regiments sent out by Benedict Arnold, who directed the left wing of Gates's army.

Shortly after one o'clock in the afternoon, Morgan's corps, with the aid of Arnold's Continentals, opened a brisk fire that compelled the British to withdraw into a pine grove to the north. But when the Continentals attempted to occupy the farmyard, they were swept back by an enemy bayonet charge. The riflemen, whose weapons were not equipped to carry bayonets, seem to have stayed behind cover throughout the afternoon. Climbing trees, Morgan's marksmen took a heavy toll in officers and artillerymen. They were likewise "sedulous" in hitting the Tories, a "misfortune" that "accelerated their estrangement from our cause," as one redcoat sergeant put it.[9]

Though neither side could gain a decisive advantage in the bloody clearing, Burgoyne's losses were staggering. As daylight faded into dusk, Burgoyne's center was rescued by German reinforcements from his left column. The sulphurous smoke wafted upward and the din of firearms died away. Morgan and the Continental officers retired to their own lines. They had halted the enemy, inflicting 600 casualties upon Burgoyne as opposed to 320 of their own. Accounts by British participants reveal Morgan's corps as the most successful American unit engaged that day.

✗ Gates, awaiting another thrust by Burgoyne, declined a request by Washington to return Morgan's riflemen. He wrote that "your Excellency would not wish me to part with the corps the army of General Burgoyne are most afraid of." [10] That Morgan's woodsmen continued to plague the British general is evident from his remark that not a night between September 20 and October 7 passed without harassment. For this reason, plus the arrival of chilly weather and a shortage of supplies, Burgoyne tried a second time to crush Gates in order to complete the British scheme of reaching Albany and eventually driving a wedge between New England and the states to the south.

When Burgoyne advanced toward the American left on October 7, Morgan, "with his usual sagacity," suggested that he assail the British right flank while a second American force—under General Enoch Poor—burst out on Burgoyne's left flank. Gates accepted the idea, which Colonel James Wilkinson called "the best . . . that could be devised." [11] Morgan and Poor, striking almost simultaneously, rolled up the enemy flanks. Hastily Burgoyne regrouped his command, which then occupied the middle of a wheat field. As Morgan and Poor pressed against Burgoyne's center, held mainly by German General Riedesel and his blue-coated Brunswickers, the Americans received the welcome assistance of Arnold, leading General Ebenezer Learned's brigade.

Arnold, who had quarreled with Gates and had been subsequently confined to camp, dashed onto the field without permission. He is said to have shouted that he was going to help Morgan. Though Morgan and Arnold pushed the enemy back, the Brunswickers fought stubbornly. When British General Simon Fraser rode forward with reinforcements, Morgan called on rifleman Timothy Murphy, who shot down the brave Scotsman.[12] Now Burgoyne's troops gave up the field and withdrew into the fortifications they had erected in the previous few weeks.

Not content with partial victory, the Americans smashed against the redoubts on the enemy's right and center, and overran the extreme right redoubt garrisoned by Colonel Heinrich von Breymann's Germans. As in the first battle, darkness called a halt to the contest. Even so, the end was in sight for Burgoyne, who capitulated to Gates on October 17, after an unsuccessful attempt to flee northward.[13]

Historians have spilled much ink in arguments over which of

the American leaders—Gates, Arnold, or Morgan—deserves the greatest credit for Burgoyne's humiliation. In fact, all had a significant hand in the outcome. Gates, though cautious in committing his entire army against Burgoyne, was wise: with fall approaching and the British on rough, unfamiliar terrain, he permitted Burgoyne to wear down his forces by fruitless probes. The credit for leadership in the field belongs to Arnold and Morgan. Following the engagement of October 7, the short, ruddy-faced Gates embraced the rifleman, saying, "Morgan, you have done wonders"; while in his battle report to Congress Gates wrote that "too much praise cannot be given to the Corps commanded by Col. Morgan." [14]

Washington, meanwhile, had suffered reversals at the Battles of Brandywine and Germantown and had sorely missed Morgan's riflemen. Their services were "essential" to the army in the dreary days of late 1777. When Washington's tattered legions retired to Valley Forge to take up winter quarters, Morgan's men were among them. Indeed, upon their return that fall and during the following year, Washington made frequent use of Morgan's corps—at Whitemarsh, Valley Forge, and Monmouth. Throughout this period Morgan kept advocating the importance of cavalry to act in conjunction with his light troops and stressed the need for militia and partisan forces to co-ordinate their guerrilla activities with his own command. In view of his performance in the Canadian and Saratoga campaigns, Morgan now considered himself the foremost authority in the Continental army on the use of mobile forces.

Morgan found the year 1779 to be the most trying period of his military career. His famous rifle regiment, most of its companies having previously been detached to the West for Indian fighting, was disbanded. His next permanent assignment was the colonelcy of a Virginia infantry regiment, hardly an invigorating post for an ambitious man whose laurels were no doubt greater than those of any colonel in the army. Restless and sensitive, Morgan soon learned that a large light infantry unit had been formed, and he was obsessed with the idea of leading it.

When he found the command had gone to Anthony Wayne, he resolved to present Congress his resignation. Though Wayne was an able officer and held the rank of brigadier general, Morgan had had more experience with light troops.[15]

Morgan was deeply disappointed that Washington had not supported his candidacy for the command. Only recently he had been one of the general's staunchest defenders at the time of the Conway Cabal, an alleged plot by politicians and officers to remove Washington from supreme command.[16] When Morgan confronted Washington, the latter was not disposed to show him more than moderate sympathy, nor did he offer his unhappy rifle officer any compensation such as a recommendation for promotion in rank. The fact that Morgan, like Washington, was a Virginian did him no good, for Washington bent over backward to avoid charges of being partial to men from his own state. Nevertheless, in a letter of introduction for Morgan addressed to the president of Congress, the commander-in-chief wrote that Morgan was "a very valuable officer" who had "distinguished himself upon several occasions." In Philadelphia, the congressmen agreed that Morgan had been "Neglected, but not intentionally." Nothing, however, was done in his behalf. Contrary to what historians have often written, he did not resign but accepted an "honorable furlough" until a more promising position became available.[17]

Proud and indignant but not wrathful, Morgan journeyed back to western Virginia, where he stayed for nearly a year. It was not a happy interlude, for Morgan was one of those hearty breed of men who fails to find satisfaction in "the sweets of domestic life." He was, as a contemporary is reputed to have said, "exactly fitted for the toils and pomp of war." Then, in 1780, Morgan received a letter from Horatio Gates, newly appointed commander of the Southern army. Gates had requested Morgan to head a regiment similar to the rifle unit which had performed so admirably against Burgoyne. Indeed, it seemed that the guerrilla warfare in which Morgan excelled was the only American hope of slowing the British invasion of the American southland, for during 1779 and 1780, British forces had overrun Georgia and much of South Carolina.

In the South, a land of innumerable rivers and creeks, intersected by swamps and forests, Morgan and other guerrilla fighters could be invaluable. Morgan fairly leaped at this opportunity, particularly since Gates trusted him and recognized his abilities. Aware of Morgan's concern over previous neglect, Gates promised to urge Congress to promote the frontiersman to brigadier general. Unfortunately, however, Morgan had experienced such a painful and crippling attack of sciatica, an ailment contracted earlier in the war, that he was unable to reach Gates's headquarters in North Carolina until mid-September. By then, Gates had been decisively beaten by Lord Cornwallis at the Battle of Camden, when Gates's militia, forming the American left wing, had fled without fighting, leaving the exposed Continentals to be chewed up by British regulars.[18]

Because of the Camden debacle, Morgan received a light corps much smaller than he had expected. During the dismal fall of 1780, when patriot prospects in the South were at their lowest ebb, Morgan labored with little success to make his light corps equal or superior to its British counterpart, Colonel Banastre Tarleton's Tory legion. Unlike most British units in the South, the legion specialized in mobility—especially slashing, head-on assaults that were not only effective but often brutally conceived. Cornwallis had also kept Tarleton and the legion busy in beating back patriot guerrillas and in maintaining supply lines between British outposts in South Carolina. The British general told his short, chunky, twenty-six-year-old subordinate that he wished Tarleton were three men instead of one: "We can do no good without you."

Morgan, chafing at his idleness got an opportunity for action in December of that year. Nathanael Greene, Gates's replacement as Southern commander, shared Morgan's enthusiasm for partisan-type operations. Even with a minuscule army, he intended to play the hit-and-run game against Cornwallis—the "old Fox," as Morgan called him. With his long overdue promotion now in hand, Brigadier General Daniel Morgan tramped into the South Carolina back country to sit on the enemy's left flank and rear. Greene, in the meantime, with the remainder of the Southern army advanced to Cheraw, South Carolina, to annoy the British right and front.

Morgan's sudden appearance in the hinterland unnerved Cornwallis. Rural patriots rallied to the standard, Tories deserted in droves, and Morgan's operations threatened the British post at Ninety-Six. His Lordship was not the only British military leader in the war to discover that rear areas could not be treated in the European sense—as free of enemy forces and simply as zones of communication. In the Revolutionary struggle, because of the activities of Morgan, Sumter, Pickens, Marion, and others, the front-behind-the-front became a theater of operations in its own right. Hence, before Cornwallis could launch his long-planned invasion of North Carolina and the upper South, Morgan would have to be eliminated. Cornwallis selected his best man, Tarleton, for the task.

Getting wind of Tarleton's approach, Morgan hastily fell back toward the North Carolina line. The guerrilla fighter has traditionally tried to avoid the challenge to positional combat in the open; his value lies in harassment, and often many of his men are unfamiliar with orthodox warfare. In Morgan's case, approximately half his force consisted of militia. But with Tarleton's Tory legion pursuing "like Bloodhounds" after prey, Morgan concluded that he would have to make a stand. He hoped to stop and fight somewhere beyond the Broad River in the rough terrain near Thicketty Mountain. But by the afternoon of January 16, 1781, Morgan became grimly aware that it was impossible to reach his destination. Tarleton was only a few miles behind. Even if he reached the Broad, a crossing would be difficult because of heavy rains and in the darkness Tarleton might surprise and destroy his corps.

Morgan prepared, therefore, to do battle on the west side of the Broad, at a place called the Cowpens—a grazing area well known to Carolina farmers. Historians have been fascinated by

Morgan's choice of ground. Both Morgan and Tarleton later admitted that the Cowpens, with its gently sloping ridge sparsely covered with oak and hickory, offered no protection for the American flanks. Morgan explained that he did not want his militia to have swamps or underbrush nearby for fear they would flee at the appearance of Tarleton's dragoons: with no shelter available they would be compelled to stand and fight. But this observation was made with the benefit of hindsight. Morgan probably had no alternative except the Cowpens because night was approaching.[19]

There is no higher quality of generalship than the ability to dominate a situation, no matter how difficult; bad as his situation was, Morgan resolved to make the best of it. He had utmost faith that he could devise a battle plan that would combine the particular talents of his militiamen and Continentals. Instead of entrusting his poorly trained militia with part of the main line of defense (as Gates had so foolishly done at Camden), Morgan proposed to make the most of the sharpshooting abilities of the frontier militiamen, without forcing them to stand for long in open combat. Placing his Continentals—under Colonel John E. Howard—at the crest of the elevation, he would deploy the bulk of the militia—commanded by Colonel Andrew Pickens—150 yards in advance of the regulars. Well in front of Pickens' line, however, he would station a small body of frontier riflemen in a skirmish line. The plan called for the riflemen and militia to fire one or two well-aimed volleys, then retire to the rear of Howard's troops, where they were to be re-formed and held in reserve.

The scheme was sound only if Morgan could infuse spirit and confidence in the men. Here, again, his qualities as a dynamic leader were of the utmost importance. In the darkness, moving from one campfire to another, he talked and joked with the men about the prospect of beating Tarleton. The "Old Wagoner" would crack his whip over "Ban" Tarleton, he cried, provided they would help him. Victory would bring them glory, and at home the old folks would praise them and the girls would kiss them. As the men crowded about, slapping each other on the

back, and betting on the number of legionnaires they would bag,
Major Thomas Young "was more perfectly convinced of General
Morgan's qualifications to command militia than ever . . . be-
fore. . . ." [20]

At dawn, after a sleepless night, Morgan repeated his rounds,
reminding them of Saratoga, Monmouth, Paoli, and Brandywine;
reminding them, too, that this day they could make their own
contribution to "liberty's cause." Morgan and other officers like
him led the American soldier to believe he had a personal stake
in the war; quite often this encouraged him to hold his own
against the better-trained redcoat or German who performed
merely for pay and in response to orders. Though battlefield
oratory was not uncommon in the patriot army, seldom did it
bring more striking results than at the Cowpens. [21]

When the battle began at seven in the morning, the air was
crisp and clear. To Tarleton, the riflemen and militia along the
American front must have looked like easy prey, reminding him
of his conquest at Camden. As the British advanced, the riflemen
emptied fifteen saddles. Pickens' line followed with a blast that
shook the green-jacketed legion. That was all for the militia.
They filed off to the left and passed around the end of Morgan's
main line—all the while under the protection of Morgan's small
but effective cavalry commanded by Colonel William Washington. Tarleton's troops took the irregulars' withdrawal for panic-
stricken flight. Again surging forward, they were brought up
short, this time by Howard's line of Continentals. During the
next few minutes the opposing forces dueled at point-blank
range. Howard's veterans gave the enemy a "well-directed and
incessant fire," Morgan later reported. Tarleton agreed: "The
fire on both sides was well supported and produced much
slaughter."

The climactic phase of the struggle saw the Americans cap-
italizing on luck and Morgan's quick thinking. Because of mistaken orders, Howard's line began a slow retrograde movement.
Tarleton's men, sensing victory, broke ranks to pursue their foe.
Morgan, seeing that the Continentals had maintained their own

good order, called for a sudden volley. Taken unawares, the line
of red and green staggered. Howard now called for a bayonet
charge. Morgan, almost simultaneously, threw the re-formed
militia against the unsuspecting British left and at the same time
sent Washington's cavalry smashing down on Tarleton's right.
Morgan had achieved a double envelopment, one of the most
difficult maneuvers. The legion was thrown into a "panic," admitted Tarleton, who fled with a handful of officers and horsemen. As Morgan informed a friend, "I was desirous to have a
stroke at Tarleton—my wishes are gratified," and "[I] have
given him a devil of a whipping a more compleat victory never
was obtained." He had "entirely Broke up Tarleton's Legion,"
the "flower" of Cornwallis' army; British losses in men amounted
to 110 killed and 702 captured as against Morgan's 12 killed and
60 wounded.[22]

Though Cowpens was one of the tactical masterpieces of the
war, Morgan's success would have gone for naught if Cornwallis
had overtaken his corps and released the Cowpens prisoners.
Aware of this danger, Morgan hastily retreated into central
North Carolina. That he made good his escape, with prisoners
encumbering his withdrawal and many of his own men barefoot
and nearly naked, across the swollen Catawba and Yadkin rivers,
was as remarkable as his crushing defeat of Tarleton. The British were scarcely a stone's throw away when Morgan reached
Guilford Court House, where he united with Greene's wing of the
Southern army, which had headed northward to assist against
Cornwallis.

For all practical purposes, Morgan's direct participation in the
war was at an end. Dampness and exposure had so aggravated
his sciatica that he was compelled to return to Virginia to recover
his health. Yet Morgan, whose performance had vindicated
Greene's bold strategy of dividing the Southern army in the
face of a superior foe, was to exert further influence. On his way
homeward he wrote Greene to resort to the tactics used at Cowpens in the event of a full-scale encounter. Greene followed
Morgan's advice in the Battle of Guilford Court House; and

though the British emerged victorious, the action was a costly one for Cornwallis. "Great generals are scarce," Greene assured his former subordinate; "there are few Morgan's to be found." [23]

The spring and summer months of 1781 were agonizing for Morgan, who exploded in helpless frustration in writing his friends. To be sure, the war in the South became high drama, with Greene mopping up South Carolina and Georgia, and Cornwallis opening a major theater in Virginia. Morgan briefly took the field with Lafayette in Virginia, but his sciatic condition caused a sudden return home. He came so close to death, he reported, that he "literally peeped . . . into the other world." If the end must come, the Old Wagoner preferred to die "more gloriously" in combat.[24] But he realized he was too late; Washington's rapid move into Virginia had spelled Cornwallis' doom.

Morgan had lost none of his respect for Washington in spite of their earlier differences. In the numerous references to Washington in Morgan's papers, there is not the slightest intimation of criticism or doubt of the commander-in-chief. To Morgan, Washington was the sustaining force of the Revolution; without him the cause would collapse. Morgan's steadfast loyalty was all the more remarkable because the rifleman must have known that Washington had criticized him for leaving the service because of dissatisfaction over rank and command. Uncertain of Washington's feeling toward him at this time, and aware of his superior's consuming duties on the Virginia peninsula, Morgan was clearly hesitant about writing to the commander-in-chief. But, as he apologetically explained in a lengthy letter, "the feelings of my heart will not permit me to be silent. . . ." It had been his "particular fate" never to have served directly under Washington in an important contest, "a misfortune I have ever sincerely lamented." Nothing on earth would have given Morgan more pleasure than to have performed in the Yorktown campaign "under your excellency's eye, to have shared the danger, and let me add, the glory too." [25] Washington was touched and replied in a generous vein. Morgan, he wrote, breathed "the Spirit and Ardor of a Veteran Soldier, who, tho impaired in the Service of his Country, yet retains the Sentiments of a Soldier in the firmest Degree." [26]

The two generals had seen little of one another during the war and each had fought in his own fashion. While Washington, the commander-in-chief, had directed operations along the eastern seaboard of the Middle States, Morgan, the guerrilla, had found his duties in the mountainous hinterland. Washington, like Morgan, had begun his military career as a frontier soldier in the French and Indian War. If in the Revolution the commander-in-chief was confronted with the more complex problems of maneuvering large forces and fighting pitched battles somewhat along the lines of European engagements, he nevertheless retained his respect for the partisan operations of Morgan and others like him. Though never intimate, their exchange of letters shows that the Virginia aristocrat had developed a genuine admiration for the Virginia farmer.

What was the value of Morgan's kind of guerrilla warfare in the Revolution? It goes without saying that it was highly successful when the British left the coastal plains and plunged into the interior, a region largely unsuited to European combat and inhabited by men who fought according to their own rules. In fact, Clausewitz might have given our struggle for independence as his prime example when he wrote that rarely indeed are orthodox forces ever successful against guerrillas. Partisans, however, seldom bring about total victory in war. Though they may weaken the enemy and make him increasingly vulnerable, the final blow is generally delivered by large, well-organized armies, working in smooth harmony. In this case, French and American forces in co-operation with the French fleet trapped Cornwallis at Yorktown and hammered him into submission.

Morgan, of course, would have been out of his element at Yorktown: the partisan leader generally has little understanding of grand strategy or the administration of large divisions. Fortunately, Morgan never was thrust into a position beyond his training or talents, as were Lincoln, Putnam, and a number of other Revolutionary generals. Morgan was admirably suited for every command he held.[27]

Retirement posed difficulties for the military hero. Though up to his "Head and ears" managing a grist mill and speculating in western lands during the postwar years, Morgan manifested a restlessness, a longing to "Keep a loose foot." Despite a new home, a more comfortable way of life, and greater respectability in the Valley of Virginia, the old soldier still craved excitement. Memories of his illustrious past weighed heavily upon him, and he felt he was growing "very rusty." Morgan, whose prose did not rival that of "pope, Voltiere or Shakespear," corresponded frequently with his "old swords," former army friends, and a number of them visited the Morgan home—"Saratoga."

In the 1790's, Morgan's letters turned from Revolutionary reminiscences to the subject of political combat. An ardent Federalist and supporter of President Washington's policies, Morgan was convinced that the Jeffersonian Republicans were trying to destroy the Constitution, "the Envy and wonder of the surrounding world." The Whisky Rebellion, an outburst against the Federalists' excise tax, brought Morgan into the field once more in 1794, as the commander of a Virginia militia detachment. Though Morgan felt "as Hearty as I ever was" and could "undergo the fatigues of two or three campaigns," he won no new laurels; the whisky rebels in Pennsylvania capitulated without firing a shot.

If the Republicans would not meet him on the field of battle in Pennsylvania, Morgan would assault them in the halls of Congress. In 1797, he ran on the Federalist ticket and won a seat in the House of Representatives. He served a single term, and on one occasion threatened to call out his Virginia militiamen against the "seditious" Jeffersonians within his own state.

Advancing age, complicated by years of sciatica and eventually crippling arthritis, had reduced his mighty frame to near helplessness, but mentally he remained alert. Nothing could have been more in character with the colorful old veteran than a remark to his physician shortly before his death on July 6, 1802:

"Doctor," said the general, "if I could be the man I was when I was twenty-one years of age, I would be willing to be stripped stark naked on the top of Allegheny Mountain, to run for my life with a pack of dogs at my heels." [28]

Mighty of spirit, independent of mind, resourceful and self-reliant, a man who rose from humble immigrant stock to military fame, modest wealth, and national political office, Morgan symbolized Crèvecoeur's image of the American—a wholly "new" man.

FOOTNOTES

1. Though the nucleus of this essay is derived from my *Daniel Morgan: Revolutionary Rifleman* (Chapel Hill, 1961), I have placed greater emphasis on the guerrilla theme here than I did in the biography. I have benefited especially from the increasing interest of historians in guerrilla warfare a trend that doubtless reflects our desire to gain a fuller understanding of the partisan-type operations carried on in South Vietnam and other so-called backward areas of Asia and Africa.

2. [Joseph Graham], "A Recollection of the American Revolutionary War," *Virginia Historical Register*, VI (1853), 211; "Notes from . . . Benjamin Berry . . . in Relation to General Daniel Morgan," Ludwell–Lee Papers, Virginia Historical Society; James Graham, *The Life of General Daniel Morgan* . . . (New York, 1856), pp. 29–30, contains an account of the whipping that is not completely accurate.

3. See John K. Mahon, "Anglo-American Methods of Indian Warfare, 1676–1794," *Mississippi Valley Historical Review*, XLV (September, 1958), 254–75, which discusses the strengths and weaknesses of colonial tactics and strategy on the frontier.

4. Franklin B. Dexter, ed., *The Literary Diary of Ezra Stiles* (New York, 1901), I, 601.

5. Journal of Joseph Henry, in Kenneth Roberts, ed., *March to Quebec* (New York, 1938), pp. 229, 335–36.

6. Journals of Henry and George Morison, in *ibid.*, pp. 378, 537–38.

7. Graham, *Morgan*, pp. 102–03.

8. For the formation of the rifle corps, see John C. Fitzpatrick, ed., *The Writings of George Washington* (Washington, D.C., 1931–44), VI, 128 and VIII, 235–37, 246; hereinafter, Washington,

Mount Prospect
Public Library

Writings; "Orderly Book of Major William Heth," *Virginia Historical Society Proceedings 1891,* X, 332–76.

9. R. Lamb, *Memoirs of His Own Life* (Dublin, 1809), p. 199.

10. Jared Sparks, ed., *Correspondence of the Revolution* (Boston, 1853), I, 437.

11. James Wilkinson, *Memoirs of My Own Times* (Philadelphia, 1816), I, 268.

12. Morgan told the story of Fraser's death to a British officer. [Graham], "A Recollection of the American Revolutionary War," p. 210. It also appears in William L. Stone, *Burgoyne's Campaign and St. Leger's Expedition* (Albany, 1877), pp. 324–25.

13. Only recently another British account of the campaign has come to light: S. Sydney Bradford, ed., "Lord Francis Napier's Journal of the Burgoyne Campaign," *Maryland Historical Magazine,* LVII (December, 1962), 285–333.

14. Gates to John Hancock, October 12, 1777, Papers of the Continental Congress, No. 154, I, 272, National Archives.

15. For evaluations of the rifle and light infantry, see the articles by John W. Wright: "The Rifle in the American Revolution," *American Historical Review,* XXIX (January, 1924), 293–99; "The Corps of Light Infantry in the Continental Army," *ibid.,* XXXI (April, 1926), 454–61.

16. Higginbotham, *Morgan,* pp. 82–84.

17. Washington, *Writings,* XV, 342; Morgan to William Woodford, July 22, 1779, Chicago Historical Society.

18. I have found no sound evidence to support the old story—still repeated—that Gates tried to draw Morgan into a plot against Washington after Saratoga, that Gates failed to accord Morgan full recognition for his part in Burgoyne's defeat, and that consequently Morgan initially refused to assist Gates in the South. To be sure, Gates and Morgan had an excellent relationship in 1780.

19. Henry "Light-Horse Harry" Lee maintained that Morgan turned on Tarleton and fought in an "irritation of temper." *Memoirs of the War in the Southern Department . . .* (Philadelphia, 1812), I, 253–54. Lee's view has received little support.

20. Joseph Johnson, *Traditions and Reminiscences Chiefly of the American Revolution in the South* (Charleston, 1851), p. 449.

21. Higginbotham, *Morgan,* pp. 95, 136, 211.

22. The most detailed account of this battle is by Hugh F. Rankin, "Cowpens: Prelude to Yorktown," *North Carolina Historical Review,* XXXI (July, 1954), 336–69. A number of Morgan's letters written during the Southern campaign are printed in Graham,

Morgan. Morgan's graphic description of the outcome at Cowpens is in a long letter to William Snickers, dated January 26, 1781, now in the Gates Papers, New York Historical Society.
23. Graham, *Morgan,* p. 395.
24. Morgan to Richard Butler, January 17, 1782, Lyman C. Draper Papers, 27CC69, State Historical Society of Wisconsin.
25. Graham, *Morgan,* p. 399.
26. Washington, *Writings,* XXIII, 174.
27. Several valuable articles point out the importance of American guerrilla warfare in the South: Eric Robson, "British Light Infantry in the Eighteenth Century: the Effect of American Conditions," *Army Quarterly,* LXII, No. 2 (1950), 209–22; Robert C. Pugh, "The Revolutionary Militia in the Southern Campaigns, 1780–1781," *William and Mary Quarterly,* 3rd series, XIV (April, 1957), 154–75; Jac Weller, "The Irregular War in the South," *Military Affairs,* XXIV (Fall, 1960), 124–36.
28. David H. Conrad, "Early History of Winchester," *Winchester, Va., Historical Society Annual Papers* (1931), I, 172.

BIBLIOGRAPHY

Bass, Robert D., *The Green Dragoon: The Lives of Banastre Tarleton and Mary Robinson.* New York, 1957. Contains a wealth of recently unearthed material on Tarleton's American service and his subsequent mistress Mary Robinson, a London socialite.
Blacker, I. R., ed., *Irregulars, Partisans, Guerrillas: Great Stories from Rogers' Rangers to the Haganah.* New York, 1954. Provides a valuable introduction to this subject.
Callahan, North, *Daniel Morgan: Ranger of the Revolution.* New York, 1961. Takes a life-and-times approach.
Graham, James, *The Life of General Daniel Morgan of the Virginia Line of the Army of the United States.* New York, 1856. Still retains a large number of letters printed in full.
Hart, Freeman H., *The Valley of Virginia in the American Revolution.* Chapel Hill, 1942. Offers a sound and readable description of frontier Virginia in Morgan's formative years.
Higginbotham, Don, *Daniel Morgan: Revolutionary Rifleman.* Chapel Hill, 1961. Stresses the uniqueness of American eighteenth-century warfare.
Nickerson, Hoffman, *The Turning Point of the Revolution.* Boston, 1928. Continues to be the standard work on the Saratoga campaign.

Robson, Eric, *The American Revolution in its Political and Military Aspects*. London, 1955. Emphasizes the importance of New World conditions and American fighting methods in bringing about British defeat.

Smith, Justin H., *Our Struggle for the Fourteenth Colony*, 2 vols. New York, 1907. Presents an exhaustive account of the campaigns of Montgomery and Arnold against Canada.

INDEX

317

military training, 193; relations with Washington, 195, 209; attitude toward militia, 196, 200; command of Southern Department, 197; relations with Congress, 201

Lincoln, Benjamin (father), 193

Lincoln, Benjamin, Jr., 204

Lincoln, Elizabeth (mother), 193

Lincoln, Mary (wife), née Cushing, 193

Livermore, Samuel, 138

Livingston family, 83

Long, Col., 67

Long Island, Battle of, 6, 9, 32, 112, 139, 142-145, 155, 194, 243

Lord Dunmore's War, 293

Louisbourg, 24

Louisiana, 235, 287

Louis Philippe, 235

Louis XVI, 201, 224, 233

Lovell, James, 5, 117

Lowndes, Pres., 198

Loyalists, 29-30, 37-38, 40, 68, 92, 101, 122, 124, 157, 167, 177, 184-188, 194, 200, 203-205, 240, 275, 284-301, 305-306

Luzerne, Chevalier de la, 159

Macaulay, Catherine, 27

McClellan, Gen. George B., 17

McCrea, Jane, 92

McDonald, Maj. Angus, 293

McHenry, Dr. James, 228

Madrid, 287

Magaw, Col. Robert, 113

Mahan, Alfred Thayer, 177

Maine, 138, 169-171, 177, 257, 295

Malden, England, 80

Malvern Hill, 231

Manchester, Vt., 196

Manhattan Island, 3, 32-33, 112, 142, 242-244

Marblehead, Mass., 245

Marion, Gen. Francis, 124, 132, 306

Martinique, 82

Maryland, 29, 121, 129-130, 292

Massachusetts, 27, 38, 62, 99, 117, 165-166, 168, 193-195, 205-207, 209, 240-241, 248, 256-257

Maurepas, Jean Frédéric, Comte de, 224-225

Maxwell, Gen. William, 262, 265

Mercer, Gen. Hugh, 112

Mes Rêveries, 252

Middlebrook, 115

Mifflin, Gen. Thomas, 14, 118, 269

Militia, as opposed to Continental army, xv, 11, 27, 33-34, 37-38, 42, 54, 68, 84-85, 97-105 passim, 121, 123-132 passim, 138, 149, 154, 165, 180, 193-196, 200, 202-203, 205-209, 216, 228-229, 232, 256, 262, 293, 307-309, 312. See also Washington, Gates, Lee, Lincoln.

Minden, Battle of, 213

Mississippi River, 235

Mohawk Valley, 57, 69-70, 73, 91, 99, 156, 180, 300

Moldavia, 25

Monckton, Robert, 81-82

Money, 100, 118-119, 122, 169, 179, 184-188, 225, 233, 277, 280, 284-286

Monmouth, Battle of, 5, 7, 9, 119, 222, 252-253, 270-272, 288, 303, 308

Monmouth's Rebellion, 6

Monongahela River, 7, 293

Monroe, Pres. James, 235

Montcalm, Louis Joseph, Marquis de, 172

Montgomery, Gen. Richard, xiii, 60-62, 169, 172, 262, 296, 299

"Montpelier," 257

Montreal, Quebec, 24, 58, 62, 75, 169, 172-175, 262, 295-297

Moravians, 218-219, 292

Morgan, Abigail (wife), née Curry, 293

Morgan, Gen. Daniel, viii, 11, 96, 123-126, 170, 173, 183, 230, 264, 272; appearance and personal qualities of, 292-293, 298, 307; as tactician, 296-303, 306-309; relations with Washington, 304, 310-311

Morris, Gouverneur, 45

Morris, Robert, 133

Morristown, 38-39, 115, 146, 225, 248, 264

Moultrie, Gen. William, 31, 199

Mount Independence, 63

Mount Kemble, 277

Mount Vernon, 234

Mud Island, 268

Muhlenberg, Gen. Peter, 219

Mulberry Grove, 133

Murphy, Timothy, 299, 302

Murray, William Vans, 287

Musgrave, Col. Thomas, 250-251